THE STATE OF ASIAN PACIFIC AMERICA

THE STATE OF ASIAN PACIFIC AMERICA:

ECONOMIC DIVERSITY,

ISSUES & POLICIES

A Public Policy Report

PAUL ONG
Editor

LEAP Asian Pacific American Public Policy Institute

and

UCLA Asian American Studies Center

1994

Leadership Education for Asian Pacifics (LEAP), 327 East Second Street, Suite 226, Los Angeles, CA 90012-4210

UCLA Asian American Studies Center, 3230 Campbell Hall, 405 Hilgard Avenue, Los Angeles, CA 90024-1546

ISBN: 0-934052-23-9

Cover design: Mary Kao

The State of Asian Pacific America:

Economic Diversity, Issues & Policies

Paul Ong, Editor

Table of Contents

Part III. Policy Essays

Preface

With this publication, our two institutions—Leadership Education for Asian Pacifics (LEAP) and the UCLA Asian American Studies Center — continue a partnership which has led to the establishment of the nation's first Asian Pacific American public policy institute. We hope this policy report, like others we have already released and those we will publish in the future, will serve to inform public discussions and shape public policy deliberations about the most important and compelling policy issue-areas facing the nation's rapidly growing and diverse Asian Pacific American population.

There is no question that economic issues are of immense interest and concern to all Americans. There has been substantial debate and speculation about the health and recovery of the American economy from various vantage points, be it from Washington, Wall Street, or South Central Los Angeles. Public opinion polls in recent years have shown that the economy is the number one concern of the majority of Americans. Indeed, the 1992 presidential campaign, which had been forecast to be a referendum on George Bush's first-term performance in the diplomatic and military arenas, became dominated by domestic economic issues like creating more jobs, reducing the federal budget deficit, and revitalizing urban cores.

This report on Asian Pacific Americans and the American economy is intended to respond to the compelling public interest on economic policy issues. Asian Pacific Americans, who now number 7.2 million nationally and are expected to grow to 20 million by 2020, have been and will continue to be important contributors to — and beneficiaries of — many different sectors of our nation's economic structure from their high visibility in advanced technology industries to their relative invisibility among the ranks of the working poor and unemployed.

Asian Pacific Americans are an extremely diverse population, and their roles in the American economy are also diverse and multifaceted. As Ong and Hee note in one of the chapters in this book, "It is impossible to distill the economic status of Asian Pacific Americans into a single statistic." Unfortunately, that happens all too often, particularly when unwarranted and simplistic conclusions are drawn from a few census indicators to label Asian Pacific Americans, in monolithic terms, as a successful or model minority group.

This report seeks to go beyond these catchy one-liners, and to provide the most comprehensive and up-to-date empirical and policy-oriented analysis of the impact, contributions, and status of Asian Pacific Americans and the changing American economy. It does this through the first-ever, in-depth examination of the growing presence and participation of Asian Pacific Americans in four major areas of the nation's economic structure — high technology, health and medical services, inner-city communities, and social welfare. This empirical analysis, which is based on a rigorous examination of 1990 Census and other economic data, provides information on Asian Pacific Americans on a national scale, as well as in relation to the three major urban concentrations in Los Angeles, San Francisco, and New York. The latter represent the top three Asian Pacific American communities in the country, and account for nearly 60 percent of all Asian Pacific Americans.

However, aside from providing accurate and full empirical findings and information, this report seeks to enhance understanding of how Asian Pacific Americans draw linkages between the realities of their own situation and the intense and varied levels of policy debate that are occurring around economic issues, be they unemployment, urban revitalization, or technological innovations. Their economic policy concerns are oftentimes overlooked, distorted, or delegitimized by the highly influential stereotype of Asian Pacific American success. This report provides important alternative policy-oriented perspectives on the major economic issues and concerns of Asian Pacific Americans by leading policy specialists.

Like our other joint policy research activities and publications, this publication reflects the special strengths and goals of our two institutions. The UCLA Asian American Studies Center, established in 1969, is one of four ethnic studies centers at UCLA, and one of the nation's oldest programs in Asian American Studies. Through its research, teaching, publishing, and public educational activities in fields ranging from literature to urban planning, the faculty, staff, and students of the Center have sought to advance scholarly and policy understanding of Asian Pacific Americans.

LEAP is a nonprofit organization founded in 1982 to develop, strengthen, and expand the leadership roles played by Asian Pacific Americans within their own communities as well as in mainstream institutions. LEAP's mission is to achieve full participation through leadership, empowerment and policy, which is being realized through the creation of the innovative Leadership Management Institute (LMI), the newly established Community Development Institute (CDI), and the nationally recognized Asian Pacific American Public Policy Institute (APA•PPI).

We would like to pay special tribute to Professor Paul Ong of the UCLA Graduate School of Architecture and Urban Planning for serving as the principal investigator of this major policy report, and for coordinating the empirical studies and policy essays that comprise this work. We are also grateful to the members of the advisory committee, whose expertise and guidance have been invaluable: Barry Bluestone, John McCormack Institute of Public Affairs, University of Massachusetts, Boston; Heidi Hartmann, Institute for Women's Policy Research, Washington, D.C.; Rebecca Morales, Center for Politics and Economics, Claremont Graduate School; and Gary Orfield, Graduate School of Education, Harvard University. We also would like to express our gratitude to the Board of Directors of LEAP and the Faculty Advisory Committee of the UCLA Asian American Studies Center for their continued support of our joint policy research center.

Finally, we would like to acknowledge the generous support of The Ford Foundation, which provided the major funding for this study. We also wish to acknowledge The James Irvine Foundation and The Carnegie Corporation of New York, who are major sponsors of the Public Policy Institute. Additional support has been provided by The GTE Foundation, The ARCO Foundation, AT & T, Kaiser Permanente, The Equitable Foundation, Time Warner, Inc., Pacific Bell, and the William Penn Foundation as well as from the following units at UCLA: the Institute of Industrial Relations, Graduate Division, Academic Senate, and the Urban Planning Program. Professor Paul Ong, in closing, would like to thank several individuals who provided invaluable support: Don Nakanishi, Tim Dong, J.D. Hokoyama, John Tateishi, Graham Finney, Glenn Omatsu, Grace Hong, Russell C. Leong, Mary Kao, Phil Okamoto, Karen Umemoto, Linda Akutagawa, Suzanne J. Hee, and Gena A. Lew.

J.D. Hokoyama
President and Executive Director
Leadership Education for Asian Pacifics

Don T. Nakanishi
Director
UCLA Asian American Studies Center

Chapter 1

Asian Pacific Americans
and Public Policy

Paul Ong

Economic changes over the last two decades have not been kind to the United States. Fluctuations in energy prices, growing international competition, and stagnant productivity have led to a restructuring that has displaced an enormous number of workers and has undermined economic growth that had previously raised the standard of living for each successive generation. The challenge facing us today is to overcome these problems by forging a new policy agenda that will reinvigorate this nation as we move into the 21st century.

Asian Pacific Americans can play a crucial and positive role in this process. During the period of harsh restructuring, this group has contributed greatly to the economy, interjecting much needed human resources and business investments. Their contributions can be readily seen in their sizeable presence among scientists, engineers and health professionals, and in their high rate of entrepreneurship. Increasingly, Asian Pacific Americans have become important in the arts and performing arts, producing plays and films that entertain and enlighten, and emerging as a force within America's premiere symphonies. With the right public policies, this growing population will contribute even more. In the drive to maximize the contributions of the highly-educated and highly-talented, we must not ignore the concerns of the segment that has been disadvantaged in our society. We must have policies that incorporate and balance the diverse issues facing all Asian Pacific Americans.

This book contains analytical studies and policy essays that form Asian Pacific American perspectives on key economic issues. This book shares the broader purpose outlined in an earlier publication, *The State of Asian Pacific America: Policy Issues to the Year 2020*, which is "to inform public discussions and shape public policy deliberations on major issues and concerns of the nation's rapidly growing and diverse Asian Pacific American population" (Hokoyama and Nakanishi, 1993, p. xiii). That book lists three major recommendations (Ong and Hune, 1993, pp. xvii-xix):

1. Promote multiculturalism and intercultural sensitivity within existing legislation, programs, and agencies;

2. Modify the concept of civil rights so protection covers the types of discriminatory practices encountered by Asian Pacific Americans; and

3. Expand programs that help Asian newcomers adjust to U.S. society in order that they can contribute to America's economic, political and social development to their fullest potential.

All three points pertain to economically oriented public policies related to upgrading the workforce, community development in the inner-city, work incentives for welfare recipients, health care reform, and research and development. There are distinct Asian Pacific American perspectives on these issues that need to be articulated.

One impetus behind this book is the phenomenal growth of the Asian Pacific American population over the last three decades. From 1960 to 1990, the numbers grew from about one million to over seven million, making Asian Pacific Americans the racial group with the highest growth rate. Projections from the Census Bureau indicate that the Asian Pacific American population will continue to grow in the following decades. By the year 2020, there will be approximately 23 million Asian Pacific Americans, comprising approximately more than 7 percent of the total population, up from 3 percent in 1990.

The perspectives of this rapidly growing group are shaped by their demographic and economic characteristics. The population is predominantly immigrant. Between the 1940s and the 1960s, when immigration was minimal, the population became increasingly dominated by U.S.-born Asian Pacific Americans. This changed with the elimination of racially biased immigration quotas in 1965. During the 1970s, the foreign-born reemerged as a large majority. According to the last census, the number of foreign-born Asian Pacific Americans stood at 4.6 million, 64 percent of the total Asian Pacific American population. Over half of the immigrants have been in this country for no more than ten years. Even though the importance of immigration relative to births will decline over the next century, the foreign-born segment will still be a majority in the year 2020 (Ong and Hee, 1993a).

Immigration has diversified Asian Pacific Americans. In the past, one group — Japanese Americans — comprised a near majority, but there is now greater balance across ethnic groups. The Japanese American population has experienced the most dramatic change. As the single largest group in 1960, Japanese Americans comprised 46 percent of all Asian Pacific Americans, but three decades later their share fell to only 12 percent. While the absolute number of Japanese Americans has grown, the growth of the other groups has been far greater. According to the 1990 Census, 23 percent were Chinese, 19 percent were Filipino, 11 percent were Asian Indian, 11 percent were Korean, and 8 percent were Vietnamese. The remaining 16 percent were divided into 21 other categories. Despite the heterogeneity revealed by census data, the statistics understate the cultural diversity. For example, among the Chinese, there are major linguistic differences among those who came from China, Taiwan and Southeast Asia. Similar differences can also be found among Filipinos and Asian Indians.

Post-1965 immigration has created not only ethnic diversity but also economic diversity. The recent wave of Asian immigration is not limited to those with limited skills, for the 1965 Immigration Act opened the way for Asians to migrate based on their potential economic contributions to this nation. Those who entered under occupational preferences include a disproportionate high number of university-educated professionals, who, along with highly-educated U.S.-born Asian Pacific Americans, have formed the foundation of a significant middle and upper-middle class. Given the diversity of background, Asian Pacific Americans can be found throughout the income spectrum of this nation.

The economic diversity is one of the most important features we need to understand in formulating public policy, but unfortunately, the image that has influenced how most decision makers view Asian Pacific Americans is the "model minority" stereotype. The "success" is overstated, as discussed in Chapter 3. After accounting for differences in regional distribution and household size, the purported economic advantage of Asian Pacific Americans relative to non-Hispanic whites disappears. Nonetheless, Asian Pacific Americans enjoy a noticeable degree of success relative to other minority populations. This latter comparison has been the basis for the pernicious "model minority" thesis, and the political implications flowing from its use and misuse are enormous.

The "model minority" argument emerged during an era that witnessed the growth of civil rights activism and minority pride. At a time when scholars and activists were arguing that a deep-seated racism caused social inequality and urban unrest, Asian Pacific Americans evoked an image of a group that had achieved extraordinary success in American society despite experiencing a long history of racial discrimination. Some have interpreted the accomplishments as validating the belief that the United States remains a land of unbounded opportunity for minorities. Implicit in the "model minority" thesis are the assertions that the way for minorities to succeed is through hard work, adherence to "traditional values," and maintenance of the family rather than relying on governmental intervention and public "hand outs." These arguments are wrong because the comparison of Asian Pacific Americans to other minorities is misleading.

The vast majority of Asian Pacific Americans, who are immigrants, have not suffered from continuous exposure to the corrosive effects of pervasive overt racism over several generations. This is not to argue that Asian Pacific Americans had not been victims of past racism. In fact, anti-Asian movements of the 19th century and early 20th century were pervasive and violent. This population was subjected to many of the same racist laws that subordinated other minority groups.

As Don Mar and Marlene Kim argue in Chapter 2, Asian Pacific Americans were the scapegoats of the economic problems of this country, particularly in the West, and were forced into narrow and less desirable occupational niches. This history of anti-Asian movements is important to understanding this country's history but is not a factor that directly defines the personal historical experience of most Asian Pacific Americans today.

The majority of today's Asian Pacific Americans have their immediate roots in the sending country, where their values and expectations were formed. Many of their social institutions are transplanted from abroad, rather than being the product of American history. The consequence of this is that the population has been isolated from the cumulative historical process that undermines the family, community institutions, and values in other minority populations. Moreover, as stated earlier, recent immigration laws and regulations have creamed the elite from Asian countries, thus producing a highly-educated and highly selected population.

Rather than focusing on the "model minority," this book illustrates the economic diversity of Asian Pacific Americans. Chapter 3 by Paul Ong and Suzanne J. Hee provides an overview. Despite the accomplishments as measured by aggregate economic measures (e.g., average household income), Asian Pacific Americans are not a homogenous group. Diversity within the Asian Pacific American population has meant sizeable affluent and impoverished segments, the "haves" and "have nots." In many ways, this population has experienced the increasing income polarization that has afflicted this nation. Chapter 3 discusses the diversity among Asian Pacific Americans by examining three major segments of the population: the highly-educated, the disadvantaged, and the entrepreneurs.

The thesis of economic diversity is further illustrated by the collection of chapters in Part II, which covers issues ranging from the inner-city poor to more advantaged professionals.[1] Chapter 5 examines four Asian Pacific American urban neighborhoods: San Francisco and New York Chinatowns, Los Angeles Koreatown, and the Cambodian community in Long Beach, also known as New Phnom Penh. The residents are predominantly immigrants or refugees. A high poverty rate is common, despite a high employment rate in three of these neighborhoods. Many are a part of the working poor, with a quarter of the employed earning less than $4.00 (1989$) per hour. The ethnic-based subeconomy, which is present in these neighborhoods, is a double-edged sword. While providing employment for at least one-third of the workers, it creates deplorable conditions: wages are low, basic benefits such as health insurance are often absent, and unfair labor practices are all too common.

Chapter 6 by Paul Ong and Evelyn Blumenberg examines Southeast Asians on welfare. Asian Pacific Americans as a percent of those on Aid to Families with Dependent Children (the nation's single largest welfare program) grew from less than 1 percent in 1975 to nearly 3 percent in 1990. Although the Asian welfare population is diverse, Southeast Asians comprise a large majority of those on public assistance and exhibit welfare usage rates that reach over 50 percent. Most of those on welfare find it difficult to find meaningful employment because they possess very limited formal education and English-language ability. Worse, programs designed to end welfare dependency appear to have limited effectiveness.

Chapter 7 by Paul Ong and Tania Azores examines health care professionals in the inner-city. While Asian Pacific Americans comprise 3 percent of the total population, they comprise over 4 percent of the registered nurses and nearly 11 percent of the nation's practicing physicians. These professionals provide a disproportionate share of the crucial services to the urban poor, particularly through public hospitals in our largest metropolitan areas. Unfortunately, they have not moved into management positions in the same proportions. There is no simple explanation for this discrepancy, but nonetheless, this pattern suggests that a change in personnel practices is in order.

The "glass ceiling" limiting upward mobility to management is also a problem in the technical fields. Chapter 8 by Paul Ong and Evelyn Blumenberg examines Asian Pacific Americans in the scientific and engineering fields, where they accounted for 7 percent of the workforce in 1990. One in five of those with doctorate degrees is Asian Pacific American. Wages of Asian Pacific American scientists and engineers are roughly comparable to those of their non-Hispanic white counterparts, but Asian Pacific Americans have experienced considerable difficulties entering top managerial positions. One interpretation for this centers on cultural and language handicaps; however, it is not clear that these factors adversely affect managerial ability. Regardless of the reason, the outcome is undesirable.

Collectively, the five analytical chapters provide insights into the breadth of the Asian Pacific American experience in the economic sphere. The authors find that this group has made enormous contributions but also faces many unresolved problems. The empirical analyses raise issues that should be addressed by public policy.

Linda C. Wing in Chapter 4 offers the broadest set of policy recommendations. Asian Pacific Americans can greatly benefit from the current effort to "reinvent" labor force policies, which include transition-to-work programs for those who do not go on to college, government-funded training programs for the unemployed and for lifelong learning for all, and private-sector training programs that are crucial for improving productivity and competitiveness. How well these programs will serve Asian Pacific Americans depends on whether their unique problems are addressed. The Asian Pacific American perspective, however, is not limited to demanding fair access to programs. Wing rightfully argues that this group has "a special vantage point from which to exercise leadership in translating the rare conceptual accord regarding the common good of education and training into concrete policies that will benefit all workers."

The four chapters in Part III offer additional policy insights. Chapter 9 by Dennis Arguelles, Chanchanit Hirunpidok and Erich Nakano examines the newly-emerging urban policy, which includes proposals to revitalize the inner-city through "Empowerment Zones" and "Enterprise Communities," greater enforcement of the Community Reinvestment Act, strengthening of community-based organizations, and partnerships with philanthropic foundations. These ventures should include the significant number of poor Asian Pacific Americans in the inner-city. Given the unique characteristics of their ethnic enclave and the role of Asian Pacific American merchants in other minority neighborhoods, programs must be structured to address ethnic-specific concerns and to take advantage of the potential contributions of Asian Pacific Americans in renewing American cities.

Chapter 10 by Joel F. Handler and Paul Ong examines the current debate over welfare reform. President Clinton promises "to end welfare as we now know it" by making public assistance a transitional program to employment for able-bodied adults. This approach has the potential of promoting economic self-sufficiency among Southeast Asians. Given the unique characteristics of Southeast Asian communities, the authors argue that strategies should go beyond targeting individual behavior to tapping collective resources found in community-based institutions, and go beyond jobs to address other forms of economic activities such as self-employment. Unfortunately, the proposal under consideration does not address the concerns of this population, thus the prevailing dismal conditions are likely to persist through neglect.

Chapter 11 by Geraldine V. Padilla and Bonnie Faherty examines the potential impacts of health care reform on Asian Pacific Americans. The authors identify four relevant issues: access to and utilization of health care services, cost of care, quality of care, and culturally sensitive care. The major recommendations, which are based on a summary of positions put forth by various Asian Pacific American organizations, include the following: provide universal access to health care for all American citizens, legal residents, undocumented workers, and illegal aliens; avoid undue financial burdens on Asian Pacific small business; increase support for community-based health agencies; and establish training and retraining programs to ensure the cultural sensitivity and relevancy of health services and consumer education.

Chapter 12 by Sheridan M. Tatsuno examines high-technology policies. With the close of the Cold War and the rise of Asian economies, this nation must rethink its technological policy. There is an opportunity to shift scarce resources to research and development that can help the United States to remain a global leader in technology and to use the technology to ensure our competitiveness in the world economy. This can be accomplished through assisting private-sector firms, and through increasing the size and improving the quality of the labor force in the technical fields. Given their sizeable presence in the scientific and engineering fields, Asian Pacific Americans can play an enormous role in helping this country achieve its technological objectives for the next century.

While the policy essays contain ethnic-specific recommendations, the authors also recognize that the Asian Pacific American perspective on public policy should not be based solely on staking a claim to public resources and programs. There is an underlying concern with policies that enable this nation to achieve the broader goal of creating a multiethnic society that recognizes the importance and dignity of everyone.

Notes

1. Unfortunately, other important topics and issues could not be covered given our limited resources. The reader might want to consult two other sources for more information and data: *1990 Census of the Population, Asian and Pacific Islanders in the United States* by the U.S. Bureau of the Census (1993) and *Asians and Pacific Islanders in the United States* by Herbert Barringer, Robert Gardner and Michael Levin (1993).

Part I

Overviews

Chapter 2

Historical Trends

Don Mar and Marlene Kim

The history of most Americans — especially minorities and immigrants — has been subject to legal and political restrictions as well as by economic forces. Nowhere is this more apparent than among Asian Pacific Americans. Their fortunes, livelihoods, and lifestyles have been shaped by immigration laws curtailing their arrival, laws proscribing where they could live and what livelihoods they could pursue, and labor shortages or surpluses that have either beckoned to them or refused their passage to America. This chapter provides an overview of how the state of the economy and formal and informal sanctions shaped the lives of Asian Pacific Americans. Rather than provide an exhaustive analysis, we summarize how political and economic constraints shaped Asian Americans' experiences in the economy. As a result, there are some topics that will have limited coverage due to considerations of brevity. For example, there is relatively little discussion of "push" factors that led Asians to escape from their home countries.

We discuss these factors during three time periods: the period covering 1850 to World War II, from the World War II to 1965, and the post-1965 period. The first period focuses on the stories of early immigrants and the severe restrictions they faced during a period of major conflict between labor and capital. The second period discusses the decline of some of these restrictions and the entrance of large numbers of American-born Asians into a mature industrial economy with the U.S. as the world economic leader. The final period discusses the consequences of having new immigrant workers enter the U.S. during the relative decline and restructuring of the U.S. economy. This chapter closes with a discussion of future labor market prospects for Asian Pacific Americans.

The Early Immigrant Experience: Pre-World War II

From 1850 to World War II, Asians were subject to the whims of a rapidly developing industrialized economy. Massive changes swept the U.S. economy: production evolved from the traditional craft method of production to factory production with labor specialization and wage labor predominant (Gordon, Edwards, and Reich, 1982; Braverman, 1974); small, regionally diverse markets were connected by transportation innovations allowing the growth of large, nationally integrated markets (Davis et al., 1972); mechanization and specialization in agriculture created larger farms with single cash crops (Hughes and Cain, 1994); increased labor productivity created pressure for U.S. expansion into world markets (Williams, 1969).

U.S. race relations also underwent a dramatic change in the late 19th century. The end of slavery ushered in a new set of racial institutions such as Jim Crow, laws segregating workers based on race, and laws demarcating the place of nonwhites in society. These new racial restrictions arose in the midst of societal conflict — largely between capital and labor during American industrialization (Reich, 1981) — that severely circumscribed the labor market opportunities of early Asian immigrants.

Against this tumultuous background, Chinese immigrants were hired to build the industrial and agricultural infrastructures on the West Coast during the 19th century. Although the initial arrival of Chinese in the 1850s was the result of the Gold Rush in the Sierra Nevada, the Foreign Miners' Tax in 1853 discouraged Chinese from continuing in mining (Chan, 1991, p. 28), scattering them into a host of occupations. Chinese workers, recruited by the Central Pacific Railroad, were responsible for constructing the western half of the first transcontinental railroad that was essential for integrating U.S. markets and providing a passageway to Pacific markets. The Chinese also built the spur lines that fed the transcontinental railroad and constructed the dikes and levees that allowed the Sacramento river delta to be reclaimed as farmland (Melendy, 1984, p. 51). They became urban businessmen, specializing in laundries, dry goods, and restaurants and established themselves in small-scale manufacturing industries such as textiles and woolens, boot and shoe making, and cigar making in the urban areas. By the 1880s, over 100,000 Chinese resided in the United States, mainly in the West and primarily composed of prime-age working men.

Formal and informal restrictions placed on Asians during this time period were prevalent and severe. Legal restrictions on occupations, citizenship, and immigration severely limited Asian American opportunities in the economy. Formal and informal sanctions against the Chinese began as early as the 1850s (Daniels, 1988, pp. 29-76). Informal sanctions included anti-Chinese marches, formation of anti-coolie clubs, demonstrations, and violence. Daniels (1988) and Saxton (1971) discuss the role of labor supporting and developing the anti-Chinese movement. Although several individuals in the labor movement often spoke out against Chinese discrimination, elements of the labor movement often supported the anti-Chinese movement. Ong (1981) argues that the conflict between labor and capital in the latter part of the 19th century led to the exclusion of Chinese workers from the high-paying, dynamic sectors of the economy. Formal social and occupational sanctions raised against the Chinese were numerous. Social sanctions included the inadmissibility of Chinese testimony in courts and anti-miscegenation laws. The California Foreign Miners' Tax (1850) and the 14 San Francisco Laundry Ordinances (1873-1884) were all targeted to exclude Chinese from certain occupations. In general, many of these formal sanctions were restrictions instituted at the local and state levels.

The conflict between labor and capital during industrialization ultimately resulted in national legislation to end Chinese immigration to the United States (Ong and Liu, 1993). The 1882 Immigration Act, which was renewed in subsequent decades, effectively ended Chinese immigration to the United States. The results of these formal and informal sanctions were to exclude new Chinese immigration and to circumscribe economic opportunities for Chinese residing in the United

States. In fact, by the end of the 19th century, the restrictions against the Chinese were so onerous that many left the U.S., decreasing the population of Chinese in the mainland United States from approximately 100,000 in 1880 to 80,000 by 1900.

The chronic shortage of labor in the West made it difficult for West Coast agriculture to expand at the end of the 19th century. West Coast agriculture in wheat and other specialty crops became increasingly important to the national economy during the latter part of the 19th century. During the 1890s, Japanese laborers were recruited to fill these agricultural jobs. By the early 20th century, many Japanese made the transition from agricultural worker to tenant farmer (O'Brien and Fujita, 1991). Given the relatively small size of Japanese farms, farmers grew labor intensive, high value added, specialty crops such as berries, celery, onions, and sugar beets.

Japanese immigration to the United States differed markedly from the earlier Chinese immigration due to a greater number of female immigrants. The higher number of women allowed more family formation among the Japanese compared to the Chinese. Family labor was critical in providing labor for Japanese enterprises, primarily the family farm and, to a lesser degree, in family retailing businesses in the early part of the 20th century. By the 1920s and 1930s, Japanese women had also extended their employment outside ethnic enterprises into urban service occupations (Glenn, 1986).

The Japanese, like the Chinese, faced both informal and formal sanctions. By the early 1900s, numerous groups and individuals such as the Asiatic Exclusion League (Daniels, 1988, p. 118) were calling for an end Japanese immigration. In an attempt to curtail Japanese, and to a lesser degree Chinese, expansion into small farms, various land acts were passed to prevent Japanese farmers from owning land. In California (1913) and Washington (1921), state alien land acts were enacted, banning land ownership by foreign nationals. Although the passage of these acts did discourage some Japanese from entering farming, the overall impact was minimal as the Japanese found numerous means to circumvent the law. Japanese exclusion became national policy with the passage of the 1924 Immigration Act, which set a numerical quota on immigration based on the number of each nationality's population in the U.S. as of 1880. As there were few Japanese residing in the United States in 1880, the Act effectively ended Japanese immigration to the U.S.

Like the Chinese, the Japanese began to diversify into small businesses, particularly hotels, grocery stores, and restaurants. However, the Japanese remained predominantly involved in agriculture throughout most of the pre-war period. As a result, the Japanese were not as urbanized as the Chinese during the 1920s and 1930s. The numbers of Japanese Americans continued to increase after the 1924 Immigration Act due to the birth of the Nisei (the second generation). By 1940, the population of Japanese in the United States was approximately 127,000, while the Chinese population numbered 77,500.

The shortage of agricultural labor in the West Coast also contributed to the arrival of Filipinos into the United States. American colonization of the Philippines allowed large numbers of Filipinos to circumvent the 1924 Immigration Act as migrant farm workers harvesting sugar beets, lettuce, asparagus, and fruits (Melendy, 1984). Unlike the earlier Chinese and Japanese immigrants, the Filipinos did not move into ethnic enterprises or farm ownership. Falling agricultural prices, combined with informal sanctions, limited employment opportunities and wages for Filipino workers during the 1920s and 1930s. With the granting of commonwealth status to the Philippines in 1935, Filipino immigration was limited to 50 persons per year. By the end of the 1930s, the population of Filipinos numbered approximately 100,000 with the majority consisting of single men employed primarily in agriculture.

Asians provided agricultural labor not only for California but also Hawaii. The "Great Mahele" of 1848 allowed Hawaiian lands to be bought and sold by private individuals, creating large land holdings with no adequate labor force to work the land (Kent, 1983). The native Hawaiians were decimated by contact with Western civilization and proved to be an inadequate labor force for plantation owners (Takaki, 1983). Chinese farm workers initially formed the backbone of the plantation labor force during most of the 19th century. However, by the end of the 19th century, sugar planters began recruiting laborers from Japan in large numbers. By 1902, Japanese laborers made up 73 percent of the plantation workforce. The passage of the Gentleman's Agreement in 1907 curtailed further immigration of Japanese into Hawaii. Planters then recruited workers from the Philippines, as well as the rest of the world, beginning large-scale immigration of Filipinos into Hawaii such that by 1920, Filipinos accounted for almost 30 percent of the agricultural labor force.

By the end of the Depression, the Japanese and Filipinos were largely employed in agriculture, whereas the Chinese had become predominantly urban workers. In 1940, over 20 percent of Japanese males on the mainland were employed as farm managers or farm owners. In addition, one in four Japanese workers was employed as an agricultural worker. Almost half the Filipino workers in the mainland U.S. were employed in agriculture. However, unlike the Japanese, Filipinos were rarely owners of the farms they worked. The Chinese were heavily urbanized by 1940 and were largely employed as operatives in the garment industry and food service sector. A large number of Chinese were also self-employed as small shop-keepers in the retail, restaurant, and service industries (see Table 1).

The First American-Born Generation:
The Post-War Period until 1965

World War II brought several changes to the American economy. By the end of World War II, the U.S. economy had completed the transition from a relatively small industrial economy to the preeminent urban industrial economy. High-paying semi-skilled jobs abounded in the manufacturing sector with the dominance of U.S. manufacturing in the world economy. The infrastructure development and housing boom of the post-war period also generated construction jobs throughout the national economy. The increasing U.S. military role around the world provided high-wage jobs in the defense industry. Finally, the expanding role of both the local and federal government generated relatively high-paying white collar jobs (Duboff, 1989). As a result, labor markets were relatively tight during this period with unemployment averaging between 4 to 7 percent.

Race relations improved considerably during this period, as

Table 1. Occupational Distribution of Chinese, Japanese, and Filipinos Compared to All U.S. Workers - 1940

Occupation	All U.S.	Chinese	Japanese	Filipino
Men				
Professional & Technical	6%	2%	4%	1%
Managerial, Official, & Proprietor	10%	21%	13%	-
Sales & Clerical	13%	10%	9%	2%
Craft	15%	1%	3%	2%
Operative	18%	22%	7%	6%
Service	6%	31%	7%	22%
Private Household	-	6%	5%	6%
Farmers & Farm Managers	15%	1%	21%	5%
Farm Laborer	8%	3%	27%	49%
Laborer	9%	2%	6%	7%
Not reported	1%	1%	1%	1%
Women				
Professional & Technical	13%	8%	3%	
Managerial, Official, & Proprietor	4%	9%	5%	
Sales & Clerical	28%	26%	20%	
Craft	1%	-	-	
Operative	18%	26%	9%	
Service	11%	19%	11%	
Private Household	18%	10%	19%	
Farmers & Farm Managers	1%	-	2%	
Farm Laborer	3%	1%	28%	
Laborer	1%	1%	2%	
Not reported	2%	1%	-	

Source: U.S. Bureau of Census, 1940 1% Public Use Microdata Sample.

is usual during boom periods. With plentiful jobs, legal restrictions based on race became less acceptable, although informal sanctions remained. As evidence of this change, Roosevelt ended employment discrimination in the federal government with the signing of Executive Order 8802 in 1941. By the 1950s, the Civil Rights Movement had begun formal challenges to the pattern of racial segregation in schools, politics, and society in general that had been instituted since slavery. The easing of tensions between organized labor and management in the post-war period also meant that race was less likely to emerge as a political issue. Moreover, the emergence of the United States as a leader in the world economy meant that the U.S. could no longer formally pursue racial segregation as a state policy in order to remain credible as a world leader to the non-European nations (Ong and Liu, 1993).

As a result of the changes in race relations and the strength of the U.S. economy, Asian Pacific American workers, particularly the U.S.-born, were able to expand their occupational choices in the post-war period. Income differences between Asian Pacific Americans and non-Hispanic whites narrowed. These same factors affected all racial minorities in the United States, as African Americans were also able to narrow the differential in incomes (Smith and Welch, 1989).

The war had an immediate and severe economic impact on Japanese Americans via the internment. The internment hastened the end of a concentration in the ethnic niches of agriculture and small businesses. Although these niches still provided employment in 1950, occupational diversification of Japanese Americans occurred in the wake of the internment. Two additional reasons account for the increasing occupational diversification of Japanese Americans in the post-war period. First, more of the Nisei (the second generation) came of age after the war and were finally able to use their American educations as overt racial discrimination lessened. Second, the post-war job expansion created opportunities in engineering, medical, and white collar sales and clerical occupations for both men and women (see Table 2).

Although the post-war expansion allowed Japanese Americans access to a broader range of occupations, they were not able to fully participate in all areas of the labor market. For example, higher-paying blue collar manufacturing jobs and

Table 2. Occupational Distribution of Chinese, Japanese, and Filipinos Compared to All U.S. Workers - 1960

Occupation	All U.S.	Chinese	Japanese	Filipino
Men				
Professional & Technical	10%	18%	14%	8%
Managerial, Official, & Proprietor	11%	16%	10%	2%
Sales & Clerical	14%	4%	15%	6%
Craft	20%	7%	17%	10%
Operative	20%	16%	10%	16%
Service	6%	23%	6%	22%
Private Household	-	1%	1%	1%
Farmers & Farm Managers	6%	1%	11%	11%
Farm Laborer	3%	-	8%	22%
Laborer	7%	2%	9%	11%
Not reported	5%	7%	-	-
Women				
Professional & Technical	13%	17%	11%	16%
Managerial, Official, & Proprietor	4%	6%	3%	1%
Sales & Clerical	38%	38%	36%	33%
Craft	1%	1%	1%	2%
Operative	15%	21%	20%	19%
Service	13%	9%	13%	18%
Private Household	8%	2%	8%	3%
Farmers & Farm Managers	1%	-	2%	-
Farm Laborer	1%	-	5%	8%
Laborer	1%	-	-	-
Not reported	6%	6%	-	-

Source: U.S. Bureau of Census, 1960 1% Public Use Microdata Sample.

construction jobs were generally not available. Moreover, earnings for Japanese continued to lag behind whites. Daniels (1988) cites a 1965 California Fair Employment Practices Commission report which found that Japanese males received only $43 for every $51 made by white males.

The second generation Chinese Americans also moved away from the traditional pre-war occupations, although at a slower pace. Without the shock of the internment, a greater number of Chinese ethnic businesses survived through the war with less disruption. The survival of these ethnic enterprises meant the continuation of employment in restaurant services and in low-paying garment work for the aging immigrants. However, substantial numbers of American-born men and women in-creased their employment in professional and technical occupations, again concentrating in engineering and medical fields. Like the Japanese, Chinese Americans were denied ac-cess to higher-paying manufacturing and craft jobs. And like the Japanese, Chinese American earnings lagged behind that of whites in 1960.

As few Filipinas immigrated prior to the war, there was not a significant number of American-born Filipino workers entering the post-war labor market. Some immigrant Filipino workers did leave farm work as a result of the economic expansion, but most remained in low-paying service or manufacturing occupations. These included jobs in restaurants and food processing. Still, by 1960, almost a third of Filipino workers were employed in agriculture compared to just 9 percent of the overall U.S. population.

Japanese and Chinese American women entered the labor force in larger numbers during the post-war period. Although the post-war period is marked by the increasing labor force participation of all U.S. women, Chinese and Japanese women entered the labor force in even greater numbers. In 1940, approximately 32 percent of all Japanese American women between the ages of 14 and 65 were in the labor force. By 1960, the percentage of Japanese American women had increased to 47 percent. For Chinese American women, the comparable figures are 24 percent and 42 percent. By comparison, only 34 percent of all U.S. women were in the labor force.

By the end of this second period, the segregation of Asian

Americans in the labor market had diminished. Legal restrictions against Asian Pacific Americans were falling due to the relatively affluent times and the growing Civil Rights Movement. American-born Chinese and Japanese were able to find employment within the growing professional and technical occupations. However, the American-born did not fully benefit from the growth of high-paying craft and manufacturing jobs as these jobs were still not available. Although the differential in earnings had narrowed, Asian American earnings still lagged behind white incomes. The immigrant Japanese, Chinese, and Filipinos largely remained employed in the occupational niches from the first period, although there was some diversification into low-paying service occupations.

New Immigrants and Civil Rights: The Post-1965 Period

The passage of the 1965 Immigration Act marked a turning point in U.S. immigration policy by ending the 1924 National Origins Act that had effectively curtailed Asian immigration to the U.S. for the preceding decades. The 1965 Act established new quotas of 20,000 immigrants per year and provisions for non-quota immigrants, and instituted a preference system for immigrants which determined who could emigrate to the United States. These preference categories emphasized family reunification and immigrants with special job skills. The 1965 Immigration Act, plus the subsequent refugee acts in 1975 and 1980, allowed for renewed large-scale immigration of Filipinos, Koreans, Chinese, and Southeast Asians to the United States. In the period from 1971 to 1990, approximately 855,500 Filipinos, 610,800 Koreans, 576,100 Chinese, and 581,100 Vietnamese entered the United States (*Statistical Abstract of the United States*, 1992).

These new immigrants entered a U.S. labor market that, while still growing, encountered difficulties by the end of the 1960s. The post-war dominance of the U.S. economy in the world economy had eroded, adversely affecting the domestic labor market. For example, unemployment increased from an annual average of 4.8 percent in the 1960s to 7.3 percent in the 1980s. Real wage growth also decreased dramatically, falling from an annual average increase of 1.7 percent in the decade from 1955 to 1965 to an annual decrease of -0.1 percent during the 1975 to 1985 decade.

Structural change in occupations altered the labor market in this period with the number of high-paying manufacturing jobs decreasing and the number of lower-paying service jobs increasing (see, for example, Eitzen and Zinn, 1989). The U.S. share of total world manufacturing declined from 29 percent in 1953 to 13 percent in 1976. U.S. productivity slowed considerably with productivity increasing by only 12 percent from 1967 to 1978, compared to Japan's 95 percent increase and West Germany's 55 percent increase, making U.S. products less competitive in world markets. These factors meant a continual weakening of the manufacturing sector in the United States that had provided the bulk of high-paying semi-skilled jobs in the post-war expansion.

Race relations in the United States were transformed during this period. The Civil Rights Movement worked to end *de jure* segregation in the United States, as well as *de facto* segregation. Not only did the Civil Rights Movement ask for the end of state supported racial segregation, it made claims to the state to remedy the entire history of racial discrimination. Affirmative action programs, political redistricting, community action and urban renewal programs were instituted in response to these new demands for state remedies. Instead of a homogeneous American society, the "politics of difference" moved to redefine the meaning of race in American society (Omi and Winant, 1983).

Recent Filipino immigration to the United States was largely influenced by U.S. immigration laws which gave preference to immigrants with professional and technical skills (Pido, 1986). As a result, recent Filipino immigrants have higher levels of education then previous Filipino immigrants. Over one in five Filipinas have professional occupations, primarily in the health care field. Filipino men are also heavily employed in professional and technical occupations (Pido, 1986). However, not all Filipinos are employed in higher paying occupations. Due to the family reunification preferences, many Filipinos follow the purely economic immigrants. Many of these immigrants are concentrated in low-paying service occupations (see Table 3).

Immigration laws have also shaped the pattern of Korean immigration. Although there is controversy over the degree to which the professional preference category selected Korean immigrants with higher skill levels (Baringer and Cho, 1989), we find significant numbers of Koreans in the higher-paying professional occupations in 1980 and today, particularly among men. Like the Filipinos, large number of recent Korean immigrants are also employed as low-paid service and garment workers.

Korean immigrants demonstrate a significant amount of self-employment in ethnic enterprises. Many of these ethnic

Table 3. Occupational Distribution, Selected Asian Americans Compared to All U.S. Workers - 1990

Occupation	All	Chinese	Japanese	Filipino	Koreans	Vietnamese
Men						
Managerial	13%	15%	20%	10%	15%	5%
Professional	12%	24%	20%	12%	16%	13%
Technical, Sales	15%	18%	17%	15%	29%	18%
Admin Support	7%	8%	9%	16%	6%	8%
Service	10%	19%	9%	16%	10%	12%
Fish, Forest	4%	<1%	4%	2%	1%	2%
Prod,craft	19%	8%	12%	12%	12%	19%
Operators	20%	9%	8%	15%	12%	22%
Women						
Managerial	11%	15%	14%	10%	9%	7%
Professional	17%	17%	19%	20%	11%	9%
Technical, Sales	16%	17%	16%	16%	25%	17%
Admin Support	28%	21%	28%	25%	14%	18%
Service	17%	14%	14%	17%	20%	19%
Fish, Forest	1%	<1%	1%	1%	<1%	<1%
Prod,craft	2%	3%	3%	3%	6%	10%
Operators	8%	13%	5%	7%	14%	20%

Source: U.S. Bureau of Census, *Asian and Pacific Islanders in the United States 1990*, CP-3-5, August 1993.

enterprises are the result of limited job alternatives available for high-skill immigrants. In 1982, there were over 31,000 Korean businesses with combined sales of $2.7 billion dollars (U.S. Bureau of the Census, *Survey of Minority-Owned Business Enterprises*, 1986). The majority of these firms were small retail establishments, restaurants, or providers of personal services.

The impact of these ethnic enterprises on Asian immigrant earnings, particularly among Chinese, Koreans, and Vietnamese, is often debated. For example, Portes and Bach (1987) and Zhou and Logan (1989) argue that ethnic enterprises reduce unemployment among new immigrants as well as provide a path of economic mobility for immigrant entrepreneurs. Sanders and Nee (1985) and Mar (1991) argue that ethnic enterprises do provide jobs for immigrant workers, but at extremely low wages with little mobility via future self-employment for workers in the ethnic economy.

Recent Chinese immigration resembles the Korean pattern with large percentages of both highly-skilled and relatively low-skilled immigrants (see Table 3). Ethnic enterprises have also increased among the Chinese with almost 52,000 firms and receipts of six billion dollars in 1982. Again, like the Koreans, large numbers of recent Chinese immigrants are concentrated in lower paying service and manufacturing jobs.

The general involuntary nature of Vietnamese immigration to the United States has severely affected their labor market experience. Borjas (1990) argues that involuntary immigrants are usually significantly worse off in the labor market due to lack of preparation, savings, and other factors. Vietnamese occupations are largely concentrated in the lower paying service and manufacturing occupations. The Vietnamese have also made significant entries into ethnic enterprises, although these businesses are generally smaller in scale and concentrated in food and personal services.

In contrast to earlier immigration patterns of predominantly males, recent immigration includes equal numbers of women. Due to lower spousal earnings, the majority of recent immigrant women have entered the labor force. In 1980, for married immigrant women between the ages of 25 and 64 years of age, 61 percent of Korean women, 65 percent of Chinese women, and 83 percent of Filipino women were in the labor force (Duleep and Sanders, 1993).

Although American-born Asians have made substantial progress in earnings, the degree of economic parity achieved by Asian Americans is still controversial. Numerous studies demonstrate that earnings problems still exist for most American-born Asians. Studies by Duleep and Sanders (1992) and Cabezas and Kawaguchi (1988) argue that due to regional location, different rates of returns to education, and different occupations of employment, even Japanese and Chinese Americans have not achieved earnings parity with non-Hispanic whites. Moreover, these studies argue that Asian Americans have particular difficulties in obtaining managerial and executive positions. Other studies (Hirschman and Wong, 1984; Chiswick, 1983) argue that American-born Japanese and Chinese have achieved parity with non-Hispanic whites. However, most studies show that post-1965 immigrants are still experiencing earnings discrimination in the labor market. Finally, many of the recent immigrant groups have a high incidence of poverty. Ong and Hee in Chapter 3 find that 46 percent of Southeast Asian, 25 percent of Vietnamese, 15 percent of Korean, and 14 percent of Chinese households fell below the poverty line in 1990.

The passage of the 1965 Immigration Act was clearly a watershed for Asian Pacific American labor in the United States. Immigration vastly increased the numbers of Asians as well as allowing immigrants from other Asian countries into the U.S. These immigrant workers joined the American-born in a labor market undergoing a sweeping transformation due to structural change and the decline of the U.S. in the world economy. In addition, the Civil Rights Movement entered a new phase, seeking remedies from the government for past injustices. This change in race relations completed the removal of the legal restrictions to Asian Pacific workers in the labor market.

Future Prospects

Our discussion of the future prospects of Asian Pacific Americans in the labor market is based on many of the same factors that shaped their earlier experience. We focus our discussion on the impact of the U.S. economy, immigration policy, demographic changes in the Asian Pacific workforce, and race relations.

We assume that the U.S. economy will continue to experience structural change in the labor market. High-paying jobs in the future will require increasingly higher skill and education levels. At the same time, the economy will generate low-paying service jobs filled by low-skilled workers. For example, the Bureau of Labor Statistics estimates that the occupations with the highest projected job growth in 2005 will be either high-skilled jobs, such as systems analysts, computer scientists, health care professionals and technicians, or semi-skilled, low-paying service jobs, such as home health aides, home care workers, medical secretaries, human service workers, and child care workers (U.S. Bureau of the Census, *Statistical Abstract*, 1992). The relatively high-paying, semi-skilled jobs that were important to the U.S. economy during the golden age of the 1950s and 1960s will continue to disappear. Increasing worldwide competition means that workers will have to be flexible in retraining for different jobs over their career lifetime. Finally, the slower growth of the U.S. economy over the next decade will likely affect race relations policy as well as immigration policy in the United States as less attention and resources will be directed towards racial equity programs.

We also assume immigration to the United States from Asia will largely continue as described previously. Although there is increasing political pressure to limit future immigration to the U.S., there has been no political mandate to change immigration laws. This means that the preference categories favoring high-skill occupations and family reunification will continue to shape who comes into the United States. Highly-educated, highly-skilled immigrants are likely to continue to do well in the future U.S. economy. However, low-skilled workers rejoining families, as well as Asian Pacific refugees, will face increasing difficulty in the labor market as the economy produces less high-paying, semi-skilled occupations. Anti-poverty programs will therefore be of increasing importance to these immigrant workers as they face more unemployment and lower wages. In addition, given the continued importance of ethnic enterprises among recent immigrants, programs to assist small minority businesses diversifying out of low-wage industries will be important.

Even if immigration laws change to limit future Asian immigration, the previous cohort of Asian Pacific immigrants will give birth to a second generation of American-born. By most accounts, this American-born generation is likely to continue to achieve high levels of educational attainment (Ong and Hee, 1993a). As a result, they are likely to fare well in the future labor market. However, this generation of American-born will face difficulties different from the earlier American-born generation. One, they enter a much more competitive labor market when the U.S. economy is no longer dominant in the world economy. Two, the fiscal crises of the federal and state governments have decreased financial assistance to all levels of education, but particularly for higher education. Three, the current retrenchment in affirmative action programs allows the continuation of employment difficulties for Asian Pacific Americans in obtaining managerial and executive positions. The economic "success" of this American-born generation is not guaranteed.

Future race relations are likely to be fluid. Although American race relations are unlikely to return to anything resembling race relations prior to the Civil Rights era, there is increasing conflict over race in the United States as the "politics of difference" continues to be waged. The economic slowdown and dislocation have contributed to a resurgence of violence against Asian Pacific Americans as well as growing hostility towards Civil Rights programs such as affirmative action, equal employment opportunity, and community economic development.

Asian Pacific Americans will become a critical part of the future U.S. workforce. Projections by Ong and Hee (1993a) estimate that the Asian Pacific American workforce will grow from 3.2 million in 1990 (2.5 percent of the workforce) to perhaps 10.2 million by 2020, tripling the number of Asian Pacific Americans in the workforce over the next three decades. As it is unlikely that the entire U.S. workforce will grow by 300 percent, Asian Pacific Americans will have a growing impact on the future U.S. labor market.

We have argued that the labor market experience of Asians in America has been impacted by formal sanctions, informal sanctions, and the U.S. economy. The early, pre-World War II experience of Asians was largely constrained by immigration laws, state and local restrictions on economic activities, and informal sanctions in the context of an industrializing economy. After World War II, American-born Asians faced a lessening of these institutional restrictions. Prime working-age American-born Chinese and Japanese entered the labor force at a time termed by many economists as the "Golden Age" of the U.S. economy where American economic power was predominant in the world market place and when high-paying jobs were relatively plentiful. As such, the American-born were able to considerably narrow the gap with non-Hispanic whites in terms of occupational differences and earnings.

The 1965 Immigration Act ushered in a new period of Asian immigration. The Immigration Act dictated preference categories for immigrants that emphasized family reunification and professional and technical occupations. As a result, the skills and social composition of immigrants are markedly different from the earlier period. On one hand, among many immigrants, there exists a group of highly-educated professional workers. On the other hand, immigrants rejoining family members in the United States do not necessarily have the same level of skills and training. As these new immigrants enter the labor market when the U.S. economy is no longer dominant and is experiencing structural change, their economic opportunities are constrained to low-paying service and manufacturing jobs. Studies also suggest that discrimination still persists.

We believe that the future labor market experience of both new immigrants and the American-born continues to be shaped by race relations, immigration legislation, and the restructuring of the U.S. economy. Policy surrounding immigration, race relations, poverty, small business development, and education must be developed within these confines as Asian Pacific Americans play a greater role in the future workforce.

Chapter 3

Economic Diversity

Paul Ong and Suzanne J. Hee

It is impossible to distill the economic status of Asian Pacific Americans into a single statistic. The prevailing and pervasive stereotype is one of a "model minority," which depicts the population as having successfully overcome numerous obstacles. There is no question that relative to other minority populations and even to the dominant population, Asian Pacific Americans have experienced a noticeable degree of economic success as indicated by measures such as average household or family income. While these indices in their simplest form overstate the relative economic position of Asian Pacific Americans, this population nonetheless has experienced a remarkable degree of economic success. This "success" is rooted in a pattern of selective immigration that has attracted some of the most highly-educated and economically mobile from Asia.

Despite the accomplishments as measured by aggregate numbers, Asian Pacific Americans are not free from poverty and other economic problems. Diversity within the population has meant sizeable affluent and impoverished segments, the "haves" and "have nots." In many ways, this population has experienced the increasing income polarization that has afflicted this nation,[1] which is driven by disparate outcomes in labor-market status and earnings. For convenience, we divided the population into three categories: the highly-educated, the disadvantaged, and the entrepreneurs. These are not mutually exclusive categories nor are they exhaustive, but they represent perhaps the most important groupings.

The economic diversity among Asian Pacific American workers and entrepreneurs is the product of both immigration and a changing structure of opportunity. The 1965 Immigration Act and a restructuring of the economy brought a large number of Asians, from low-skilled to highly-educated, to this country, creating a bimodalism. Many of those with extensive education have filled the high-wage professional ranks, while those with less skills have filled the low-wage menial positions. For some, operating a business has provided a means to make a livelihood. Restaurants, groceries, gardening, and laundries are still very much a part of Asian-owned businesses, but the range of activities along with financial rewards are much more diverse today.

Our discussion of the economic status of Asian Pacific Americans is organized into four sections: the overall income levels and distribution, the highly-educated, the disadvantaged, and the entrepreneurs.

Overall Income Levels and Distributions

One broad and widely used measure of economic status is the average income, and this measure for households and families shows that Asian Pacific Americans are doing well. While identical statistics are not readily available for every decade, existing statistics reveal a consistent picture of Asian Pacific Americans faring the same as or better than whites, which we can take initially as the standard for comparison. According to the 1970 Census, the median[2] family income of whites was approximately $10,000 compared to $10,600 for Chinese, $12,500 for Japanese, and $9,300 for Filipinos (U.S. Bureau of the Census, 1973). In 1980, the median family income for Asian Pacific Americans was $22,700, higher than that of whites at $20,800.[3] A decade later, the difference was greater, both in absolute and relative terms. The 1992 Current Population Survey shows a similar difference in terms of median family income: $40,350 for Asian Pacific Americans and $35,975 for whites (1992, p. 66).

Mainstream media has used these averages to paint an image of a "model minority." Starting in the 1960s, Asian Pacific Americans have been depicted as a "model minority," the non-white group that has "made it" in American society through hard work, dedication, and strong family networks. For example, the December 1966 issue of U.S. News and World Report stated that "the nation's 300,000 Chinese Americans is winning wealth and respect by dint of its own hard work" (p. 1). This image of relative affluence was restated in 1982 by Newsweek, which stated "despite years of discrimination — much of it enforced by the federal government — the difficulties of acculturation and a recent backlash against their burgeoning numbers, Asian Americans now enjoy the nation's highest median income" (Kasindorf, p. 39).

More recently, *Commentary* reported that "according to most socioeconomic indicators — income, labor force participation, education, occupational status, family stability and structure — Asian-Americans were now the equals of, or had surpassed, mainstream America" (Winnick, 1990, p. 24). Another report states "like immigrating Jews of earlier generations, they have parlayed cultural emphases on education and hard work into brilliant attainments" (Walsh, 1993, p. 55). Of course, the "model minority" thesis is based on more than just economic status, but nonetheless economic status is one of the most important, if not single most important, point.

A simple comparison of average household income, however, does not account for a number of factors that lead to an overestimate of the overall economic standing of Asian Pacific Americans. Because of the method used by the Census to collect information, the racial category "white" contains Latinos, whose population has grown tremendously over the last few decades. A far better bench mark is the non-Hispanic white (NH-white) population. Because Latinos who are classified as whites fare worse economically than NH-whites, income statistics for whites tend to be lower than that for NH-whites. This discrepancy has grown over time, and is particularly sizeable in geographic areas with large Latino populations.[4]

The national statistics cited are also misleading because they compare populations that are not identically distributed across geographic regions. Asian Pacific Americans are highly concentrated in large metropolitan areas where the cost of living tends to be higher; consequently, it takes more income to maintain a comparable standard of living in these areas. Our market economy operates in such a fashion that the higher cost is partially compensated by higher wages.

Table 1 shows the economic status of Asian Pacific Americans relative to NH-whites and other minority groups, nationally and for the four metropolitan areas with the largest Asian Pacific American populations (Los Angeles, San Francisco,

Oakland, and New York, which together house approximately 30 percent of all Asian Pacific Americans). While the estimated median household income for Asian Pacific Americans at the national level is higher than NH-whites ($36,000 versus $31,000), the opposite is true for the combined four metropolitan areas ($37,200 versus $40,000).

Even the comparison with NH-white households in the four metropolitan areas overstates the relative economic position of Asian Pacific Americans, who tend to have larger households and whose income does not go as far on a per person basis; consequently, median per person income at a national level for

Table 1. Income and Poverty Levels – 1990

	NH-white	Asian Pacific American	African American	Latino
National				
Median Income	$31,100	$36,000	$19,000	$24,000
Median Per Person	$12,000	$10,500	$6,600	$6,200
% above $75,000	10%	16%	3%	5%
% below $10,000	13%	14%	30%	20%
Poverty Rate	9%	14%	29%	25%
4 Metro Areas				
Median Income	$40,000	$37,200	$24,100	$25,600
Median Per Person	$17,600	$10,800	$8,600	$6,300
% above $75,000	20%	16%	6%	6%
% below $10,000	11%	13%	25%	19%
Poverty Rate	7%	13%	22%	24%

Source: Estimates based on observations drawn from the U.S. Bureau of the Census, 1990 1% Public Use Microdata Sample. NH-whites were sampled at a rate of 1 in 10, and African Americans and Latinos were sampled at a rate of 1 in 2.

Asian Pacific Americans is lower than that for NH-whites ($10,500 versus $12,000). For the four metropolitan areas, the difference is even larger — $17,600 for NH-whites and $10,800 for Asian Pacific Americans. While Asian Pacific Americans still have higher per capita income than blacks and Latinos, their earnings are closer to other minority groups than to NH-whites. The lower per capita income of Asian Pacific Americans cannot be explained merely as a choice to have larger families, although it is true that Asian Pacific families tend to be larger than NH-white families. The larger number per household also represents efforts to pool limited resources. Many households have multiple wage earners because the earnings of each tends to be limited.

Average income statistics give a partial picture, but they mask very important differences among Asian Pacific Americans. For every Asian Pacific American household with an annual income of $75,000 or more, there is roughly another with an annual income below $10,000. While the proportion of Asian Pacific American households that can be classified as low-income is of the same magnitude as the proportion of NH-white households, the percentage of Asian Pacific Americans that can be classified as being impoverished is substantially higher. The most widely used measure of impoverishment is the poverty line, roughly three times the cost of the economy food plan, which is the minimum needed for adequate nutrition. The poverty line varies by family size and composition, but not by geographic region. For a family of four, the average poverty line was $12,674 in 1989, with the number being slightly lower for units with more children than adults. Using the official poverty line, 14 percent of the Asian Pacific American population lived in households with an income below the poverty line in 1989, about one-and-a-half times higher than the rate for NH-whites. The difference is even greater in the four metropolitan areas, where the Asian Pacific American rate is approximately twice as high that for NH-whites.

Median household incomes vary across ethnic and native lines within the Asian Pacific American population. As Table 2 shows, Filipinos and Asian Indians have the highest median household income, both at approximately $43,000 each. In addition, Asian Indians have a fifth of their households with incomes of $75,000 and above, which is the highest among all Asian Pacific ethnic groups. On the low end of the income distribution are Southeast Asians with a median household income of $18,300. Not surprisingly, they also have the highest percentage of Asian Pacific American households with incomes below $10,000 and the highest rate of persons living below poverty, 26 percent and 46

Table 2. Household Income and Poverty Levels
by Ethnicity and Year of Immigration – 1990

	Median Income	% Income <$10,000	% Income >$75,000	Below Poverty*
Ethnicity				
Chinese	$37,600	15%	19%	14%
Filipino	$43,300	6%	18%	7%
Japanese	$42,800	9%	19%	7%
Asian Indian	$43,000	8%	22%	10%
Korean	$30,600	17%	11%	15%
Vietnamese	$31,300	16%	11%	25%
SE Asian	$18,300	26%	4%	46%
Other Asian	$32,000	15%	12%	17%
Pac. Islander	$32,900	13%	10%	20%
Year of Immigration				
US-Born	$43,000	9%	19%	11%
1985 to 1990	$23,000	25%	7%	26%
1980 to 1984	$32,000	13%	11%	17%
1975 to 1979	$41,100	9%	16%	11%
1970 to 1974	$46,000	7%	23%	7%
1965 to 1969	$54,000	5%	28%	5%
Pre 1965	$44,000	10%	21%	7%

* Poverty rate is based on the proportion of the population that resides in a family with an income below the official poverty line.

Source: Compiled by authors from 1990 1% Public Use Microdata Sample.

percent, respectively.

Household income also varies according to place of birth and year of immigration to the United States. Asian Pacific Americans who entered between the years of 1965 and 1969 have the highest household income at $54,000, and the highest percentage, 28 percent, of households with incomes of $75,000 and above. More recent immigrants, those who entered between 1985 and 1990, have the lowest median income ($23,000), the highest percentage of households with incomes below $10,000 (25 percent) and the highest number of persons living below the poverty line (26 percent).

To understand the diversity in income, it is necessary to examine how Asian Pacific Americans are performing in the U.S. economy as workers and entrepreneurs. The next section begins this analysis by examining the highly-educated population.

The Highly-Educated

One factor for the proportionately large numbers of Asian Pacific American households with above average incomes is the relatively large number of highly-educated persons. According to the 1990 Census, 37 percent of all Asian Pacific Americans 25 years of age and over had at least a bachelor's degree, and 14 percent had a graduate or professional degree. This is considerably higher than the figures for NH-whites (22 percent and 8 percent, respectively). This high level of educational attainment translates into a population of highly-educated working-age Asian Pacific Americans (24 to 64) of 1.5 million persons, of which 63 percent had only a bachelor's degree, 31 percent had a master's or professional degree, and 6 percent had a doctorate degree. Because of the high employment rates, this highly-educated group constitutes a labor force of 1.3 million workers.

Understanding the source of this highly-educated population is important to examining the accomplishments of Asian Pacific students. One is tempted to point to the high educational achievement among Asian Pacific American students. They are portrayed by the popular media as super students surging to the top of their class. The statistics on school enrollment rates support this image. Compared to other groups, they are more likely to pursue an undergraduate education as indicated by enrollment rates among those 20 to 21 years of age: 71 percent are enrolled as compared to 42 percent for the total population. Asian Pacific Americans are also more likely to pursue a graduate degree. For those between the ages of 22 and 24, 51 percent of Asian Pacific American and 20 percent of the total population are enrolled. While these statistics include foreign students, it is important to note that roughly two-thirds of those attending school are either U.S.-born or immigrants who were raised in the U.S. Asian Pacific American students are disproportionately overrepresented in the elite public and private universities. For example, they comprise approximately 30 percent of the undergraduates at the University of California, Berkeley, and 34 percent at UCLA. Although the percentages are lower in the private universities, Asian Pacific American students nonetheless have a strong presence. At Harvard and Stanford, they comprise 20 and 22 percent of the undergraduate student population, respectively.

Despite the high numbers attending colleges and universities, the U.S.-born or U.S.-raised do not account for the majority of the highly-educated Asian Pacific American adult population. A far more important source of this highly-educated population is immigration. The 1965 Immigration Act created occupational preferences for highly-skilled workers, which usually meant the highly-educated, particularly those in the engineering and scientific fields, and in the health fields, such as doctors, nurses, and health technicians. (Chapters 7 and 8 provide more details on these immigrants.) While the number of Asians entering through the labor categories accounts for only a small share of total immigration, initial occupational migration set into motion a new chain migration that favors the highly-educated even among those entering through the family reunification provisions (Liu, Ong, and Rosenstein, 1991).

Of course, the 1965 Immigration Act is a necessary but not sufficient factor for the extensive migration of the highly-educated. Forces within the sending country have played a major role. In the case of India, for example, an economic slowdown, the lack of access to domestic higher education, and the inability of that country to fully employ its highly trained labor force all have contributed to the emigration of skilled professionals to the United States (Mazumdar, 1993). To varying degrees, these factors have been present in other Asian Pacific countries. As a result, most of these countries experienced a "brain drain," where many of their most talented individuals emigrated to the United States seeking better economic opportunity (Ong, Cheng, and Evans, 1993). Some of the highly-educated came with their college and university degrees in hand. We estimate that roughly half of those with only a bachelor's or with a master's or professional degree fall into this category, while only about a quarter of those with a doctorate do.[5] However, there are also large numbers who initially came as foreign students in higher education, and then adjusted to status as permanent immigrants. While probably only a small fraction of those with only a bachelor's degree and about a quarter of those with a master's or professional degree chose this route, as many as half with a doctorate degree did. When taken together, the foreign-educated and immigrants who started as foreign students constitute about two-thirds to three-quarters of the highly-educated Asian Pacific American population. In other words, selective post-1965 immigration is the primary factor in creating the highly-educated Asian Pacific American group.

The post-1965 immigration of the highly-educated also had indirect effects in expanding the highly-educated population. Immigrant parents with college or university degrees are likely to instill in their children the desire and drive to be academically successful. Moreover, their influence is likely to extend beyond the immediate family, for their presence and prestige provide a model and standard for families where the parents are less well educated. The highly-educated reinforces and validates those norms and values that promote schooling.

College and university training opens the door to participation in the U.S. economy. The labor force participation rate of highly-educated adults is 84 percent.[6] Their civilian unemployment rate[7] is 3 percent, which is essentially frictional unemployment,[8] and two-thirds of the labor force works full-time, full-year. Table 3 provides additional statistics by educational attainment and gender.[9]

Although the level of economic activity of highly-educated Asian Pacific Americans is high, they do not always receive salaries that are commensurate with their level of education. At a national level for 1990, Asian Pacific American adult males

Table 3. Asian Pacific American Educational Attainment – 1990

	Bachelor's Degree	MA/Prof Degree	Doctoral Degree
Male			
Number	457,800	299,100	69,800
% Recent Imm.	24%	26%	18%
% Employed	87%	88%	94%
% FT/FY* among the empl.	64%	62%	70%
Unempl. Rate	3%	2%	1%
Earnings of FT/FY*			
Median	$33,000	$45,700	$50,000
% >50K	22%	45%	53%
Earnings of All			
Median	$29,900	$40,000	$45,000
% >50K	18%	37%	44%
Female			
Number	519,600	185,600	16,100
% Recent Imm.	24%	22%	25%
% Employed	73%	76%	83%
% FT/FY* among the empl.	43%	42%	56%
Unempl. Rate	3%	4%	4%
Earnings of FT/FY*			
Median	$27,000	$35,000	$34,400
% >50K	7%	24%	23%
Earnings of All			
Median	$22,100	$27,000	$33,000
% >50K	5%	17%	18%

* Full-Time/Full-Year Worker

Source: Compiled by authors from 1990 1% Public Use Microdata Sample.

who work full-time, full-year, earn about 10 percent less than white males, and for the West, the difference is 12 percent (U.S. Bureau of the Census, 1992, P20-459, Table 5). This may understate the difference because Asian Pacific Americans are more likely to have a graduate degree than whites. While there is essentially no difference between highly-educated Asian Pacific American females and their white counterparts, both suffer from a gender gap, earning about 70 percent of income of white males.

The gender difference can be seen in the figures in Table 3. While both sexes have comparable and relatively low rates of unemployment, there is a large gap in median income for each level of education. Males with a doctoral degree earn a median income of $50,000, whereas the median income for females is merely $34,400. In addition, the percentage of males with the higher degree who earn $50,000 and above is 53; the percentage for females is 23. Furthermore, there tends to be a higher percentage of males (31 percent) in the professional and managerial class than that of females (24 percent).

Along with the variations in earnings, there are substantial occupational differences. While the proportion of the highly-educated in professional occupations is roughly the same for Asian Pacific American males and white males (38 percent and 36 percent, respectively), whites are considerably more likely to hold a job as an executive, administrator, or manager (31 percent versus 23 percent) (U.S. Bureau of the Census, 1992, P20-459, Table 4). Among highly-educated females, 31 percent of Asian Pacific Americans were professionals compared to 48 percent for whites, and 19 percent of Asian Pacific Americans were in the managerial class compared to 23 percent for whites.

The discrepancy in earnings and occupational standings between Asian Pacific Americans and NH-whites is due to three factors: limited-English-speaking ability, lack of transferable skills into the U.S. labor market, and differential treatment based on race. Because a high percentage of the highly-educated received an education abroad, it is not surprising that only 71 percent are either native-English speakers or speak English very well. On the other hand, only 6 percent have a poor command of the English language (either do not speak English well or not at all). The language problem, then, is a hurdle rather than an absolute barrier; however, the hurdle can lower the odds of receiving a professional license and can limit promotions, particularly to managerial positions.

In many cases, the educational training received in their home country is not comparable to that in the United States. Asian Pacific immigrants may not be able to transfer their skills to the

U.S. labor market. In fields such as law and some of the social sciences, the knowledge is specific to each country. The demand for such knowledge is very limited in the United States, although greater economic integration with Pacific Rim countries may increase the demand in the future. As a result of the lack of transferability, this population suffers downward occupational mobility, taking relatively low-paying and low-skilled positions.

Finally, there is discriminatory treatment based on race. It is difficult to isolate the effects of race on employment outcomes from other factors such as English language ability, transferability of knowledge, and variations in the quality of education. One way is to use comparable populations, such as those receiving their undergraduate education in the United States.[10] One study which examines a group of 1983-84 BA/BS graduates and controls for several important factors (e.g., major, school attended, grades), found that Asian Pacific American males earned 10 percent less than white males, and Asian Pacific American females earned 11 to 12 percent less than white males.[11] The findings can be interpreted as discriminatory practice, although there may be other unobserved factors correlated with race that influence outcomes.

The limitations encountered by the highly-educated can be summarized by the term "glass ceiling," a promotional barrier against minorities and women. As we have seen, many Asian Pacific Americans, especially the post-1965 immigrants, have experienced "downward occupational mobility," which is in part responsible for their lower income. Despite their educational attainment, they occupy lower status, lower salary positions, most of which are in the technical fields. For others, there are barriers that hinder their progress into the higher ranks of the professional and managerial class.[12] Cracking this glass ceiling has been difficult due to the debates over affirmative action and employment policies. The cost of this barrier is not limited to the individuals for there is also a tremendous loss to the economy as a whole.

The Disadvantaged

Coexisting with the highly-educated is a sizeable population that is disadvantaged. Nationally, 23 percent of Asian Pacific Americans, age 25 and over, have less than a high school degree, while 21 percent of non-Hispanic whites do. For analysis, this disadvantaged population can be categorized into three groups according to deficiencies in human capital: those with limited English; those with limited education; and those limited by both language and education. Limited English is defined as speaking English not well or not well at all, and limited education is defined as having less than a high school degree. Nationally, there are over a million disadvantaged Asian Pacific American adults, and the size of the three categories is approximately equal.

Although figures show that Asian Pacific Americans have achieved greater levels of education than the general population, there is a large percent with minimal educational training. The difference is even greater in the four metropolitan regions: 24 percent of Asian Pacific Americans have low educational levels, compared to 15 percent for non-Hispanic whites. It is not only low-education attainment that serves as a disadvantage. Over two-thirds of a million adults are handicapped by not having a command of the English language.

As with the highly-educated population, the disadvantaged population is largely a product of immigration. Nine-tenths are immigrants, approximately two-thirds entered this country when they were adults (25 years and older),[13] and approximately one-third have been in the country five years or less. These percentages are higher than the corresponding percentages for the whole Asian Pacific American population. There is ethnic variation in the proportion of adults who are disadvantaged, with Southeast Asians having the highest percentage with less than a high school degree (64 percent) and with limited-English-speaking ability (55 percent). Although they comprise only a fifth of all disadvantaged Asian Pacific Americans, they are a population with unique problems. They came as political refugees who suffer from additional problems associated with their flight. Chapter 6 examines this group in detail.

The deficiencies in human capital greatly hinder economic opportunities. Compared to the highly-educated, the propor-tion of disadvantaged Asian Pacific American adults not in the labor force is over twice as high (37 percent versus 16 percent). Among those in the labor market, the civilian unemployment of disadvantaged adults is nearly three times higher (3 percent versus 8 percent). While a majority (54 percent) of all highly-educated Asian Pacific Americans work full-time/full-year, only a third (32 percent) of all disadvantaged do.

The jobs that disadvantaged workers take are largely limited to low-skill occupations. Among the disadvantaged labor force, 10 percent are in sales occupations, 8 percent are in clerical

Table 4. Profile of Disadvantaged
Asian Pacific Americans – 1990

	Limited English and Education	Limited English	Limited Education
Male			
Number	135,000	159,000	161,000
% Recent Imm.	36%	46%	19%
% Employed	64%	77%	76%
% FT/FY*	35%	46%	47%
Unempl. Rate	10%	4%	7%
Earnings of FT/FY*			
Median	$14,800	$20,000	$18,000
% <10K	21%	11%	12%
Earnings of All			
Median	$12,000	$17,000	$15,000
% <10K	38%	25%	25%
Female			
Number	232,000	196,000	231,000
% Recent Imm.	37%	47%	16%
% Employed	40%	47%	55%
% FT/FY*	19%	23%	31%
Unempl. Rate	11%	9%	8%
Earnings of FT/FY*			
Median	$12,000	$15,600	$15,000
% <10K	32%	20%	14%
Earnings of All			
Median	$9,000	$10,700	$12,000
% <10K	54%	43%	39%

* Full-Time/Full-Year Worker

Source: Compiled by authors from 1990 1% Public Use Microdata Sample.

occupations, 17 percent in restaurant-related occupations such as waiters and cooks, 5 percent are in the menial cleaning occupations (e.g., janitors), and 9 percent work as apparel machine operators. Although a few rise to managerial positions (6 percent), most of these jobs are in the retailing sector.

As Table 4 illustrates, the median income for those with limited English is $20,000 for males and $15,600 for females.[14] Similarly, figures are relatively low for males and females with less than a high school degree: $18,000 and $15,000, respectively. In contrast, persons with both limited-English-speaking ability and low levels of education suffer the most. For a disturbing portion of this population, even working full-time, full-year brings in less than $10,000 in earnings.

Joblessness and low wages are not merely the result of low skills. Macro-level changes have increasingly placed those with limited skills at a disadvantage. Increased global competition in manufacturing from developing and newly industrialized economies, including Asian Pacific countries, has pushed down real wages for industrial workers, and where there is increasing demand, it has meant low-wage service jobs. As labor markets have became less regulated due to decreasing union strength and state enforcement of working conditions, firms have incorporated more immigrants (legal and undocumented) as new sources of cheap labor. These changes have led to a real decline in wages in the 1980s of all workers with limited education and job skills (Murphy and Welch, 1993).

It is unknown how many disadvantaged Asian Pacific Americans are trapped at the bottom. Given that this population is primarily immigrant, and disproportionately recent immigrant, acculturation that occurs over time should improve their skills and understanding of the U.S. labor market. We certainly have examples of dramatic improvement within the first few years of living in the United States. Many newly-arrived immigrants are initially dependent on family and friends in finding work, which often translates into the worst jobs within an ethnically defined economy. Within a year or two, they become acquainted with a broader range of employment opportunities and the laws that protect workers, and acquire skills more appropriate to the U.S. economy. Unfortunately, there are limits to how much disadvantaged workers can improve their basic skills.

One indication of these limits is the lack of change in the disadvantaged Asian Pacific American population during the 1980s. In 1980, there were 243,000 immigrants between the ages of 25 and 54 who had less than a high school education, and ten years later, 229,000, or 93 percent of this group, still did not have at least a high school degree.[15] There was improvement in terms of English language proficiency. Of the 232,000 immigrants between the ages of 25 and 54 who did not speak English or spoke it poorly in 1980, only 73 percent fell into this category in 1990. While this drop does indicate that acculturation is occurring, the statistics also reveal that acculturation is very limited, certainly not enough to qualitatively improve the employment opportunities of most immigrants.

There are four factors that limit the opportunities of many Asian Pacific American immigrants.[16] One is the lack of time to learn new skills. Many of the disadvantaged are struggling to survive economically. Consequently, their time is constrained, and they have very little energy after putting in long hours of work and attending to household responsibilities. Second, there is a lack of programs available to these immigrants. Although many are constrained, even those who can find the time and energy often discover a limited number of effective programs. English-language and adult training programs are often oversubscribed, forcing applicants to wait, which could demoralize them. Even the programs that do exist are not always appropriate for Asian Pacific Americans. Third, there are structural barriers that devalue the type of improvements that can be reasonably made by the most disadvantaged. Many operate in an ethnically defined labor market that limits daily on-the-job contact with non-immigrants, which can be important in improving language and other skills. Finally, economic restructuring has raised the hurdles for the disadvantaged. As the returns to a high-school education decline, the economic incentive to acquire this level of education also decreases.

Despite their economic holdings, disadvantaged Asian Pacific Americans retain a value system that stresses schooling and education. Much like the highly-educated families, immigrants in the lower economic sector are likely to instill in their children the drive for academic success. However, while highly-educated parents build their influence upon a foundation of material and tangible wealth, the parents of disadvantaged families base their influence upon aspirations.

The Entrepreneurs

Along with average income and educational attainment, entrepreneurship has been depicted as a part of the Asian Pacific American success story. For some, self-employment serves as a way to circumvent the limitations of the labor market. Owning a business requires hard work and sacrifice — approximately 42 percent work 50 hours or more per week, and 26 percent work 60 or more hours per week. For some, the payoff is a considerable monetary return; however, for others, financial rewards are problematic. For every Asian Pacific American business person who makes a fortune, there are those who struggle daily to eke out a living.[17]

The number of Asian Pacific American-owned businesses has grown phenomenally, particularly compared to other minority groups (see Table 5). Asian Pacific American businesses grew nearly ten-fold between 1972 and 1987, far outpacing the growth of the Asian Pacific American population, which increased approximately five times from 1970 to 1990. By 1987, the number of Asian Pacific American businesses was rapidly approaching the number of Latino and African American businesses, and in terms of sales and employees, Asian Pacific-owned businesses fared better.

Despite the phenomenal growth, Asian Pacific Americans are not super entrepreneurs. A more careful examination of the data shows that the outcomes are mixed. The self-employment rate for Asian Pacific Americans is of the same magnitude as that for NH-whites, both at 11 percent in 1990.[18] Asian Pacific American firms accounted for 2.6 percent of all firms in 1987 but only 1.7 percent of all receipts (U.S. Bureau of the Census, 1991). This is due in large part to the smallness of Asian Pacific firms, which had an average receipt of less than $10,000 in 1987, approximately half the average receipt for businesses owned by non-minority males. Although smaller in size, the total earnings for self-employed Asian Pacific Americans as reported in the 1990 Census is $23,000, which is slightly higher than for NH-whites ($20,000). Further, 14 percent of Asian Pacific Americans

Table 5. Minority-Owned Businesses

Year	Asian Pacific American	Latino	African American
1972			
# of estab	33,114	120,108	194,986
sales (millions)	$2,533	$5,306	$7,168
employees (x1000)	68.7	149.7	196.6
1987			
# of estab	355,331	422,373	424,165
sales (millions)	$33,125	$24,732	$19,763
employees (x1000)	351.3	220.5	264.8
% growth			
# of estab	973%	252%	118%
sales	121%	366%	176%
employees	411%	47%	35%

Source: U.S. Bureau of the Census, *1987 Survey of Minority-Owned Business Enterprises*.

who are self-employed earned $75,000 and more, while only 12 percent of NH-whites fell into this income category. The relative numbers at the lower end of the scale are approximately the same. One-quarter of each group earned less than $30,000.

Table 6 shows that Asian Pacific Americans share some characteristics with other groups.[19] For example, a sizeable minority of all entrepreneurs had some exposure to the business world through relatives prior to owning their business, either by having a close relative who owned a business or was self-employed, or by having worked for such a relative. Like other groups, the vast majority of Asian Pacific Americans start small, with 53 percent requiring less than $10,000 in startup capital. When capital is needed Asian Pacific Americans, like others, use a combination of personal savings, personal loans, and commercial loans to raise the startup capital.

However, Asian Pacific Americans also have relied on family and ethnic ties to help raise funds, promote cooperation and

Table 6. Characteristics of Business Owners

	Asian Pacific American	Latino	African American	White Males
Have Entrepreneur Relative	35.3%	30.7%	27.8%	48.0%
Worked for Entrepreneur Relative	17.0%	12.1%	10.0%	23.7%
Required Startup Capital	81.6%	69.4%	69.5%	75.3%
Personal Loans for Startup*	8.5%	5.5%	5.4%	4.1%
Had Commercial Startup Loan	12.2%	8.7%	9.5%	16.0%
Borrowed from Relative(s)	12.3%	6.7%	3.3%	7.2%
Borrowed from Friend(s)	7.7%	2.5%	2.0%	1.7%
Borrowed from Prior Owner	3.9%	0.9%	0.6%	1.9%
Purchased Business	19.1%	9.9%	9.2%	15.4%
Sales to other firms	18.0%	17.0%	12.1%	25.0%

* Personal loans include loans from spouses, personal credit, and refinancing of homes.

Source: U.S. Bureau of the Census, *Characteristics of Business Owners*, 1992.

training between owners and workers, and facilitate transactions among firms of the same ethnicity (Light, 1972; Sowell, 1983; Waldinger, 1985; Kim, 1981). Compared to other minority groups, they appear to have more varied sources to borrow capital needed to start a business. Asian Pacific American entrepreneurs are more likely to have a commercial loan than other minorities, although white males fare even better. Asian Pacific Americans are more likely to borrow from relatives or friends. Where intra-ethnic interactions appear to be important is in the sale and purchase of businesses. Asian Pacific Americans are more likely to have purchased their businesses from a previous owner, and more likely to have received a loan from the seller. Asian Pacific American entrepreneurs also utilize ethnic banks and international investment networks that have played a large role in spurring ethnic entrepreneurial activity in recent years (Horton, 1992; Goldberg 1985; Gold, 1994).

The data indicate that vertical linkages — trade among firms — within the Asian Pacific American community exist but are not extensive. If inter-firm transactions were extensive among Asian Pacific Americans, then we should see a high percentage of firms with sales primarily to other firms. While the proportionate number of Asian Pacific American firms that sell primarily to other firms is higher than that for Hispanic and black firms, it is still considerably lower than for white firms. Unfortunately, there are few Asian Pacific American manufacturers and producers. Vertical linkage is predominantly between wholesalers and retailers.

While familial and social resources are important to Asian Pacific Americans, the statistics reveal that racial differences are a matter of degree than kind. One must acknowledge the unique resources of Asian Pacific Americans, which may help explain their relative economic advantages, but we should not overplay these factors. These resources have not been sufficient to eliminate barriers that keep many operations marginal. Some limitations will be overcome with time. The smallness is due, in part, to the newness of many firms, and the lack of business experience of the owners. As many become more established, they will grow in size and profitability. However, underlying factors will prevent many others from becoming anything more than mom-and-pop operations.

The limitations, as well as the potentials, are defined by the characteristics of Asian Pacific American entrepreneurs. The vast majority of the self-employed (85 percent) are immigrants.[20] While the rate of self-employment generally increases with time in the U.S., the greatest increase occurs within the first ten years. The rate is only 6 percent among those who have lived in the country five years or less, but is twice as high among those with between six and ten years of residence. For those with more than ten years of residence, the self-employment rate is around 15 percent. It is reasonable to assume that over time the economic returns from being self-employed increase as individuals become more experienced. This can be seen in the percent of the self-employed who earn at least $70,000 a year: 7 percent for those in the country ten years or less, compared to 27 percent for those in the country for 25 or more years. However, it should be noted that 33 percent of the latter group had total earnings below $20,000. This is substantially lower than the percentage for the more recent immigrants (54 percent), but the statistics indicate that time itself cannot lift all Asian Pacific American businesses to prosperity.

One limitation is education. The self-employed is a very diverse group that includes not only the highly-educated but also those disadvantaged by a lack of education and, to a lesser extent, by a lack of English language proficiency. While one in five has a graduate or professional degree, one in six lacks a high school education. Less than two-thirds are proficient in English (native English speakers or speak English very well). In terms of our combined measure of ability, 43 percent fall into the high category, while 25 percent fall into the low category. Education and language skills have a strong influence on earnings. The typical self-employed with low-income (under $20,000) has a little more than a high school education and is not proficient in English, while the typical self-employed with high-income ($70,000 and over) has a graduate degree and a strong command of English.

Many Asian Pacific American businesses are also limited by market forces. Because of limited capital and skills, many go into highly competitive, marginally profitable industries such as small markets and restaurants. In fact, one-third of the self-employed are in the retailing sector, with restaurants being the most common operations. Although manufacturing firms are rare for Asian Pacific Americans, the single largest cluster is in apparel. Personal service firms, which includes hotels and laundries, account for over a tenth of all Asian Pacific American self-employed. Investing in these industries is not only risky, but also offers few opportunities for growth into larger, more profitable operations. Three-quarters of Asian Pacific American firms do not have a single employee — the typical store is a single person or family operation.

Concluding Remarks

The "model minority" image of Asian Pacific Americans is not entirely false, but it does paint a misleading picture. The data show that not all are faring well. Along with more affluent households, there are large numbers of low-income and impoverished ones. While educational attainment helps many move into the professional ranks, others are not rewarded commensurate to their level of education and skill and still others suffer from "downward mobility" and the "glass ceiling." Despite the high number of entrepreneurs and because of the limitations of small business ownership, few Asian Pacific American business persons have been invited into the boardrooms of corporate America. Among the Fortune 1000 publicly-held companies, Asian Pacific Americans hold only 0.4 percent of the seats on the board of directors (Marumoto, 1993). At the same time, large numbers of disadvantaged workers are trapped in low-wage and low-skilled positions, with a slim chance of moving up the socioeconomic ladder due to limited educational training and English-speaking ability.

The economic diversity within the Asian Pacific American community, with a sizeable bottom end, led Bob Suzuki, one of the earliest critics of the model minority thesis, to argue that "the upward mobility of Asian Americans has been limited by the effects of racism and most of them have been channeled into lower-echelon white collar jobs having little or no decision making authority, low mobility and low public contact" (1977). More recently, Henry Der stated that Asian Pacific Americans "still lag behind whites economically ... per capita income of Asian Pacific Islanders is lower than that of whites; the poverty and unemployment rates are consistently higher" (1993). Indeed, when one looks at the hard numbers, there is strong evidence supporting this position — Asian Pacific Americans are not free from the troubling problems of poverty, social and cultural isolation, and crime. While we should recognize and honor Asian Pacific American economic accomplishments, we should not be blind to the myriad of problems and unfulfilled potentials.

As Asian Pacific Americans become more visible in all areas of mainstream society, including corporate boardrooms and welfare rolls, policymakers need to grapple with changing demographics and economic diversity. While some Asian Pacific Americans make contributions to this society, there are also low-income, low-skilled individuals.

Asian Pacific Americans are an increasingly diverse group, both demographically and economically. To respond to this growing population, policymakers must address the needs and problems of all Asian Pacific Americans in the areas of education, welfare, health, employment, and labor. By doing so, all Asian Pacific Americans will become fully productive members of our society.

Notes

1. For a discussion on this polarization, see Harrison and Bluestone, 1988.

2. The mean is the weighted algebraic average and is equal to the total income divided by the total number of households or families. The median is the level where half of the households or families have less income and half have more income.

3. This pattern also holds true for median household income. The 1980 figures show that Asian Pacific Americans have median household income of $20,000 compared to $17,000 for whites.

4. In the Census, race and Hispanic origins are not mutually exclusive categories. For example, it is possible for a Latino to be white, black or Asian. This creates two problems: 1) double counting when data are presented by both race and Hispanic origins, and 2) potentially downwardly biased estimates of the economic status of the dominant non-minority group, the non-Hispanic whites. The second problem is not severe at a national level because the number of Hispanic whites is relatively small compared to the total white population. But for some areas such as Los Angeles, the statistics for whites are poor substitutes for non-Hispanic whites. When possible, we present statistics separately for non-Hispanic-whites.

5. The Census does not contain data on place of education. We estimate the number of foreign-educated persons by first imputing the age of individuals at the time of entry into the United States. The Census provides information on the exact age at the time of the enumeration but not at time of entry. Information on the number of years in the United States can be used to calculate age at time of entry (age at time of entry = age minus years in the U.S.), but unfortunately, year of entry is recorded by periods that cover two to ten years. We use the midpoint of each category to estimate the number of years in the United States, and then use that to impute the age at time of entry. Based on this method, 59 percent of those with only a bachelor's degree entered this country when they were at least 22-years old, and 50 percent entered when they were at least 24-years old. It is likely that a majority had received their bachelor's degree by age 22, and certainly by age 24. For those with a master's or professional degree, 51 percent were at least 25-years old at the time of entry to this country, and 38 percent were at least 27-years old. For those with a doctorate, 29 percent were at least 30-years old at the time of entry, and 23 percent were at least 32-years old.

6. The labor force consists of those that are employed and unemployed. The labor force participation rate is the number of people currently in the labor force divided by the total population.

7. The unemployment ratio is the number of people unemployed divided by the total number of people who are employed and unemployed in the labor force. Unemployed persons are those who are not working but actively seeking employment.

8. Frictional employment is associated with job changes, inter-firm mobility, new entrants and re-entrants to the labor market, and job search that are all inherent parts of a dynamic economy.

9. The statistics are based on data for persons 24 to 64 years of age. Full-time/full-year (FT/FY) is defined as working 50 or more weeks per year, and 36 or more hours per week. Earnings data for the "all" workers category are based on those who worked at least 100 hours in 1989. Recent immigrants are defined as in the U.S. five years or less. The unemployment rate is based on the civilian labor force.

10. Weinberger (1993) and other studies that use census data to examine this issue have found that American-born Asian men earned less than white men in 1969 (Chiswick, 1983), and that highly-educated American-born Asian men earned less than white men in 1979 after controlling for both personal characteristics and employment sector (industry and occupation) (Duleep and Sanders, 1992).

11. Interestingly, these racial/gender gaps experienced by Asian Pacific Americans are very similar to those experienced by African Americans (10 percent for males and 13 percent for females). However, this is not to say that both groups face the same problems. These racial/gender gaps are based on otherwise similar individuals. Unfortunately, African Americans are highly underrepresented in our

colleges and universities, particularly the more elite, and in majors that lead to higher earnings. One of the major problems facing African Americans, then, is the lack of access to higher education.

12. This is consistent with the findings by Duleep and Sanders (1992) that Asian Pacific American men are less likely than white men to be in managerial positions after controlling for observable personal characteristics, although Asian Pacific Americans are more likely to be in professional occupations. Their study does not look at relative rankings within the professional category.

13. To estimate this statistic, we use the same method used to estimate the place of education for the highly-educated. The estimated number of years in the United States is based on the midpoint of period of immigration, and the age at time of entry is the difference between the reported age in 1990 minus the estimated number of years in the United States.

14. The statistics are based on data for persons 24 to 64 years of age. Full-time/full-year (FT/FY) is defined as working 50 or more weeks per year, and 36 or more hours per week. Earnings data for the "all" workers category are based on those who worked at least 100 hours in 1989. Recent immigrants are defined as in the U.S. five years or less. The unemployment rate is based on the civilian labor force.

15. Although cross-sectional data (data for one point in time) shows that those in the United States tend to have better skills, the difference can be due to either acculturation or systematic differences in the characteristics of groups by time of entry. It is far better to compare cohorts over time, that is, trace changes in skill levels for the same population over two different points in time. Unfortunately, there is no longitudinal data set that allows us to do this for Asian Pacific Americans, but we can use 1980 and 1990 Census data as panel data. The analysis is based on immigrants who entered in 1980 or earlier. To compare roughly the same group, we used those between the ages of 25 and 54 in 1980, and those between the ages of 35 and 64 in 1990. The 1990 sample is smaller, in part because of deaths and outmigration. Nonetheless, the two groups have similar distributions in terms of year of entry and age.

16. This is based on the research reported in Ong et al., 1993.

17. One indicator of the diversity is the variation in income of self-employed Asian Pacific Americans as reported in the 1990 Census. We use total earnings rather than just self-employment income because many of those who own an incorporated firm receive a salary rather than self-employment income as compensation. The data show that the median annual income is $23,000, but a quarter earn $10,400 or less. While a quarter earn at least $47,000, only 1 percent earn over $200,000.

18.   These rates are based upon 1% PUMS sample for 1990 and included workers age 24 to 64 at the time of the Census. The rates for blacks and Latinos are 4 and 7 percent, respectively.

19.   Unless otherwise noted, the statistics for the following discussion come from the report, *Characteristics of Business Owners*, U.S. Bureau of the Census, 1992. Unfortunately, this report does not report data for Asian Pacific Americans separately, but instead places this group with "others." However, Asian Pacific Americans owned 93 percent of the firms in this residual category, thus we use the statistics for this category as statistics for Asian Pacific Americans.

20.   The statistics on self-employment are based on employed persons between the ages of 24 and 64.

Chapter 4

Workforce Policies

Linda C. Wing

International trade and information technology have combined to bring about a new American economy. In the new
economy, the number of jobs, the wages of jobs, the skills that
jobs require, job security, and the distribution of jobs across
occupations, firms, industries, and geographies are all changing. Moreover, a different political economy is operative, as the
first Democratic president to be elected in 12 years attempts to
"reinvent" labor force policies. How will a new American
economy, workforce, and a new American president affect
Asian Pacific Americans, both those in the labor market now
and those who will enter it in the future?

As detailed by Ong and Hee in Chapter 3, Asian Pacific
American workers are not fully incorporated into the current
United States economy. The wage and occupational problems
encountered by Asian Pacific workers are due in part to their
immigrant background. Immigrants account for nearly all of
the educationally disadvantaged, and a majority of the highly-
educated consists of immigrants who obtained most or all of
their schooling in their native countries. Depending upon the
field of study, college education obtained abroad may not be
completely transferable to American work settings. Asian
Pacific immigrants with imperfectly generalizable educations
are likely to experience downward economic mobility in the
U.S. Lack of full English proficiency also characterizes many
Asian Pacific immigrants. Those who are highly-educated but
who have not attained expert English skills may lose out on
promotions to management positions. Those lacking both
English proficiency and a high school education have extremely
limited opportunities to obtain good jobs.

It is unquestionably the case, however, that opportunities to obtain relevant education and training would enable Asian Pacific American workers to overcome the obstacles that impede their progress in the current economy. Given the emergence of a new economy that will demand even higher performance from its workers, access to appropriate education and training programs is crucial not only to workers who want to break the "glass ceiling" or escape low-wage jobs, but also to those who want to remain the most competitive. Therefore, the key policy question for Asian Pacific American workers is whether the United States will invest in their human capital development.

In this chapter, I explore how progress of Asian Pacific Americans in the new United States economy would be facilitated by increased national attention to human capital development. I look in particular at the implications for Asian Pacific workers of possible changes in work-related education policy, public sector job training policy, and private sector job training policy.

The Rising Significance of Human Capital Investment

Asian Pacific Americans have reason to be sanguine about the prospects for obtaining new education and training opportunities. On no other current issue is there such unanimous agreement: education and training pay off in terms of individual earnings and national productivity. However, cautious optimism is in order, since the special needs of Asian Pacific Americans have historically been ignored in workforce policy discourse, policymaking, and policy implementation.

Since 1929, policy analysts have known that the ability of firms to make better use of human capital accounts for substantial productivity improvements. Yet human capital development was given relatively short shrift in terms of the national agenda until recently. Today, investments in worker training are touted as more effective in boosting company performance than the introduction of new technologies or increases in research and development budgets. "Learning to earn" programs for high school youth have catapulted from virtual ignominy to prominence in state and federal efforts to foster a high performance workforce.

The turnabout in the attention paid to human capital development began in 1987, when the Hudson Institute issued the first of what has become a steady stream of high-profile policy advocacy reports depicting demographic changes in the American workforce, the new competitive standards of the global marketplace, and the merits of investing in the education and training of "knowledge workers." Reports such as *America's Choice: High Skills or Low Wages* maintain that significant investments in the human capital development of knowledge workers are crucial to reversing the slowdown in the growth of the nation's productivity and therefore to maintaining the United States' leadership position in the changing world economy (National Center on Education and the Economy, 1990). Although most jobs in the new economy will not require more than a top-quality high school education, all workers who want good wages will have to be lifelong learners, periodically obtaining additional knowledge and skills through formal and informal job training. The highest-paying and fastest-growing jobs in the best performing sectors of the economy will require workers who possess both a high level of formal education and a high level of access to ongoing workplace training. These scenarios have been given weight by recent research findings:

- During the 1980s, the difference between the earnings of high school graduates and college graduates widened. Between 1980 and 1988, the advantage of college-educated workers over high school-educated workers had jumped from 31 percent to 86 percent for men with ten years work experience and from 37 percent to 60 percent for women with the same work experience (Carnevale, 1991). The returns to education are even higher for college-educated workers employed in high technology companies (Lillard and Tan, 1986).

- Workers with less than a high school education and a low level of training are significantly more likely to experience periods of unemployment than workers with higher levels of education and training. Those with less than 12 years of education and a low level of training also experience longer spells of unemployment (Vaughan and Berryman, 1989).

The confluence of advocacy and research has resulted in a remarkable consensus of opinion about the high priority that should be placed upon human capital development in the national economic policy agenda. Given the declining size of the overall American workforce and the growing proportions who are Asian Pacific Americans and other minorities, the United States has the unprecedented opportunity to address this economic imperative by finally fulfilling its social and political commitment to insure equal education and training opportunity for all of its people. Indeed, several blueprints for comprehensive approaches to human capital development — lifelong learning systems for all American workers — have been put forward by leaders in education, business, and government, including President Clinton.

Clients of a new lifelong learning system would include up to 90 percent of all American workers. Only the occupational elite working in high performance organizations — the "symbolic analysts" in Robert Reich's parlance (1992) — already have access to excellent, ongoing education and training opportunities. Employees of Motorola, for example, currently receive 40 hours each of classroom training per year, and the company plans to quadruple training time by the turn of the century (*Business Week*, March 28, 1994). Meanwhile, the vast majority of the American labor force has no access to workplace training or high-quality work-related education and training provided in other venues. For them, the downsizing of corporate giants, the movement of blue collar work offshore, and defense-related layoffs are harsh realities. Their unemployment spells are becoming longer and more frequent.

For the average American worker, a comprehensive human capital development system would appear to be a compelling proposition. In the new economy, the average person will make six major job changes. Lifelong access to education and training would enable a worker to acquire the skills needed to move from job to job. However, there is inherent peril in any broad-based proposal intended to reach 90 percent of the workforce. The average American worker exists only as a statistic, not as flesh and blood. Thus, a large-scale system designed to meet the needs of the average worker could easily miss its real mark. In the process of enacting the necessary policies and programs at the federal, state, and local levels, decision-makers would face innumerable possibilities to miscalibrate the fine line between a universal human capital development system that truly serves everyone and a universal human capital development system that actually serves no one, least of all educationally disadvantaged Asian Pacific Americans at the margins of the labor force and highly-educated Asian Pacific Americans whose labor force needs are masked by the myth of the "model minority.

It is important that Asian Pacific American voices be included in policy discussions if we as a nation are to formulate a comprehensive human capital investment strategy that is capable of addressing the specific needs of some workers as well as the general needs of all workers. The active involvement of Asian Pacific Americans in workforce policy development is especially essential during a time when more than 60 percent of the American public believes that immigrants take jobs away from other Americans (*Business Week*, July 13, 1992; Morganthau, 1993). It is not that we as Asian Pacific Americans need to protect our own self-interests as a largely immigrant workforce. Rather, having historically experienced exclusion from this country as a result of immigration law, and having a culture that places extraordinary value on learning, we have a special vantage point from which to exercise leadership in translating the rare conceptual accord regarding the common good of education and training into concrete policies that will benefit all workers.

Work-Related Education Policy

The first area of workforce policy that warrants Asian Pacific American attention pertains to future labor market entrants — high school youth. Three-fourths of American youth enter the workforce without a college degree. In the old economic order, such workers could find steady employment. In the new economic order, individuals with high school educations face limited job opportunities. Fewer than one in ten large companies hires new high school graduates. Non-college-educated youth drift from low-paying job to low-paying job and suffer frequent periods of unemployment. Half of all high school graduates are not able to find a steady job by the age of 30 (Olson, 1994b). High school dropouts fare even worse in the labor market.

SCHOOL-TO-WORK POLICIES

Policymakers have now decided to remedy the fact that ours is the only industrialized country in the world that does not facilitate the transition of youth from school to work. Fifteen states have recently instituted school-to-work programs and the House and Senate are currently working out differences in their respective versions of the Clinton administration's School-to-Work Opportunities Act.

The best thinking of school-to-work advocates is captured by the provisions of the School-to-Work Opportunities Act proposed jointly by the U.S. Department of Labor and the U.S. Department of Education. The provisions provide incentives to high schools to upgrade both the academic curriculum and the vocational curriculum through new programs that combine classroom-based education with workplace-based education. Such programs are to be designed by educators in collaboration with employers and are to begin no later than the 11th grade. At the workplace, paid work experience, workplace mentoring and workplace instruction are all to be provided to students. At the school site, a curriculum to enable students to meet rigorous academic standards, career exploration activities, and career counseling are all to be offered. In addition to high school diplomas, skill certificates are to be awarded to students upon program completion. These certificates must be portable and recognized by industry so that they will help students get good first jobs on career tracks. School-to-work programs must also establish partnerships with colleges in order to provide a bridge to postsecondary education for students who choose not to go directly into the labor market.

When finally approved by Congress, the School-to-Work Opportunities Act will provide $300 million in seed money to states during its first year of operation, fiscal year 1995. Programs funded under this legislation will join other school-to-work programs variously called youth apprenticeships, career academies, tech-prep programs, school-based enterprises, and cooperative education. All share the same purpose of linking school-based learning with workplace-based learning, but use different approaches (see Appendix 1). The purpose of the most comprehensive approaches, such as that encompassed by the School-to-Work Opportunities Act, is not only to help prepare a more productive workforce, but also to transform high school learning.

In the ideal comprehensive school-to-work program, learning would take place in a real-world context. Students would have opportunities to observe how experts approach and solve problems, and they would receive coaching on how to carry out similar tasks themselves. Student learning would be intrinsically motivated, for it would serve an authentic purpose. As students achieve mastery, they would be provided with less and less scaffolding for learning. They would gradually become self-directed members of a community of practice, figuring out the applications of what they have learned to other situations.

Learning of this kind, called cognitive apprenticeship learning by some, requires a reconstitution of both the organization of school and the organization of work (Berryman, 1991). That is, both the school site and the workplace would necessarily abandon the low-skill, low-wage, factory model of production in favor of facilitating learning to work and working to learn. It is highly doubtful that federal and state governments are in a position to provide financial incentives of the magnitude needed to foster dramatic restructuring of this kind. As it is, there appear to be inadequate incentives for companies to provide workplace training at all, regardless of how they organize the production process. The big cost of workplace training is on the employer side of the equation — a single youth apprenticeship can cost an employer up to $30,000 — and companies, especially small firms, are likely to want tax credits to offset their costs before joining in school-to-work enterprises. Despite this very real obstacle to putting comprehensive school-to-work programs in place, interest in school-to-work policy continues to be intense. The policy discourse seems to have the desired effect on the school side of the equation. Educators are reexamining their beliefs about the role of youth in our society, and they are looking at concepts such as learning in genuine settings to inform their pedagogy and change the way they structure schools.

IMPLICATIONS FOR ASIAN PACIFIC AMERICANS

What are the implications of school-to-work proposals for Asian Pacific youth? While all Asian Pacific American youth would profit from participation in school-to-work programs, there are grounds for giving priority to those who are potential dropouts or who do not aspire to college. Preliminary assessments indicate that the positive effects of school-to-work programs are mainly school-related. They improve students' attendance, raise their college aspirations and increase the amount of academic course work they take. There are no available data on the characteristics of non-college-bound Asian Pacific American youth, but there is suggestive evidence compiled by the U.S. Commission on Civil Rights (1992) that the dropout rates of Southeast Asian youth are high and their post-high school aspirations are low. In 1986-87, over half of Laotian students in Lowell, Massachusetts, dropped out of the public schools. Laotian and Cambodian students in San Diego not only drop out at high rates, but are also more likely to aspire to low-status jobs. Limited English proficiency and recent arrival in the United States undoubtedly contribute to the educational experiences of these students. New school-to-work programs, if customized to meet the special needs of Southeast Asian youth, might significantly alter their life prospects. In particular, the opportunity to learn in a real-world context, if structured properly, promises to facilitate their English language acquisition. There is a purposefulness about speaking, reading, and writing in order to accomplish job tasks that increases the motivation to learn these skills. Additionally, the sociology of work — people working with other people — means that students can call upon multiple sources of support and guidance for learning.

At issue is whether or not school-to-work programs will in fact be inclusive of Asian Pacific American and other youth who are immigrants and/or who are limited English proficient. State-funded career academies in California are legislatively mandated to serve their needs, and the federal School-to-Work Opportunities Act contains language specifying that students "with limited English proficiency" and students "of diverse racial, ethnic, and cultural backgrounds" are among "all students" who may participate. However, there is reason to predict that implementation will fall short of legislative mandates. The overall level of educational services currently being provided to limited-English-proficient students in the United States is abysmally low. Only 36 percent of all students in the nation identified as limited English proficient have been assessed by their schools as such, and a stunning two-thirds of those who have been assessed receive no special language services at all (Council of Chief State School Officers, 1990).

Even if educators were suddenly to provide appropriate school-based teaching and learning opportunities to limited-English-proficient Asian Pacific youth, the issue of finding high-quality workplace experiences for them would remain. Historically, employers who have participated in federal job training programs for disadvantaged adults have been reluctant to provide on-the-job training to anyone other than relatively skilled white men suffering from temporary unemployment. When employers have agreed to provide on-the-job training to limited-English-proficient immigrant men, the placements have typically been in undesirable low-wage jobs where little English and few skills are required. These workplace training issues are likely to be exacerbated when youth are concerned, and educators are ill-prepared to take leadership in devising creative approaches to workplace learning.

These concerns are made real by two recent studies, one of tech-prep programs and one of traditional vocational education programs. Tech-prep programs combine the last two years of high school with the first two years of college. Graduates earn an occupational skill certificate and an associate's degree in a technical field. The National Center for Research in Vocational Education surveyed 228 tech-prep programs and found that few serve special needs students, particularly those who are non-English-speaking. Only one-third of 120 programs in operation for one year or more reported having special activities for any category of at-risk students (Sommerfeld, 1993).

Traditional vocational education programs are school-based programs and do not typically offer workplace training. They are not known for academic rigor, although reforms are being put into place to strengthen their adherence to high academic standards. The National Assessment of Vocational Education found evidence that traditional vocational programs have become a dumping ground for special needs students (Olson, 1994a). In 1992, students who were limited English proficient, disabled, or educationally or economically disadvantaged represented 34 percent of all high school graduates but earned 43 percent of all vocational credits. They were likely to be concentrated in training for low-skill occupations such as food service work. Special needs students in general earned fewer academic credits than other students, and limited-English-proficient students in particular were no more likely to be employed than their counterparts not enrolled in vocational education.

These studies indicate that elite school-to-work programs may be unlikely to serve Asian Pacific students who are not college bound. Instead, these students may be channeled into second-class vocational programs where they are treated as cast-offs. Unless more concerted policy and programmatic attention is devoted to finding ways of identifying and meeting the special needs of Asian Pacific American youth under the rubric of new school-to-work policies, their educational disadvantages may very well continue to turn into economic disadvantages when they leave school and enter the labor market. A concrete step that needs to be taken immediately to inform not only school-to-work policy but also overall educational policy is the systematic collection and analysis of detailed data on the number, characteristics, and condition of Asian Pacific American youth in our nation's public schools.

Public Sector Training Policy

The second area of workforce policy that demands Asian Pacific American attention concerns the training of unemployed workers. For the past 30 years, the United States has offered federal job training programs to workers experiencing troubled times. These programs are particularly appropriate given that we live in a period of economic disruption. The U.S. Department of Labor estimates that two million workers are permanently laid-off each year due to structural changes in the economy. About one-fourth may be unemployed as long as six-to-twelve months. Unemployment is hitting every sector of the labor market, including the middle-class and middle management. The large concentration of Asian Pacific Americans in California and other areas where defense-related industries and giant corporations are in the process of downsizing and restructuring suggests that some number of highly-educated Asian Pacific Americans are among those suffering from layoffs and extended spells of unemployment. Their capacity to relocate to areas where their skills might be in demand, or to retool their skills for different jobs, would be enhanced by public sector job search assistance and job training. The current state of the economy means also that many newly-arrived immigrants and refugees find it extraordinarily difficult to find good-paying jobs. Some endure unemployment while searching for decent jobs for which they are qualified because they lack the job search skills appropriate for the American labor market. Others experience unemployment due to lack of skills appropriate for American jobs. In both cases, public sector job assistance and job training programs could offer critical help. Lacking access to such training, a large proportion of immigrants and refugees are forced to take low-paying jobs in order to make ends meet. As described by Ong and Umemoto in Chapter 5, these individuals constitute the 25 percent plus of workers in the inner-city communities of San Francisco Chinatown, New York Chinatown, Los Angeles Koreatown, and Little Phnom Penh in Long Beach who earn less than $4.00 per hour.

THE REEMPLOYMENT POLICY PROPOSAL

In March 1994, President Clinton introduced a bill to address the needs of unemployed workers. Called the Reemployment Act of 1994, the five-year $13 billion program would have three main components (U.S. Office of the President, 1994a and 1994c). The first component would consist of the establishment of a network of "one-stop shopping centers" that would provide the latest national data on job openings and opportunities to obtain job training, job counseling and job search assistance. The second component would entail the offering of long-term education and training opportunities. Individuals undergoing long-term training, defined as 18 months of training, would be eligible for income support such as extended unemployment benefits or loans. The third component would put into place reforms of the unemployment insurance system. For example, it would be permissible for workers to receive jobless benefits up front in order to start new businesses. To fund the Reemployment Act, the Clinton administration announced it will consolidate, eliminate, or cut back on the 150 job training programs currently administered by 14 different federal agencies. In total, the 150 programs currently cost the federal government $24 billion each year.

The future of the reemployment bill in Congress is open to debate. Drawing upon studies of past and current federal job training efforts, we can inform the policy discussion by outlining our best thinking about public sector job training in general and public sector job training as it pertains specifically to Asian Pacific Americans.

LESSONS LEARNED FROM CETA AND JTPA

The federal government has provided job training to disadvantaged and dislocated workers for the last 20 years (see Appendix 2). For ten years, programs operated under the auspices of the 1973 Comprehensive Employment and Training Act (CETA); current programs function under the authorization of the 1982 Job Training Partnership Act (JTPA). What impact have these programs had on workers? What program short-comings should be remedied in the development of new job training policy?

Evaluations of CETA indicate some positive benefits, particularly for women; classroom training increased the earnings of participants by a tenth in the year after program termination, while on-the-job training yielded increments nearly twice as large (Taggart, 1981). Classroom training appears to have a long-term effect as indicated by additional gains two years after leaving the program. Women accounted for one-half of the participants in classroom training but four-fifths of the beneficiaries of post-program gains from such training. This gender difference also appears in a 1982 study done by the Congressional Budget Office (CBO) which found that CETA substantially increased the average post-program earnings of women when matched against a comparison group of non-participants, but had no similar effect on the earnings of men.

These studies found there were consistent differences between the impact of CETA training on minority participants compared to non-minority participants — that long-term training had substantial earnings benefits, and that those with the least previous labor market experience received the biggest earnings payoff from CETA participation.

The effects of training provided under the Job Training Partnership Act (JTPA) are similar to those evidenced under CETA. One study found that compared to a control group, JTPA women increased their chances of employment by 2 percent and their earnings by one dollar per day. JTPA men increased their changes of employment compared to a control group, but did not experience earnings gains (Bowman, 1993). Another national study of JTPA indicated that compared to control groups, both women and men increased their earnings in the 30 months after they completed training. Again, women benefited more than men. They increased their salaries by an average of 15 percent, compared to an average of 8 percent, for men (Olson, 1994d).

Despite the positive outcomes, there are major concerns about both CETA and JTPA centered on limited scope of service, creaming, and little or no provision of new skills. CETA never had the capacity to serve more than a relatively meager number of disadvantaged workers. In Fiscal Year 1980, CETA participants represented one-twentieth of the unemployed and less than one-tenth of the working poor (Taggart, 1981). Only 5 percent of the eligible adult and youth population was served in 1989 under JTPA's provision for the basic training of disadvantaged workers.

Creaming is thought to be encouraged by JTPA for two main reasons. First, local JTPA providers are subject to performance-based contracting. They must meet federally determined standards for the job placement of participants at program termination. By definition, the most employable are the easiest to place in jobs. Second, JTPA restricts support services to participants. CETA provided a stipend equal to the state or federal minimum wage, whichever was higher, and, in many cases, child care, a transportation allowance, a meal allowance, and in some cases, medical and dental care. JTPA does not allow the payment of stipends, although "needs based payments" and support services to enable individuals to participate are allowed. Lack of stipends might result in disadvantaged workers, especially women, self-selecting out of JTPA. For example, without having access to child care, poor women may not be able to participate in JTPA.

Despite engaging in practices such as creaming, neither JTPA nor CETA has enabled participants to increase their skills to a scale recognizable in the labor market. A case in point concerns CETA women, who benefitted more than their male counterparts. In the period before entering CETA, women consistently earned less than comparison group members. After leaving CETA, the women's average earnings jumped above those of their comparison group and stayed above for at least three years. The average annual post-program earnings increase for a woman was $800 to $1300. About 80 percent of this increase can be attributed to a greater amount of time worked and the remaining 20 percent can be attributed to increased wage rates. Since only a small portion of the earnings gain was due to increased wage rates, it is unlikely that CETA training substantially improved the women's job skills (U.S. Congressional Budget Office, 1982). In other words, the principal role of CETA was a job placement service.

CETA programs were simply too brief in duration to make a difference in the skills level of disadvantaged participants. It was permissible to provide training for as long as two-and-one-half years, yet the average training program was 20 weeks long, the equivalent of one semester. There are very few occupations where the necessary skills can be taught in one semester, where the newly-acquired skills can be certified or tested at the hiring door, and where there are lots of jobs available. Although it is almost universally agreed that training pays off the most when it is long enough to enable participants to acquire competencies that are rewarded in the labor market, CETA evolved instead into a short-term palliative.

The prospects for acquiring new skills under JTPA are equally dismal. The emphasis on placement rates not only encourages creaming, but also short-term training activities. To find and get a job, the most employable workers may be able to get by with only short-term training or job search assistance. Short-term training and job search assistance are both less costly than long-term training, therefore program dollars can be stretched to reach a greater number of workers. The average duration of CETA training was 20 weeks. JTPA training is even more short-term. On average, classroom training lasts 18 weeks; on-the-job training lasts only 14 weeks.

A New Vision

The impact and shortcomings of CETA and JTPA offer in reverse a new vision of an effective federal job training policy. This new vision has five components.

The first element of a new vision involves the targeting of people, not places (Taggart, 1981). Funds are currently allocated to state and local areas with the greatest number of workers in need, but those areas tend to be where educational institutions are overburdened and ill-positioned to develop new capacities to provide job training. Funds should instead be allocated to individual workers in the form of portable career investment accounts. These accounts, which would work like vouchers, would be used for intensive remediation, career training, or postsecondary education equivalent to the costs of two years of college in any location where there is high-quality training available and where the job opportunities are greatest.

The second element of a new vision calls for reliance upon mainstream institutions for the provision of education and training. Employers cannot determine the value of a job applicant's completion of a training program unless the training has either been obtained from an established institution with its own reputation and standards or has resulted in an outside-referenced certificate. Mainstream institutions such as community colleges are better positioned to give workers more rigorous preparation leading to the acquisition of job skills. They are also able to offer a wider choice of career training options. The validity of this recommendation is supported by a recent National Bureau of Economic Research study (*Business Week*, May 24, 1993). Going to community college pays off in terms of future earnings. For every year of credits earned, a college student earns 5 percent more than a high school graduate, whether the student is enrolled at a two-year or a four-year institution.

The third element of a new vision for federal job training policy focuses on the establishment of occupational skill standards, the criteria for selecting training methods and curricula with which to impart occupational skills, and the means of measuring and certifying skills that meet the standards. In March 1994, a concrete step was taken in line with this recommendation when the American Electronics Association issued the first industry-wide occupational skills standards. With $300,000 in support from the U.S. Department of Labor and $1.5 million in in-kind contributions from its members, the association developed standards for three occupational areas: manufacturing specialist, administrative and information services support, and pre- and post-sales (Olson, 1994e). The next steps are to validate the standards so that they can be used for hiring and certification and to identify the knowledge and skills needed to attain the standards so that an appropriate training curriculum can be developed.

The fourth element of a new vision involves the creation of a career development system offering a "one-stop, comprehensive, full-services approach for all career investment activities" (Taggart, 1981, p. 342). This system, consisting of a realignment of existing, currently separate federal, state, and local services, should outreach to individuals needing help in utilizing their career development accounts, exercise oversight responsibility for the quality of institutions accepting vouchers, and provide incentives for the development of new institutions or new institutional capacities to meet needs where voids exist. The Clinton administration's reemployment bill incorporates a one-stop concept whose exact outlines will be defined as a result of the legislative process. Secretary Reich has indicated that state-chartered centers consisting of consortia of community colleges and other entities is one option favored by the U.S. Department of Labor.

The fifth component of a new vision for public sector job training calls for customizing services to client needs, with priority given to the most severely disadvantaged. Job search assistance, for example, should be directed to middle-class workers who have been temporarily laid off. Long-term training, on the other hand, should be directed to workers most in need, such as those who are limited English proficient.

The Reemployment Act appears to some observers to be pitched to the middle class (Salwen, 1994). The Clinton administration's support of more and better training for the hard-to-employ may manifest itself only in terms of its call for increased Job Corps funding. The Job Corps is a residential youth training program whose typical client is a minority male who is a high school dropout, who comes from a poor family, who reads at a low level, and who has never held a full-time job. On the other hand, Secretary Reich has cited the Center for Employment Training (CET) as a model for programs that might be developed under the Reemployment Act (U.S. Office of the President, 1994b). CET's mission is to train the disadvantaged, including high school dropouts and limited-English-proficient immigrants. About half of its clients nationwide are migrant workers or former migrant workers; 80 percent are Latinos.

In sum, a new vision for a public sector training system calls for setting up individual career development accounts that would finance the equivalent of two years of college; reliance upon established, mainstream institutions to provide education and training; the development of national skills standards to guide the objectives, content, and methods of education and training; and the award of a skills certificate upon graduation. The system would additionally offer a "one-stop, full services" array of related education and training services. It would tailor services to workers depending on their needs, and priority would be given to the most severely disadvantaged. Although it is too early to tell, the Clinton administration's proposed Reemployment Act seems to be in line with some but not all of the recommended components. An especially important un-answered question is the degree to which the bill is intended to serve the hard-to-employ.

IMPLICATIONS FOR ASIAN PACIFIC AMERICANS

What little is known about the experiences of Asian Pacific American participants in past and current federal job training programs mirrors the overall findings. First, the demand for training exceeds the supply of training slots. For every one limited-English-proficient Asian Pacific immigrant admitted to a federal job training program, four are typically turned away. Second, both Asian Pacific men and women find employment after training, but women experience higher earnings as well. The higher earnings are associated with greater labor force participation, not higher wages. Especially given their limited English proficiency, Asian Pacific Americans have not had access to training of adequate duration or quality to enable them to develop marketable skills. Third, Asian Pacific Americans who have been able to leverage job training into real careers in, for example, the financial services industry, tend to be young women, part of whose training took place in community colleges where the quality of English instruction was of relatively high quality and long duration, and where there were options to take accounting and similar courses. In contrast, men are more likely to be assigned to on-the-job training in occupations that do not require high-level English skills and provide no opportunity to acquire English informally on the job.

If both Asian Pacific men and women are to be well-served by a new federal job training policy, then decision-makers need to critically analyze the flaws of past policies and focus specifically on how to fully incorporate immigrants and other limited-English-proficient workers into the labor market. A major reform of the current system is needed. Otherwise disadvantaged Asian Pacific American workers will continue to be left behind in the new economy.

Private Sector Training Policy

The third area of workforce policy that deserves Asian Pacific American attention involves employer-sponsored training. Employer-sponsored training is a potent form of human capital investment. Workers who are the recipients of company training have a 30 percent earnings advantage over those who are not. Company-trained workers are also relatively advantaged in terms of job security. The current consensus of opinion is that American companies should significantly increase their overall annual investment of $30 billion in employee training. The policy discourse focuses on the relative merits and political feasibility of the federal government providing tax credits or issuing mandates in order to spur a higher level of private sector job training. Because the present incidence and distribution of employer-sponsored training may very well contribute to the "glass ceiling" that seems to limit the promotions of many Asian Pacific American professionals, it is important to explore the possible influence of future employer-sponsored training policy directions on Asian Pacific Americans.

THE BENEFITS OF EMPLOYER-SPONSORED TRAINING

From the firm point of view, productivity is increased by inducting new workers and upgrading the skills of existing workers through training. Improving managerial skills through training has an impact on the efficiency of production as well. From the worker point of view, those who receive company training tend to earn more and experience less unemployment than untrained workers. The benefits of company training appear to be portable from job to job. In short, both employers and employees receive a payoff to investments in company training (Lillard and Tan, 1986; Vaughan and Berryman, 1989; Vaughan, 1990).

Of particular interest here are the benefits to workers. Among employees with less than 12 years of work experience, trained workers earn wages that are almost 10 percent higher than those of untrained workers, all else being equal. For those with more than 12 years of work experience, trained workers earn wages approximately 3.5 percent higher than those who are untrained. The impact of training on wages endures for more than a decade. With the exception of managerial employees, trained workers are less likely to be laid off and experience shorter periods of unemployment when they are laid off. The reduced probability of unemployment endures for 12 years.

Company training from previous jobs has a statistically significant effect on workers' wages in current jobs, indicating that they received generic skills as well as company-specific skills. Moreover, workers trained by one employer are more likely to be trained by subsequent employers and to enjoy longer tenure in those subsequent jobs. Since two-thirds of the nation's labor force get their first jobs in small businesses, and since small businesses tend not to provide their employees with any training, the chances of small business workers being trained by future employers is less than other workers.

The productivity of trained workers appears to increase twice as much as wages (Vaughan and Berryman, 1989; *Business Week*, February 22, 1993). One study found that companies that initiated formal training programs experienced a 17 percent larger jump in productivity compared to companies that did not (Reich, 1993). Companies who train their employees have a more stable workforce. Trained workers are less likely to leave companies for other jobs. Despite the benefits of employer-sponsored training, less than one-half of the nation's workers currently receive training from their employers. Those with lower levels of educational attainment, minorities, women, and employees of small businesses all tend to receive less company training than highly-educated white men and employees of large corporations (Lillard and Tan, 1986; Vaughan and Berryman, 1989; *The Wall Street Journal*, November 9, 1993).

Moreover, company-trained workers are not widely distributed across firms. Ninety percent of the $30 billion invested each year on employee training is spent by only one-half of 1 percent of all employers (Vaughan, 1990), and these tend to be large corporations. A study by the Small Business Administration found that only 9 percent of workers in firms with 50 to 99 employees received any training in their first three months on the job, compared to 29 percent of workers in firms with 500 to 2,000 employees. Overall, only 20 percent of the workers in small businesses ever get any training at all (Committee for Economic Development, 1990).

The Policy Debate

As a presidential candidate, Bill Clinton advocated a federal mandate requiring employers with 50 or more workers to spend 1.5 percent of their payrolls on company training. Firms in many foreign countries are already obliged to make this level of investment; German firms, in fact, spend even more. In the Clinton scenario, employers not meeting this target would pay an equivalent amount into regional training funds. These funds would provide training to disadvantaged workers whose skill development employers would probably not otherwise underwrite. It is estimated that a 1.5 percent level of investment would generate $63 billion in new economic activity and 2.5 million new jobs over a three-to-five year period (*Business Week*, February 22, 1993).

Organizations such as the American Society for Training and Development and the National Alliance for Business agree in principle that firms must substantially raise their training expenditures in order to remain competitive in the global economy. However, business looks askance at the $21 billion per year in added training costs that a federal mandate would require. Instead, groups such as the Commission on Workforce Quality and Labor Market Efficiency (1989) and the Committee for Economic Development (1990) have proposed that a federal tax credit be legislated as an incentive to expand business investments in training. They point to a federal tax credit for research and development which resulted in new investments that equaled the amount of the credit. If a tax credit for training had the same impact, and if it covered 20 percent of the costs of new training, then employer spending on training could potentially be increased by six billion dollars to a total of $36 billion per year (Committee for Economic Development, 1990).

To date, there has been no legislative proposal from the Clinton administration concerning employer-sponsored training, although Labor Secretary Robert Reich is said to remain convinced of its importance as a policy focus. Employer-sponsored training remains, nonetheless, a central part of the national conversation on economic development. The business press keeps a keen eye on the training initiatives of leading-edge companies like General Electric and Motorola; and states such as California, Illinois, New Jersey, and Texas are taking concrete steps to provide financial help to corporations for worker training.

IMPLICATIONS FOR ASIAN PACIFIC AMERICANS

Until the equity implications of employer-sponsored training are better understood, the lack of any major policy proposal on the table at the moment may be just as well. About 55 percent of the total U.S. labor force works for small businesses with fewer than 50 employees. These firms would not be touched by a 1.5 percent payroll scenario, but their current level of investment in human capital development is low. Companies that do provide employee training tend to select the best-educated workers for development. As a result of training, these highly-educated workers, already well rewarded in terms of wages, become even more economically advantaged relative to workers with lower educational attainment. Minorities and women — including highly-educated minorities and highly-educated women — do not receive training to the same degree as men. A policy that would increase the level of company training in workers without attending to the possible impact on equal employment opportunities would thus have the effect of exacerbating wage differentials related to race, gender, and education.

In terms of educational attainment and occupational background, Asian Pacific Americans fit the profile of those who should be the prime beneficiaries of company training. Among working-age Asian Pacific Americans, 63 percent have a bachelor's degree as a terminal degree, 31 percent have a master's or professional degree, and 6 percent have a doctoral degree. More than 30 percent are employed in professional occupations. Yet the economic condition of highly-educated Asian Pacific Americans suggests they are not the recipients of employer-sponsored training to the degree that would be expected. Put another way, a low level of access to employer-sponsored training may account in part for the earnings differentials between highly-educated Asian Pacific American men and highly-educated white non-Hispanic men, as well as between highly-educated Asian Pacific women and all highly-educated men. The relatively low proportions of Asian Pacific men and women employed in managerial positions, despite high proportions being employed as professionals, may also be connected to their level of access to company training.

Research on the relationship between company training and the promotional and earnings inequities that characterize the work of Asian Pacific professionals is needed to inform future policy development affecting employer-sponsored training. There is a general paucity of policy research on employer-sponsored training, and the specific study of the company training of Asian Pacific professionals may be completely uncharted territory. Data on, and the analysis of, the observable behaviors entailed in company training may provide some clues as to how to break the "glass ceiling." The role of race in corporate America would also be illuminated.

Concluding Remarks

Learning is a value in itself. It can, however, be used as a lever, a means to another end. Asian Pacific Americans have used the lever of learning to make their way in the U.S. labor market. The schooling of highly-educated Asian Pacific workers has paid off in earnings and occupational status. The long queues of Asian Pacific immigrants awaiting access to English classes and job training programs represent the same confidence placed in the lever of learning as a means of overcoming disadvantages to find good jobs and earn decent wages.

Yet for highly-educated Asian Pacific Americans, formal schooling is not enough to continuously advance in the new economy. As Carnevale (1991) has pointed out, "people with the most education and access to learning on the job are doing the best." Asian Pacific Americans with the "most education" may be hitting a glass ceiling in terms of access to learning on the job through company training programs.

For educationally disadvantaged Asian Pacific Americans, job training programs like CETA and JTPA have provided a limited "helping hand" to securing employment. Not made available by these programs are the long-term education and training needed to become proficient in English and other skills required by the labor market for sustained success.

Asian Pacific American youth stand at a crossroads. If they are given access to new school-to-work programs that promise to transform both learning and work, they may escape the limited career paths of their highly-educated and educationally disadvantaged predecessors. Lacking access, they may become yet another generation of Asian Pacific workers unable to develop their skills in order to add full value to, and gain full value from, the labor market.

Polls show that a majority of Americans want more government involvement in the preparation of youth for jobs and more job training for adults already in the labor market, even if it means higher taxes for employers and employees (*Business Week*, January 24, 1994; *Education Week*, January 26,

1994). The national support for larger investments in human capital provides an opportunity for Asian Pacific Americans to influence policies and programs to meet their special needs and the needs of the common good at one and the same time. In his first address before a joint session of Congress, President Clinton said "lifelong learning will benefit workers throughout their careers" under his administration. The United States, if it is to remain one nation indivisible, much less continue to be competitive in the global marketplace, must make good on this promise for all its diverse peoples.

Appendix 1: School-to-Work Programs

School-to-work programs exist in many forms. Career academies are schools within large comprehensive high schools. Students and teachers stay together for up to four years, and the curriculum is focused on a broad career theme such as financial services. It is estimated that more than 200 high school career academies exist nationwide. High schools place cooperative education students in part-time jobs with a relatively loosely structured plan for learning at work. School personnel visit the job site to monitor the training done by the job supervisor. Approximately 400,000 students in the United States are involved in cooperative education programs.

School-based enterprises are programs in which students offer goods or services for sale. Auto repair shops and restaurants are examples of school-based enterprises. About one-fifth of the nation's high schools operate some variation of such enterprises. Tech-prep programs usually combine the last two years of high school with the first two years of college in an integrated program of study. Graduates earn an associate's degree in a technical field as well as an occupational skill certificate. The Carl D. Perkins Vocational and Applied Tech-nology Act of 1990 encourages states to establish such programs. Up to 100,000 students are said to participate in tech-prep programs across the country.

Youth apprenticeships begin in high school and include some postsecondary education. Students spend part of the time at school and part of the time at a work site. The curriculum is quite structured and is industry-specific. Academics are learned in the context of work. Students have work site mentors and usually receive a wage. A high school diploma and a skill certificate are awarded to graduates. About 3,000 students in the United States are youth apprentices.

Appendix 2: Manpower Programs

The Comprehensive Employment and Training Act (CETA), under which workers were trained between 1973 and 1983, was designed as a comprehensive approach to worker training. It was originally intended to offer long-term training, defined as up to two-and-one-half years long, and it offered stipends to participants during training.

For economically disadvantaged adult workers, CETA provided specific occupational training, general exposure to work, job search assistance, and basic education training. Basic education training could include preparation for the GED, as well as English-as-a-Second-Language (ESL) instruction. Any of the four types of job training and services could be combined, either in sequence or simultaneously. ESL instruction could, for example, precede specific occupational training. CETA participants were enrolled in classroom training, on-the-job training, or work experience. Although training could take place over an extended period, its average duration was only 20 weeks, whether delivered in the classroom, on the job, or through work experience.

For youth, CETA offered pre-employment services and Job Corps training. For experienced, skilled workers experiencing temporary setbacks, it offered fully subsidized public service employment. In 1980, 47 percent of CETA participants were enrolled in classroom training, 13 percent in on-the-job training, and 40 percent in work experience (U.S. Congressional Budget Office and the National Commission on Employment Policy, 1982, hereafter referred to as U.S. CBO, 1982). Classroom training mainly focused on entry-level clerical work, while on-the-job training offered craft and operative work such as automotive repair or machine tooling. Work experience, although offered mainly in the context of clerical or service work, was intended to impart general work habits, not occupation-specific skills.

Women, minorities, high school dropouts, single parents and individuals with limited-English-speaking ability were likely to be assigned to classroom training. On-the-job training tended to be the reserve of the most employable — white males with previous labor market experience (Taggart, 1981). In Fiscal Year 1980, men constituted 62 percent of the participants in on-the-job training, while minorities were only 38.5 percent (U.S. CBO, 1982).

Total CETA spending ranged from $2.9 billion in 1975 to a peak of $9.5 billion in 1978. During this time, its appropriations kept pace with inflation. When it expired in 1982, CETA had been cut back to a funding level of $4.4 billion. In fiscal year 1980, at least 16 million persons were eligible for CETA programs, but only 760,000 served (U.S. CBO, 1982).

The Job Training Partnership Act (JTPA) was enacted by Congress in 1982, took effect in 1983, and continues to be operative today. JTPA is primarily intended to address the needs of economically disadvantaged workers, but includes provisions for permanently laid-off workers. As its name advertises, JTPA emphasizes partnerships with state officials and promotes private sector leadership at both the state and local levels.

JTPA requires that program success be determined by performance standards "determined by the Secretary of Labor and accepted or modified by Governors." Public service employment is prohibited, and there are restrictions on support services to participants and on administrative costs.

JTPA funding has averaged around $3.5 billion per year since its inception. In Program Year 1985, 752,900 individuals received JTPA services for the economically disadvantaged (National Commission for Employment Policy, 1987, hereafter referred to as NCEP, 1987). They represented approximately 9 percent of the nation's unemployed.

JTPA closely resembles CETA in terms of the occupations for which services are offered. Training is provided for clerical work such as keyboarding, service work such as food service, and craft and operative work such as auto mechanics and welding.

In Program Year 1985, 37 percent of JTPA participants were enrolled in classroom training, 22 percent in on-the-job training, 22 percent in job search assistance; 8 percent in work experience, and 11 percent in other training (NCEP, 1987). Similar to CETA,

JTPA permits the provision of basic education skills, such as English-as-a-Second-Language instruction, either as a precursor or adjunct to classroom training. Compared to CETA participants, a higher percentage of JTPA participants apparently do not receive training in occupation-specific skills, but general job search help instead. A higher percentage of JTPA participants than CETA participants is involved with on-the-job training.

JTPA terminates participants from classroom training after an average of 18 weeks and from on-the-job training after an average of 14.2 weeks (NCEP, 1987). In comparison, the average length of CETA classroom and on-the-job training was 20 weeks each.

Part II

Case Studies

Chapter 5

Life and Work

in the Inner-City

Paul Ong and Karen Umemoto

Asian Pacific Americans play an increasingly significant role in the economy of America's inner-cities. For many Americans living in suburbs and small cities, the inner-city has become synonymous with a multitude of social and economic problems plaguing this nation — poverty, drug abuse, crime, welfare dependency and physical blight. These problems are the products of a cumulative process of abandonment that marginalizes and alienates an ever increasing number of people. A disproportionately large number of inner-city residents are African American, a testimony to the powerful and pervasive role of racism. However, America's older urban areas and their problems should not be seen as endemic to only one racial group. The particular hardships of inner-city life affect others, including Asian Pacific Americans.

Asian Pacific Americans play multiple roles in the economy of the urban core — as residents, workers and entrepreneurs. Residents live in neighborhoods populated largely by immigrants or refugees. A high poverty rate is common, despite the fact that a high employment rate is the norm in many of these neighborhoods. In others, a high rate of joblessness prevails. Many are part of the working poor or find employment in an ethnically defined subeconomy. Ethnic entrepreneurs play a strong role in the enclave economy, but have also emerged as prominent "middleman" merchants in other low-income neighborhoods. They fill a void created by the absence of mainstream retailers and producers. At the same time, their presence has generated new sources of interracial tensions.

Asian Pacific Americans will influence the way this nation pursues urban revitalization. Certainly, low-income Asian Pacific neighborhoods share many of the problems facing other inner-city neighborhoods; consequently, the corresponding urban policies and programs must involve Asian Pacific Americans along with other groups. At the same time, there are features unique to the development of Asian Pacific enclaves in the inner-city. These bring with them specific sets of problems as well as potential contributions that Asian Pacific Americans can offer under informed public policy.

We begin this chapter by first discussing the larger process of urban decline and how it has created communities of high poverty. We place the general development of Asian Pacific inner-city neighborhoods in this historical context and profile several communities for illustrative purposes.[1] We have selected four urban neighborhoods, two that are older enclaves and two that have emerged with the arrival of post-1965 immigrants and refugees from Asia. The neighborhoods are: San Francisco and New York Chinatowns, Los Angeles Koreatown, and the Cambodian community in Long Beach, also known as New Phnom Penh. We then look at the role of Asian Pacific entrepreneurs in non-Asian Pacific inner-city communities. We conclude by summarizing the problems facing Asian Pacific Americans in the inner-city and the prospects concerning their role in urban revitalization.

Inner-City Communities and Urban Decline

Inner-city neighborhoods are not new to this nation. Immigrant tenements existed in the great industrial cities of the manufacturing belt that stretched from the Northeast to the Midwest around the turn of the century. Employment, health, and housing problems in these slums were horrendous (Ward, 1975). In later decades, minorities and African Americans, in particular, became a growing share of the population in aging inner-city areas. Today, America's racial ghettos have been characterized by the social ills associated with being economically marginalized, such as high rates of crime, substance abuse, teen pregnancy, welfare dependency, school drop-out, and long-term unemployment.

These problems have grown in severity as poverty has become more concentrated in major urban centers. Between 1959 and 1985, the percentage of the nation's poor residing in metropolitan central cities grew from 27 percent to 43 percent (Kasarda, 1993). This increased concentration has transformed the neighborhoods. Between 1970 and 1990, the total number of persons living in a metropolitan census tract in which the poverty rate was greater than 40 percent increased steadily from less than four million to nine million (Mincy and Wiener, 1993, Table 1; Tobin, 1993, Table 5.2).

The residents of extremely poor inner-city neighborhoods are predominantly nonwhite. In the largest metropolitan areas, non-Hispanic blacks comprised 52 percent of the 1990 population residing in concentrated poverty areas (tracts where the poverty level was at least 40 percent); they were followed by Hispanics (36 percent), non-Hispanic whites (9 percent), and "others" (3 percent) (Mincy, 1993, Table 3c). An increasing percentage of those living in poverty are immigrants. In 1990, foreign-born residents constituted 10 percent of all those living in concentrated poverty areas, up from 3.5 percent two decades earlier (Mincy and Wiener, 1993, Table 6).

The growth of inner-city poverty can be traced to an exodus of jobs driven by three phenomena: 1) suburbanization, 2) regional realignment, and 3) global competition. Suburbanization, which dates back to at least the last century, occurs as firms relocate to the outer edges of the city in response to rising land costs within the urban center and to changes in the cost of transportation and public services. Firms also take advantage of prior suburbanization by following the labor force and consumers outwards (Mills 1989; Mills and Price, 1984; Mieszkowski and Mills, 1993). The building of efficient transportation systems accelerates suburbanization, as the cost and time required to transport goods declines. Federal government policies after World War II contributed to the process by subsidizing highway construction and homeownership. Race plays a role in suburbanization, as studies indicate that the presence of a large minority population in the central city, relative to the number of minorities in the suburbs, accelerates the exodus of both white residents and jobs (Mills, 1985; Mills and Price, 1984).

The flight of jobs from the urban center is not solely a result of suburbanization. During the late 1960s and through most of the 1970s, the shift in production and jobs from the older industrial "frost belt" of the Midwest and Northeast to the "sunbelt" of the South and Southwest has also contributed to employment losses (Harrison and Bluestone, 1988). The rise of the sunbelt took place gradually, but several factors accelerated its emergence. Public policy, particularly in the form of defense spending, facilitated the industrial development of this region (Markusen, 1984). Rising oil prices during this period favored firm relocation to the sunbelt, where energy costs and energy requirements were lower. Lower labor costs and weaker unions also attracted established firms and new capital investments. Moreover, a more moderate climate, a lower cost of living, and lower land prices lulled residents, insuring a growing labor pool for expanding businesses (Sawers and Tabb, 1984). The net result of the regional shift was the disappearance of hundreds of thousands of manufacturing jobs from the older industrial cities.

International competition is a third factor. Over the last two decades, U.S. manufacturers have increasingly found themselves competing against both developed and developing nations which are able to produce and sell goods at lower prices. The significance of imports can be traced to the late 1960s, but the effects became pronounced in later years. Imports as a percentage of the gross domestic product grew modestly in the 1970s, from 7 percent in 1969 to 8 percent in 1979, but jumped to 11 percent by the end of the 1980s. One reaction to competition has been to cut labor costs through layoffs, wage and benefit reductions, and the relocation of production to low-wage areas both within the United States and abroad (Sassen, 1988; Smith and Feagin, 1987; Mollenkompf and Castells, 1991). These changes have been supported by deregulation and federal tax laws which favor corporate restructuring and speculative strategies (Goldsmith and Blakely, 1992).

In urban centers, the above three phenomena have transformed the composition of employment. Higher-paying jobs in manufacturing have been replaced by lower-paying jobs in services and retailing. At the same time, the demand for the highly-educated and highly-skilled expanded in finance, insurance, and real estate (FIRE), and in professional services, which together created a new class of well-paid urban workers. Consequently, urban labor markets across metropolitan regions have sharply divided, with increasing disparity between high-paying, upwardly mobile, stable jobs and jobs which are low-paying, unstable, with little job mobility (Sassen, 1988; Goldsmith and Blakely, 1992; Harrison and Bluestone, 1988).

The economic transformation had a devastating effect on African Americans. Blacks held a disproportionate share of the jobs that were lost, with many of those displaced unable to find equivalent employment. Discrimination and lack of affordable housing in many suburban areas prevented many from following the outmigration of jobs (Massey and Denton, 1993). Additionally, the lack of education and training created a "mismatch" between the skills possessed by inner-city residents and those required for emerging jobs (Kain, 1968; Kasarda, 1989). The employment problems created by the mismatch were aggravated by racial discrimination in hiring by employers (Moss and Tilly, 1993a, 1993b). Some employers drew a "redline" around inner-city areas which they identified as undesirable places from which to recruit (Kirschenman and Neckerman, 1991).

In some African American neighborhoods, the structural changes and resulting joblessness led to a cumulative decline that undermined social and community institutions, leaving behind what William Julius Wilson labeled the urban underclass (1987). The "concentration effects" of poverty resulted in alienation and behavioral patterns which, in turn, reinforced their economic marginalization.[2] Although the size of the urban underclass is small, approximately 2.7 million according to one estimate (Mincy and Wiener, 1993, Table 1), its existence reveals the ultimate tragedy produced by contemporary racism.

The economic transformation also led to the growth of Latino inner-city neighborhoods. Latinos account for over one-fifth of those residing in concentrated poverty areas nationwide and one-third of those in concentrated poverty areas in the largest metropolitan cities. The poverty rates in many Latino barrios match those of the most depressed African American ghettos. The major source of poverty, however, is different. Many Latinos are immigrants or migrants who have been absorbed into the expanding low-skilled sector where poverty arises from the low level of wages as opposed to widespread joblessness (Melendez, 1993; Morales and Ong, 1993; Sassen, 1993; Betancur, Cordova, and Torres, 1993). With the exception of some Puerto Rican neighborhoods, there is not yet a clear emergence of a Latino urban underclass (Moore, 1989).

Latinos and African Americans, however, were not the only minority groups to be incorporated into the inner-city segment of the urban economy. Asian Pacific Americans have built an economic and residential niche. In the following sections, we discuss the economic characteristics of Asian Pacific communities in several inner-city metropolitan areas.[3]

Asian Pacific Urban Settlements

Asian immigrants formed some of the earliest racially defined communities in urban America. Long before the establishment of black ghettos in New York's Harlem and Chicago's South Side,[4] the Chinese were forced by racial violence and legal restrictions to retreat into Chinatowns throughout the West. The origins of land-use control and restrictive covenants, which had been the legal basis for housing segregation, can be traced to the efforts to isolate the Chinese (Ong, 1981; Warner, 1972; Vose, 1959). Subsequent waves of Asian immigrants led to the formation of enclaves such as Little Tokyo in Los Angeles, Manilatown in San Francisco, and the International District in Seattle.

Many of the older Asian communities went into decline during World War II and the first two decades following the war. Japanese American enclaves were destroyed by the mass and illegal internment of this population during the war. Although some residents did return to their pre-war neighborhoods, most dispersed throughout the nation. Urban renewal programs destroyed other residential communities, further dispersing the population.[5] With new immigration restricted by a racially biased national-origins quota and with a waning of overt state-sponsored racism, other Asian enclaves lost population. Many completely disappeared by the early 1960s.[6]

A major exception to the post-World War II decline was San Francisco's Chinatown,[7] which, as the largest and oldest Asian enclave at that time, received a large share of the limited number of new arrivals. Between 1940 and 1960, the Chinese population increased from about 16,000 to over 28,000.[8] However, this community was not destined to grow much more despite the reemergence of large-scale immigration from Asia following the enactment of the 1965 Immigration Act. This community grew slightly during the 1970s, from about 28,000 Chinese in 1960 to about 32,000 in 1970.[9] Since then, Census data indicate that the number has remained stable. This lack of a net growth is due to a limited ability to expand into adjacent neighborhoods, for Chinatown is surrounded by the financial district, Union Square (the city's major retailing district), Fisherman's Wharf, and high-income neighborhoods such as Nob Hill. Developments in these neighborhoods, along with other problems,[10] continue to threaten the future vitality of Chinatown.

Though the absolute number of residents in San Francisco Chinatown remained fairly stable over the past two decades, there is a high rate of turnover in residence. Chinatown still serves as a point of entry for new immigrants, as two-fifths (44 percent) of Chinese in Chinatown arrived between 1980 and 1990.[11] Many families have moved to more spacious quarters in less densely populated areas once they could afford to do so. San Francisco's Richmond district, which is located several miles to the west, has challenged the pre-eminence of Chinatown as the commercial and residential center of the Chinese population in that city. At the same time, there remains a stable core of elderly residents in Chinatown.[12]

Post-1965 immigration has had a far more profound impact on New York City's Chinatown, whose growth has made it the largest Chinese enclave in the United States. By 1970, its population of nearly 27,000 Chinese was nearly as large as that of San Francisco's Chinatown.[13] Unlike its West Coast counterpart, the enclave in New York is geographically less constricted. By 1990, the number of Chinese had grown to about 50,000,[14] and larger if one considers that the census enumeration missed many immigrants. The growth is driven by recent immigrants, who comprised 43 percent of the Chinese population in 1990. It is questionable whether this enclave can continue to expand at a phenomenal rate. Though less constricted than San Francisco, New York's Chinatown is similarly adjacent to financial centers and residential areas where housing prices are expensive. Already, "new Chinatowns" have emerged or expanded throughout the New York area — Sunset Park in Brooklyn, Canal Street in Manhattan, and Main Street in Queen's Flushing district.

The older Asian urban enclaves have been joined by new

ones, such as Koreatown in Los Angeles. Prior to post-1965 immigration, Koreans were concentrated in parts of South Central.[15] Today's Koreatown is located north of the original enclave centered at Western Avenue and Olympic Boulevard. This community lies within an older and centrally located section of the city, but is not directly adjacent to the downtown commercial district. In contrast to the older Chinatowns, Koreatown and other recently emerged enclaves do not have an ethnically homogeneous core. Koreans comprise only one-third of the total population in Koreatown and live alongside Latinos, who comprise the majority. The Korean population in Koreatown has rapidly grown, however, from less than 1,200 in 1970 to over 30,000 today.[16]

Los Angeles Koreatown has served as a point of entry for many who arrive to the U.S. and remains a predominantly immigrant community. Approximately two-thirds (67 percent) of its Korean residents are recent arrivals, having immigrated after 1980. Despite the low unemployment rate among Koreans living in Koreatown (4 percent), there is a high level of poverty. Over one-quarter (26 percent) of Korean residents live below the poverty level. It is also a fairly youthful population, with 20 percent under the age of 15 and only 8 percent who are age 65 and over.

The Cambodian community in Long Beach, a city located in the southern part of the Los Angeles metropolitan area, is another example of the new Asian Pacific urban enclave. As late as the spring of 1975, there were only seven Cambodian families who were reported living in Long Beach.[17] That changed rapidly with the fall of the Lon Nol government in 1975 and the subsequent mass exodus of refugees. The movement started with the assistance of several exchange students who aided the relocation of refugees from Camp Pendleton military facility to this city. In five short years, the Cambodian community expanded to over 8,000.[18] Ethnic and kinship ties and later the establishment of mutual aid organizations, churches, and services such as ESL classes attracted more residents, including "second migrants" from other parts of the country. By 1990, over 15,000 Cambodians lived in New Phnom Penh. The population is very young with an extremely high proportion of recent arrivals; 71 percent arrived to the U.S. between 1980 and

1990 and 46 percent are under 15 years of age.

The Cambodian population is distinct from the other communities profiled in this section, as it is a refugee rather than an immigrant population. Like other Southeast Asian refugee communities, the socioeconomic conditions facing Cambodians are more severe than those facing other ethnic and racial groups. This is certainly true in the case of the Long Beach enclave, where half of all Cambodians live below the poverty line. Households often include the extended family, and it is not

Table 1. 1990 Population Characteristics
Asian Pacific Americans
in Selected Urban Neighborhoods

	N. Y. Chinatown	S. F. Chinatown	L. A. Koreatown	L. B. New Phnom Penh
Age				
Youth (age <15)	15%	14%	20%	46%
Elderly (age 65+)	14%	23%	8%	3%
Nativity				
US-born	17%	23%	12%	22%
Recent immigrant	43%	44%	67%	71%
Below Poverty	25%	17%	26%	50%
Median HH Income	$18,200	$20,000	$20,000	$17,000
Mean HH Size	3.1	2.6	3.0	5.7
Homeowners	8%	18%	11%	8%

Note: Statistics for New York and San Francisco Chinatowns, Los Angeles Koreatown, and Long Beach New Phnom Penh include values for Chinese, Koreans, and Cambodians, respectively. "Recent immigrant" includes those entering the U.S. between 1980 and 1990.

Source: U.S. Bureau of the Census, Public Use Microdata Sample, 1990

uncommon for more than one nuclear family to share housing. An average of about six persons live in each Cambodian household in the Long Beach enclave, nearly twice that of the other selected neighborhoods.

These profiles do not represent the wide range of inner-city Asian Pacific communities, but they illustrate their diversity and common characteristics. First, their growth is driven by immigration, and as immigration continues these communities will remain important points of entry. Second, these communities are culturally and socially unique, providing a comfortable home for ethnic minorities and adding to the diversity of the urban milieu. And third, these communities face serious social and economic problems. These include the strains of cultural adjustment among new arrivals, economic poverty, deteriorating housing conditions, overcrowding, and special problems facing elderly, youth, and refugee populations. These communities are growing at a rapid rate during a time of fierce economic competition and global recession.

Employment of Enclave Residents

With the exception of New Phnom Penh in Long Beach, the three enclaves — San Francisco Chinatown, New York Chinatown and Los Angeles Koreatown — are characterized by a high level of economic activity among the working-age population (see Table 2). As a community of refugees, the residents of New Phnom Penh suffer from a multitude of personal and social problems that limits employment opportunities and forces many to rely on public assistance. Chapter 6 examines this phenomenon in fuller detail. In the other three enclaves, the labor force participation rates range from slightly below to well above the national rate. This has occurred despite the presence of severe deficiencies in human capital. A majority of the working-age population (61 percent) either do not speak English or speak it poorly, and nearly half (48 percent) have less than a high school level education. There are also significant differences across communities, with Koreatown having the smallest pro-portion of disadvantaged workers and New York's Chinatown having the largest proportion. There is not, however, a cor-responding difference in the labor force participation rates. For example, despite the astonishingly high proportions of adults with limited English ability and limited education in New York Chinatown, the labor force participation rate ranks first. Clearly, factors other than the observed measures of human capital influence whether or not a person works.

One explanation is that many residents, particularly those with limited skills, are immigrants with a strong work ethic that is reinforced by social pressure. For example, the typical Chinatown resident in San Francisco feels compelled to work to avoid "tarnishing his public image and, perhaps more importantly, to avoid bringing shame upon the family" (Ong, 1984, p. 50). This behavior is so strong that a large number of individuals are willing to accept very low wages rather than remain jobless. Over one-quarter of the employed in the four communities work for less than $4.00 (1989$) per hour.[19] Low wages, in fact, can have the effect of increasing the number who work because they force households to send two or more workers into the labor market in order to meet their financial needs.

The high participation rates are by no means due solely to individual characteristics. Employment occurs when there is also a demand for the workers' labor. Although many enclave residents find employment in mainstream firms, frequently in clerical and janitorial positions in adjacent retailing and office centers, others work in what is known as the ethnic economy.[20] This subeconomy can be defined by its reliance on ethnic capital and labor; ethnicity serves as a basis for pooling resources and defining employer-employee relations.[21] As discussed in Chapter 3, these resources help some Asian Pacific Americans to establish and operate businesses. While the contribution of ethnic resources to Asian Pacific entrepreneurship as a whole is limited, they can play a significant role for firms within the ethnic economy. Ethnic solidarity also supports economic functions in relation to labor. Social networks and community institutions facilitate job searches by individuals and recruitment by firms. Moreover, a common language and a shared set of values facilitate the coordination of production.

A significant segment of the ethnic economy is concentrated in the ethnic enclave. Many of these firms exist through agglomeration effects created by the presence of a multitude of economic and cultural activities. Collectively, these activities

Table 2. Economic Characteristics of Working-Age Population

	N. Y. Chinatown	S. F. Chinatown	L. A. Koreatown	L. B. New Phnom Penh
Limited English proficiency	65%	58%	56%	69%
Limited education	61%	50%	24%	68%
Labor force participation	81%	76%	69%	28%
Unemployment rate	6%	6%	4%	21%
Median earnings	$9,000	$11,000	$15,000	$12,000
Self-employed	7%	7%	27%	6%

Notes: Prime working-age population includes those between the ages of 24 and 64.

See Table 1 for definition of ethnic groups included.

The category of limited-English-speaking ability includes those who indicated they speak English "not well" or "not at all."

Source: U.S. Bureau of the Census, Public Use Microdata Sample, 1990

are able to draw in outside dollars by attracting co-ethnics from throughout the region, tourists looking for "exotic" sights, and non-Asian Pacific workers from adjacent employment centers.[22] The firms rely on a local, ethnically-bounded labor pool of low-wage workers who are limited by a lack of transportation, low skills, and low English-language proficiency. Because of limited capital and the nature of the client base, the "export" sector of the ethnic economy is often limited to activities such as curio and novelty shops, ethnic-oriented groceries, restaurants, garment assembly plants, and menial services. There is also an economic sector that caters to "domestic" needs of local residents. This sector is comprised of banks, real estate and insurance offices, health and legal services, and a variety of establishments that meet social and cultural needs. The "export" and "domestic" sectors are interlinked. The income generated from the former enlarges the latter, and the existence of "ethnically" looking establishments on the "domestic" side contributes to the ambiance that attracts outsiders. Moreover, many enclave firms actually serve both local residents and outsiders.[23]

While many residents find employment in the enclave segment of the ethnic economy, it is not a self-enclosed system. Even in San Francisco's Chinatown, which has one of the most developed enclave economies, there is considerable movement into and out of this unit. Roughly half of those working in the enclave commute from other parts of the region, while roughly half of the working residents find work outside the enclave, in both ethnic and non-ethnic firms. Nonetheless, the ethnic economy and its enclave segment play an important role in absorbing what would otherwise be excess and unemployable labor.

Although the Census does not provide information on the ethnicity of employers, which would indicate the level of employment within the ethnic economy, we can use industrial distributions of workers and other variables to estimate the relative importance of the ethnic economy. Among the working residents in the four enclaves, 15 percent are in apparel manufacturing and another 16 percent are in restaurants, two industries that are closely identified with the ethnic economy. The combined percentages vary by community, ranging from 50 percent in New York's Chinatown to only 18 percent in Koreatown. The low percentage in Koreatown is offset by an unusually high self-employment rate (27 percent), which is another economic activity that is largely based within the ethnic economy. A broader, but more ambiguous measure, is employment in wholesale and retailing. Roughly one-quarter of the employed work in this sector.

A survey of Asian Pacific households in low-income Asian Pacific communities in Los Angeles found that 40 percent of the employed respondents either had a co-ethnic employer or supervisor (Ong et al., 1993, p. 54). These numbers suggest that at least one-third of enclave workers depend on the ethnic economy. Without this internally generated demand for co-ethnic workers, it is unlikely that the labor force participation rates would be as high as observed.[24]

Ethnic economies generate benefits, but not without liabilities. These subeconomies provide employment opportunities not available elsewhere and can provide a preferable alternative to employment in the secondary labor market.[25] The ethnically-bounded labor markets shelter ethnic group members from direct interethnic and interracial competition for the same jobs. In some cases, the ethnic economy reproduces many of the desirable features of the primary labor market such as higher returns to human capital. This is possible when ethnic firms exercise monopolistic control and provide informal training which leads to greater opportunities for self employment. Finally, there are non-monetary benefits, such as the chance to work among co-ethnics and shelter from racial subordination in the workplace.

But there is an underside. Although the enclave economy may bring comparable returns to human capital for business owners, the same is not always true for their employees. Enclave businesses have a narrow economic base, face harsh competition, suffer high turnover, and earn low profits. They consequently create undesirable labor conditions. The isolation of workers often leaves workers vulnerable to unfair labor practices. Ethnic solidarity can facilitate the exploitative nature of the relationship between owner and worker, leading to harsh conditions. Wages tend to be low and benefits such as health insurance are often absent. Unfair labor practices are not uncommon, including unpaid wages, violation of worker health and safety regulations, unpaid workers' compensation, and violation of minimum wage laws.[26] Additionally, the utilization of unpaid family labor is more frequent among ethnic small businesses.

The relative balance of the positive and negative employment outcomes for enclave residents hinges on the interplay of supply and demand in the labor and product markets. The degree of competition, the supply of cheap labor, the growth of firms, and the final demand for their goods and services are key variables. Outcomes are partly dependent on market forces within the ethnic/enclave economy. The isolation of its labor market can concentrate the adverse effects of a growing supply of immigrant labor, which tends to push down wages in the absence of a concomitant growth in businesses. However, merely expanding the current set of business activities would not necessarily raise wages beyond current levels because of the pressures on firms to keep prices down.

These pressures are formed by market forces beyond the ethnic/enclave economy. Although Asian Pacific workers may not be in direct competition with other minority workers for the same jobs, there is indirect competition because the ultimate buyers have the option of purchasing from other sources. This is true in the garment industry, for example, where the extent of garment production within the Asian Pacific community is determined by the availability of non-Asian Pacific subcontractors who rely on low-wage Latino workers. Restaurants and curio shops, heavily dependent on tourism and on nearby office workers, are also sensitive to the business cycle. When the economy goes into recession, both industries take a dive.

Despite these limitations, ethnic/enclave economies are nevertheless a key factor that explains why employment outcomes differ among minority neighborhoods in the inner-city. Moreover, there are many non-economic dimensions of ethnic-based development that affect the quality of life in the inner-city. Enclaves serve as a spatial center from which members organize to facilitate social relations, promote cultural activities, and increase political leverage. Subsequently, many community-based institutions and associations play a role in local politics and have the potential to play a greater role in revitalization efforts. One segment of the community which has a large influence not only on the ethnic enclave economy, but on the economy of the inner-city at large are small business owners.

Middleman Minority

Asian Pacific entrepreneurship in the inner-city is not limited to Asian Pacific enclaves. Throughout recent American history, Asian Pacific-owned businesses could be found in various urban neighborhoods, including communities of color. Paul C.P. Siu (1987), for example, traces the existence of Chinese laundries in urban centers to the late 19th and early 20th centuries. Chinese, Japanese and Korean Americans operated retailing businesses in African American communities such as South Central Los Angeles prior to the 1960s. A few are still in business, but it is more common to find recent immigrants from the countries or from other parts of Asia — such as South Asia, Hong Kong, Taiwan, and Vietnam — running neighborhood grocery stores and restaurants, gas stations, clothing and wig boutiques, stalls in "swap" meets, and small hotels. In addition to businesses in retail and service sectors, Asian Pacific Americans are also involved, though to lesser degrees, in small-scale manufacturing, international trading, and professional services in the urban core.

The presence of Asian Pacific businesses in minority neighborhoods is a result of various factors, including their entrepreneurial drive, barriers to their employment in the mainstream labor market, barriers to entrepreneurship faced by other minority groups, and the commercial void created by the absence of mainstream firms in inner-city neighborhoods. Asian Pacific entrepreneurs have overcome some of the barriers to business ownership through such strategies as the mobilization of ethnic and family resources. Additionally, the oversaturation of businesses in many of their respective ethnic enclaves, especially in retail and service industries, has prompted entrepreneurs to venture outside of their ethnic market niche. Some, particularly those with limited funds, have opted to run businesses in low-income minority communities where the startup costs are relatively low. Most of these businesses are mom-and-pop operations, but there are also larger firms ranging from small supermarkets and retail chains to import wholesalers and medium-scale assembly or production plants.

Asian Pacific entrepreneurs have been said to fill the function of "middleman minority," which refers to their position as brokers between a racial minority clientele and non-minority business elites (Bonacich, 1973). Asian Pacific Americans are not the first to play this role and have often followed in a succession of ethnic business owners. For example, the urban riots of the 1960s prompted many Jewish merchants to sell their stores, many to newly-arrived Asian Pacific immigrants whose populations were rapidly growing during that period.[27]

At the same time, business practices among some recent

Asian Pacific groups have changed the definition of the middleman. The original concept was developed when production and wholesale distribution were controlled by a white elite. Although this pattern still persists, the global economy has added new complexity. Today, retail trade in some sectors involves ethnic wholesalers who do business directly with producers in their country of origin. Moreover, Asian Pacific entrepreneurs are not limited to retailing. Some have established production facilities that rely on minority labor. This is particularly true in labor intensive industries as in the case of garment work, where Asian Pacific immigrants act as labor contractors for U.S. producers (Bonacich, 1993). "Middleman" in reference to Asian Pacific Americans now characterizes businesses in minority neighborhoods regardless of the sources of capital, goods or services (Ong, Park, and Tong, 1993).

Although it is impossible to quantify the size of this phenomenon, we can identify issues pertinent to public policy concerning community economic development. The experiences of these entrepreneurs can be described as a bittersweet endeavor. On the one hand, operating businesses has provided Asian Pacific Americans with a means of economic survival and, in some cases, an avenue for upward mobility. At the same time, their presence in economically distressed areas has generated resentment among other racial and ethnic groups. While intergroup antagonism is not present in all situations, reports of conflict have become commonplace.[28]

Racial antagonisms often begin with complaints directed by customers towards individual merchants. At least four complaints have been repeatedly aired: 1) merchants exhibit racist attitudes and rudeness; 2) there is an inability to communicate due to language and cultural differences; 3) merchants do not hire local residents; and 4) merchants do not "give back" to the community in the form of economic or civic participation outside of profit-making. Although individual members of the various Asian Pacific groups do business with local clientele or hire local workers, the publicity over racial conflict has centered on Korean merchants. This may be due to the high proportion of Korean businesses which serve non-Korean clientele.[29]

While ethnic and racial antagonism has its economic roots, the resentments among residents are shaped by broader historical forces. Longstanding grievance• against discriminatory prac-tices on the part of financial institutions, for example, set the stage for racially based resentment by African Americans against newly-arrived immigrants who were able to establish businesses. The emergence of Asian Pacific merchants is perceived by some groups as another mechanism in a long history of racial oppression which contributes to their subordinate status in the U.S. Meanwhile, some Asian Pacific immigrant entrepreneurs hold negative stereotypes acquired in their home countries, either through the media or through limited contact with U.S. military personnel. The high crime rate in many inner-city neighborhoods has served to reinforce negative images of other minority groups and has fostered a defensive posture among Asian Pacific entrepreneurs (Ong, Park and Tong, 1993; Kim 1981). Misunderstandings as a result of language and cultural differences have often exacerbated antagonisms and hindered conflict mediation.[30]

Interracial tensions not only fester between merchants and customers, but often involve employers and employees. In Los Angeles, for example, racial tensions have arisen in the garment industry between Asian Pacific contractors and Latino workers. In this highly competitive and exploitative industry, conflict between owners and workers is endemic. Where class positions are defined along ethnic categories, the clashes are often transformed into ethnic antagonism (Bonacich, 1993).

Though ethnic and racial conflicts do not occur between all merchants and their patrons or between all employers and those they employ, conflicts between individuals can feed into intergroup tensions, transcending class and geographic boundaries. This has taken place among Korean Americans and African Americans in sections of New York, Chicago and Los Angeles. Complaints against individual merchants have become political rallying points for boycotts and demonstrations, becoming embroiled in a wider movement for racial justice and community control. Korean merchants have taken collective action to protect their economic interests in their quest to attain the "American dream." Ironically, this group solidarity has further emphasized the racial dimension of the conflict, fueling intergroup antagonism.

The escalation of tension is an interactive process involving direct participants, but is often affected by government. The widely publicized conflicts in Los Angeles illustrate this process. One case which heightened tensions between the African American and Korean American communities involved the fatal shooting of an African American girl, Latasha Harlins, by liquor store owner Soon Ja Du. The guilty verdict with the absence of a prison sentence enraged many in the African American community who saw the judicial system as valuing Korean American life over that of African Americans. The judge's action confirmed in the minds of many African Americans a prevalent view that Korean Americans are collaborating with the very system that historically victimized them.[31]

The tensions between African Americans, Latinos, and Korean Americans further escalated in the wake of the April-May 1992 civil unrest. In addition to 43 deaths, 2,383 injuries, over 16,000 arrests, and $1 billion in property losses, over 2,000 Korean-owned stores were damaged or looted, representing over $400 million in monetary losses. Many of those businesses lost were located in South Central Los Angeles (Ong and Hee, 1993). Koreans felt betrayed both by the police department which did not respond to their calls as well as by those who looted and vandalized their stores. As rebuilding proceeded, residents objected to the city permitting the reopening of liquor stores, the majority of which were owned by Korean Americans. Organizers saw these outlets as contributing to substance abuse, the deterioration of the social environment, and the lack of neighborhood control.[32] Though individual leaders within the Korean and African American communities made efforts to prevent the racialization of this controversy, the politics of the issue was racially tinged, since the majority of closed outlets were owned by Korean Americans and protestors were predominantly African American.

This controversy illuminates a dilemma facing Asian Pacific Americans operating businesses in low-income, minority communities. Although Asian Pacific Americans are not the cause of poverty and discrimination, they have become a part, albeit a relatively powerless part, of an economic system that drains meager resources from these neighborhoods. One could argue that many of the desired services would not be provided were it not for Asian Pacific entrepreneurs. But this does not negate the daily hardships faced by local residents nor does it justify the presence of undesired businesses. Occupying the middleman-minority position, many Asian Pacific merchants have become the target of rage and resentment held by those who are frustrated with the treatment received in an economically and racially polarized society.

Concluding Remarks

Asian Pacific Americans have historically been an integral part of inner-city life and continue to play an increasing role today. They occupy the roles of worker, resident, and entrepreneur. Each position is accompanied by a set of issues and concerns which have implications for urban policy. The conditions facing Asian Pacific Americans in the inner-city are important to address and provide insight into the problem of economic revitalization.

One lesson is the importance of the ethnic enclave economy in the absorption of ethnic immigrant labor. The evidence shows that the ethnic economy provides employment opportunities, but working conditions are often harsh, wages low, and benefits non-existent. For immigrants who are most disadvantaged, there is some improvement over time, but not enough to lift them into the middle class (see Chapter 3 for details). The challenge is to support the economic viability of urban ethnic enclaves in such a way as to take the particular needs and concerns of all parties into consideration.

The experience of Asian Pacific entrepreneurs in other low-income, minority communities raises serious policy questions concerning the role of entrepreneurial development in inner-city revitalization. How does business development in the inner-city benefit those who live there? Who should be given public support to do business in the inner-city? What type of business development is desirable or undesirable and from whose perspective? How should state and local government regulate business development in the inner-city in order to reach the related but distinct goals of commercial revitalization and poverty alleviation? And how can urban revitalization policies address the problem of interracial conflict?

Clearly, the root causes of poverty and inequality must be eliminated in order to fully alleviate racial group tensions.[33] However, to the extent that Asian Pacific entrepreneurs play a role in economic revitalization, there are areas in which business owners can exercise choice to maximize their contributions and minimize unnecessary intergroup conflict. The choice of business type, the employment of local residents, attention to wage scales and working conditions, investment into the overall life of the communities in which they conduct business, and the improvement of interpersonal skills and business practices are several ways that Asian Pacific business owners can affect economic and social outcomes. Entrepreneurial development is one area in which members of some Asian Pacific groups have extensive experience, expertise, and support networks. However, the potential they possess in playing a more productive role in urban revitalization has yet to be tapped by public policy instruments.

The development of small businesses, however, represents only one of a variety of ways to revitalize the economy of the inner-city. While ethnic enclave development has provided an economic livelihood for some residents, the experience of Asian Pacific Americans shows that other measures are still needed to overcome the numerous barriers to better employment. Additionally, other forms of economic development, including cooperatives, nonprofit business training projects, and alternative vehicles for economic activity merit consideration. And lastly, as changes in the global economy focus greater attention on the importance of human capital for economic survival, the education and training which inner-city residents receive is of utmost importance.

Appendix — Asian Pacific Suburban Enclaves

Not all Asian Pacific urban communities are located in the inner-city. New York's Jackson Heights/East Elmhurst area (in Queens), San Francisco's Sunset District (on the western edge and south of Golden Gate Park), and the City of Cerritos (southeast of the City of Los Angeles) are examples of newer Asian Pacific enclaves. These communities tend to be ethnically diverse. The Asian Pacific population in these areas is comprised of Chinese (40 percent), Korean (20 percent), Indian (12 percent), Filipino (15 percent), and others (13 percent) including those of Japanese, Southeast Asian, and Pacific Islander ancestries. Like other recently emerging and rapidly growing communities, a large proportion of residents (45 percent) are recent immigrants.

Located in less densely populated areas where land values are lower as compared to inner-city Asian Pacific enclaves, these areas have attracted a number of residents who can afford to purchase homes. While the home ownership rate ranges between 8 to 18 percent for the other selected neighborhoods, the home ownership rate among Asian Pacific Americans in suburban-urban areas ranges from 27 percent in Jackson Heights/East Elmhurst to 78 percent in Cerritos. Similarly,

Table 1. 1990 Population Characteristics
Asian Pacific Americans
in Selected Suburban Neighborhoods

	Jackson Heights	Cerritos	S. F. Sunset District
Age			
Youth (age <15)	19%	23%	19%
Elderly (age 65+)	5%	5%	9%
Nativity			
US-born	14%	29%	34%
Recent immigrant	61%	38%	28%
Below Poverty	16%	8%	9%
Median HH Income	$33,000	$55,460	$46,250
Mean HH Size	3.4	4.0	3.5
Homeowners	27%	78%	64%

Note: "Recent immigrant" includes those entering the U.S. between 1980 and 1990.

Source: U.S. Bureau of the Census, Public Use Microdata Sample, 1990.

while the median household income for the other selected neighborhoods ranged from $17,000 to $20,000 in 1990, the median annual household income for Asian Pacific Americans in these three suburbs ranged from $33,000 to $55,460. While the median income is higher in comparison to the other four selected neighborhoods profiled in this chapter, poverty may still remain a problem. For example, approximately 16 percent of Asian Pacific Americans in Jackson Heights/East Elmhurst live below the poverty level.

Notes

1. We view these inner-city communities in contrast to other Asian Pacific communities in large metropolitan areas, many of which remain in urban core areas but do not exhibit the same degree of economic hardship as do those highlighted in the body of this chapter. See Appendix for economic and employment data for a sampling of cities which do not fit the more commonly known characteristics of the inner-city but which are located in large metropolitan areas.

2. According to Wilson (1987), the underclass is defined by a lack of attachment to the labor force among adults, the prevalence of female headed families with children and correspondingly high welfare usage rates, high crime rates, and a youth population alienated from schools and other traditional social institutions.

3. There are other social indicators which can be used to measure the well-being of these communities. These include measures of welfare dependency, school drop-out, involvement in criminal activity, and the breakup of the nuclear family. However, due to a lack of systematic data on Asian Pacific American ethnic groups, this chapter will rely on economic indicators.

4. See Osofsky (1971) for discussion of blacks in New York City, and Spear (1967) for discussion of blacks in Chicago. Both authors date the formation of the black urban ghetto in the two respective cities to the period around the turn of the century.

5. See Okamoto, 1991; Doi, Fujita, Kawahara, Niiya, and Umemoto, 1986; and Tatsuno, 1971.

6. See Lee (1960) regarding this process for Chinatowns. See Ong and Liu (1993) for a description of the change in race-based policies.

7. Urban decline did not affect Asian Pacific Americans in Honolulu in the same way due to differences in historical conditions and population ratios.

8. The San Francisco Chinese Community Citizens' Survey & Fact Finding Committee (1969) listed a total of 28,578 persons who were neither white nor black residing in three areas: Hard Core Chinatown, Residential Chinatown, and Potential Chinatown. There was no separate count for Asian Pacific Americans or Chinese, but the

Committee stated that nearly all of the nonwhite/non-black population were Chinese. This area also contained some Filipinos, who lived in the eastern portion of greater Chinatown, which was also know as Manilatown. The 1940 figure is from Loo (1991, p. 50).

9. The latter figure is reported in Loo (1991, p. 50).

10. See also Bishop (1990). Past redevelopment projects and the encroachment of the financial district have reduced the size of Chinatown and pushed up rents. Other factors also threaten the economic viability of Chinatown businesses, including the closing of the Embarcadero Freeway damaged during the 1989 earthquake and declines in the tourist trade.

11. The data describing the population characteristics of the Asian Pacific populations have been tabulated from the 1990 U.S. Census Public Use Microdata Sample (PUMS), a sample of 5 percent of the population. We use PUMS areas, sub-metropolitan areas of at least 100,000 persons, to define our sample. The boundaries for the PUMS samples do not necessarily correspond to the boundaries of the residential ethnic enclave for each of the communities profiled in this section. Therefore, the numbers and percentages may vary slightly and are presented as approximate rather than exact totals and proportions. The use of the term "recent immigrants" refers to those entering the U.S. between 1980 and 1990.

12. San Francisco Chinatown has a more stable residential core in comparison to New York Chinatown. This is indicated by a higher proportion of elderly (23 percent as compared to 17 percent), a slightly higher median annual household income ($20,000 compared to $18,200), and a higher rate of home ownership (18 percent as compared to 8 percent) among Chinese residents in San Francisco Chinatown as compared to their cohorts in New York Chinatown.

13. 1970 and 1980 statistics are listed in Zhou (1992, p. 187, Table 8-1).

14. Using the geographic definition of what had been considered greater Chinatown in 1970, the 1990 Census listed 50,309 Asian Pacific Americans and 49,020 Chinese. However, the 1990 Census shows adajcent census tracts that contain over 1,000 additional Chinese.

15. According to Givens (1939, pp. 31-32), this settlement began with the establishment of the first Korean church in 1905. The Korean community in Los Angeles in the late 1930s was concentrated in the area between Vermont and Western Avenues and between Adams Boulevard and Slauson Avenue. These were older neighborhoods with families from a mix of racial and ethnic backgrounds who located where racial housing covenants were not strictly enforced.

16. As of 1990, there were 28,000 Koreans residing in Koreatown. With the recent growth, the number has reached an estimated 30,000. U.S. Bureau of the Census, Census of the Population, 1970 and 1990.

17. The history of this community is based on Trounson (1981); Holley (1986); and Ong et al. (1993).

18. At that time it was bounded by 7th Street on the south, Pacific Coast Highway on the north, California Avenue on the west, and Freeman Avenue on the east.

19. The hourly rate at the 25-percentile was $3.91. The minimum wage in 1989 was $3.35 per hour and moved up to $3.80 per hour in 1990.

20. Ethnic economies are not unique to Asian Pacific Americans, but also exist in other immigrant populations. For example, see Portes and Bach (1985) for a discussion on Cuban enclave economies.

21. The literature on enclave economies and working conditions in these subeconomies has grown considerably over the last few years. The following discussion is based on Zhou (1992), Light (1972), Light and Bonacich (1988), Light and Bhachu (1993), Portes and Wilson (1980), Portes and Bach (1985), Wong (1987), Portes and Jensen (1987), Zhou and Logan (1991), Mar (1991), Kim (1981), Bonacich (1987), Kwong (1987), Ong (1984), Sanders and Nee (1987), Kato (1993), Ong et al. (1993).

22. Another way of defining the enclave economy is as one part of a sequence of stages of ethnically defined business development proposed by Waldinger, Aldrich, Ward and associates (1990). In the first stage, a limited number of very small businesses arises to serve a small population of immigrant workers. As the population grows, the community undergoes a qualitative change that marks the second stage with a much broader set of social, cultural, and economic activities. This describes the ethnic enclave. The third stage involves ethnic entrepreneurial activity in communities other than their own, including the role of middleman merchants. In the last stage of this sequence, immigrant entrepreneurs assimilate and disperse over the wide range of industrial activity and become closer to the characteristics of white-owned businesses.

23. In many cases, owners themselves live outside of the inner-city enclave in which their businesses are located.

24. The low labor force participation rate of adults in New Phnom Penh may be partly explained by the lesser degree of enclave economic development within the Cambodian community relative to the other three communities.

25. Jobs in the secondary labor market, in contrast to those in the primary labor market according to dual labor market theory, are characterized by low-skill work, low wages and fringe benefits, poor working conditions, job instability, high rates of labor turnover, and little chance of upward job mobility. See the following for discussions of labor market segmentation theories: Gordon, Edwards, and Reich, 1982; Kerr et. al., 1960; Doeringer and Piore, 1971, Chapter 8.

26. For example, a recent crackdown by the U.S. Department of Labor on a random sample of restaurants in San Francisco found violations of federal minimum wage and hour, overtime, and wage reporting laws, particularly in ethnic restaurants. See *San Francisco Chronicle*, December 17, 1993. See also Kato (1993).

27. See Takahashi and Hee, n.d. For example, many store owners doing business in the Watts area of south central Los Angeles prior to the 1970s were Jewish along with early Asian immigrant groups, primarily Japanese and Chinese. Following the Watts rebellions of the late 1960s, however, many closed their businesses or relocated to other areas. This period coincided with the period of increased immigration from Asia following the 1965 Immigration Act. Many new Asian Pacific immigrants took over small businesses from established Jewish, Chinese, and Japanese merchants who were leaving the south central area.

28. Data and analyses on the conflict are drawn from Ong, Park and Tong (1994), Umemoto (1994), and Freer (1992), unless otherwise noted. There are also numerous accounts of tensions between Asian Pacific merchants and non-Asian Pacific residents in the popular media. For examples, see: *New York Times*, November 25, 1990 and July 30, 1990.

29. Waldinger and Aldrich, 1990. They refer to Illsoo Kim's findings (1981) to note that the distinguishing mark of Korean business in America, as compared to other immigrant groups, is the fact that business growth has occurred by selling non-ethnic products in the general market.

30. See also Stewart, 1989.

31. For example, collaboration was suggested by a reporter of the *Los Angeles Sentinel*, the largest West Coast African American vernacular, in an interview with Judge Karlin, who presided over the trial of Soon Ja Du. The reporter asked how the Korean community views her after the sentencing, referring to a donation reportedly made by the Korean American Grocer's Association to Karlin's reelection campaign. See *Los Angeles Sentinel*, March 18, 1992.

32. The campaign to lower the density of liquor stores had begun over nine years prior to the civil unrest. With weak and largely ineffective regulations by the alcohol and beverage control board, the relative numbers of liquor outlets flourished in neighborhoods with little political power to control zoning commission decisions and with low-income populations vulnerable to substance abuse and addiction.

33. For example, the implementation of the Community Reinvestment Act increasing capital to inner-city borrowers, ending redlining practices discriminating against inner-city economic development on the part of banks and insurance companies, implementing effective employment and training programs, ending employment and housing discrimination, improving the educational infrastructure, and other more fundamental steps need to be taken.

Chapter 6

Welfare and Work among Southeast Asians[1]

Paul Ong and Evelyn Blumenberg

Concerns over increasing poverty rates, the growth of an urban underclass, and long-term dependence on public assistance have shaped the debate over the relationship between welfare and work (Wilson, 1987; Ellwood, 1988; Murray, 1984). But despite the volume of material in this field, Asian Pacific Americans, a rapidly growing welfare population, have largely been excluded from this literature. Studies of welfare dependency typically focus on African Americans, who comprise a disproportionate percentage of those on public assistance. More recently, scholars have turned their attention to Latinos whose growing numbers on welfare have fueled a larger discussion concerning the effects of immigration and undocumented aliens on welfare usage. While these studies are useful, they are incomplete. We argue in this chapter that the experience of Asian Pacific Americans is unique and that this uniqueness can provide important insights into the welfare debate and help shape future discussion on welfare reform.

Not only are Asian Pacific Americans the fastest growing segment of those on welfare, but some Asian Pacific ethnic groups, particularly Southeast Asians, have the highest welfare dependency rates of any ethnic or racial group. In 1975, only 0.5 percent of parents on Aid to Families with Dependent Children (AFDC) (the nation's single largest welfare program) were Asian Pacific Americans, but by 1990 the percentage grew to 2.8 percent (U.S. Committee on Ways and Means, 1992, p. 670). (See Appendix for a summary of the welfare programs discussed in this chapter.) This substantial growth in the percentage of Asian Pacific welfare recipients occurred during a period when the total number of AFDC recipients remained fairly stable, increasing only slightly from 11.3 to 11.5 million (U.S. Committee on Ways and Means, 1992, p. 665). The increase in Asian Pacific Americans on welfare is driven, in part, by the growth of this population, which expanded from approximately 1.6 million in 1970[2] to 7.3 million in 1990. Population growth, however, only explains a small part of rising welfare usage rates among Asians. The key lies in the experiences of specific ethnic groups. Although the Asian Pacific AFDC population is diverse, Southeast Asians comprise a large majority and exhibit welfare dependency rates that reach over 50 percent.

Despite a paucity of studies on Southeast Asians within the welfare literature, important insights can be drawn from the substantial literature on their adaptation to the U.S. These studies have examined refugee and assimilation issues, but they have not done so in the context of a broader set of welfare issues. For example, these studies analyze the use of public assistance with little reference to ethnic and racial groups on public assistance. We believe that this is a serious limitation given the realities.

Although one could argue that a misguided refugee adjustment policy is at the root of the problems facing Southeast Asians, this population is now so enmeshed within the public assistance system that their well-being is and will be determined by this system and future reform. The question is whether current and proposed welfare policies adequately meet the needs of this unique and growing population of welfare recipients. The findings from this study suggest that existing programs fail to assist Southeast Asians in making the successful transition from welfare to work.

This chapter adds to the literature by examining welfare and work issues based on both a synthesis of existing materials, an analysis of unpublished data for California from the Public Use Microdata Samples of the U.S. Census, and specialized administrative data from California's Department of Social Services. With respect to Southeast Asians, the state of California is both representative of national welfare trends and unique. Paralleling national trends, Asian Pacific Americans residing in California experienced a faster average annual growth rate in their numbers on welfare

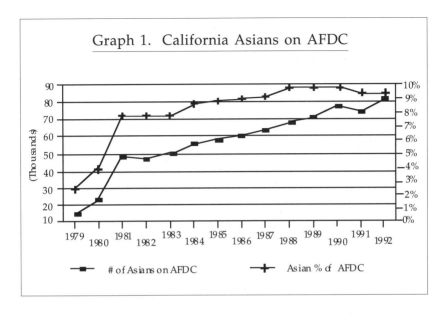

Graph 1. California Asians on AFDC

■ # of Asians on AFDC   + Asian % of AFDC

than any other ethnic or racial group. In 1979, 14,020 Asians received AFDC in California, comprising 2.6 percent of the AFDC population (California Employment Development Division, 1980). By 1992, however, the number of Asian Pacific Americans on AFDC jumped over 480 percent to 82,177, approximately 9.5 percent of the state's total AFDC population[3] (see Graph 1). Southeast Asians constitute the largest group of Asian Pacific Americans on welfare, comprising from 71 to 87 percent of the total Asian Pacific welfare population.[4] As a comparison, Southeast Asians comprise 13 percent of the total Asian Pacific population, ranking third after Chinese Americans and Filipinos.

California diverges from the rest of the states with respect to welfare dependency rates among Southeast Asians. Southeast Asians have substantially higher welfare usage in California than in any other state in the country (Bach and Carroll-Seguin, 1986). During the early 1980s, an overwhelming majority of Southeast Asian welfare recipients, perhaps over three-quarters, resided in California (Kerpen, 1985, p. 22). Although recent statistics from the U.S. Office of Refugee Resettlement include only those who had been in the country for two years or less, the data for 1989 show that among recent arrivals, 80 percent of those in California received public assistance compared to 31 percent of those in all other states (U.S. Congress, 1992, p. 230).[5] These figures would indicate that a large majority of all Southeast Asians on public assistance continue to reside in California.

The following sections of the chapter provide background information on Southeast Asian resettlement in the U.S., document their employment and welfare patterns, and review the determinants of welfare usage. The final section evaluates government sponsored efforts to transition Southeast Asians off of public assistance and into the labor market. The chapter concludes with a discussion on the broader implications of this study for public policy.

Southeast Asians in the U.S.

The U.S. Southeast Asian population is a legacy of the Vietnam War, this country's unsuccessful, military effort to eradicate communism in Indochina. In support of South Vietnamese forces, the U.S. government bombed, deployed troops, and sent millions of dollars in aid as well as hundreds of specialists, technicians, and researchers to Southeast Asia. By the early-1970s millions were refugees — homeless Laotians, Cambodians and Vietnamese who had escaped with their lives but little else. Many were living in refugee camps — crowded and unsanitary facilities.

The influx of Southeast Asians to the United States was thought to be a short-term phenomenon, the immediate consequence of the violent communist takeover that occurred in Vietnam in 1975. However, contrary to expectations, the flow of refugees did not wane; new political upheavals and natural disasters motivated Laotians, Cambodians, and ethnic Chinese to enter the U.S. during the 1980s. Between 1975 and 1991, over a million Southeast Asian refugees migrated to the U.S., arriving in two waves (U.S. Congress, 1992, p. 126) (see Graph 2). From 1975 to 1978, 178,000 refugees came to the U.S.; of these, 83 percent were Vietnamese and the remainder were largely Laotians (see Table 1). After this first wave, migration continued as Cambodians, ethnic Chinese, and Hmong entered this country in increasing numbers. North Vietnam overthrew the existing Cambodian government causing over 100,000 Cambodians to seek asylum in Thailand (Strand and Jones, Jr., 1985). Shortly

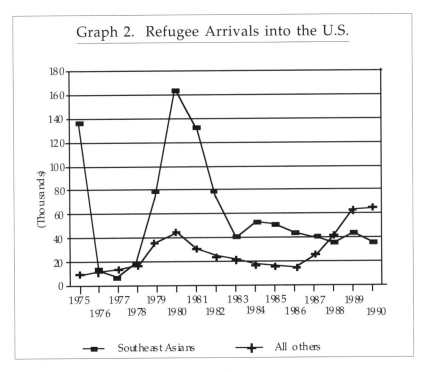

Graph 2. Refugee Arrivals into the U.S.

thereafter, a protracted Cambodian famine forced an additional 150,000 people into Thai refugee camps (Strand and Jones, Jr., 1985). Ongoing political turmoil in Vietnam motivated over 85,000 people, mainly ethnic Chinese, to risk travel in small crafts never meant for the open seas; these refugees were popularly termed "boat people" (Strand and Jones, Jr., 1985). And finally, refugees from Laos fled to Thailand as communists drove Hmong from their highland homes and seized businesses largely owned by ethnic Chinese. Rising antagonisms toward refugees in countries of first asylum such as Thailand combined with the continued massive exodus from the region prompted the U.S. government to admit additional refugees.

Southeast Asians are unevenly dispersed throughout the United States. This unevenness is derived in part by geographic variations in the number of voluntary organizations that have been willing to sponsor initial settlements, and also by the residential preferences of Southeast Asians. While U.S. policy-makers pursued a conscious plan of distributing refugees

Table 1.   Distribution of Southeast Asian Refugees by Country of Origin

	Vietnam	Laos	Cambodia
1975-1978	83.3%	11.5%	4.5%
1979-1982	59.4%	25.1%	15.4%
1983-1986	44.8%	13.1%	27.7%
1987-1990	57.5%	33.8%	5.9%

Source: 1975-1982, Le (1993, p. 170); 1983-1990, INS reports.

throughout the nation, secondary migration has led to greater concentrations in a handful of geographic areas (Forbes, 1984). Of all U.S. states, California is home to the largest Southeast Asian population. According to the 1990 Census, approximately 45 percent of those classified as Vietnamese, Laotian, Cambodian, or Hmong (both foreign- and U.S.-born) reside in this state. Other states including Texas, Washington, Minnesota, Massachusetts, Virginia, Pennsylvania, Wisconsin, New York and Florida have sizable Southeast Asian communities. State estimates from the Office of Refugee Resettlement show similar patterns (see Table 2).

Within California, Southeast Asians are geographically concentrated. Close to 40 percent of Indochinese refugees live in the Southern California counties of Los Angeles and Orange with smaller concentrations in California's other major metropolitan areas — Santa Clara, San Mateo, San Francisco/Oakland, and San Diego. Southeast Asian ethnic groups are also clustered within metropolitan areas. In Los Angeles County, for example, Vietnamese have largely settled in the San Gabriel Valley on the east side of Los Angeles, while Cambodians are located in the city of Long Beach to the south.

Changes in the circumstances and sources of the two waves of refugees have created disparities in population characteristics. The first cohort consisted largely of the more privileged segments of the population, refugees with advanced education

Table 2. Distribution of Southeast Asians in the U.S.

State	1990 Census		Office of Refugee Resettlement	
	Total Number	Percent of Total	Total Number	Percent of Total
California	453,363	45.3%	398,200	39.8%
Texas	85,029	8.5%	75,100	7.5%
Washington	36,724	3.7%	46,800	4.7%
Minnesota	36,459	3.6%	36,600	3.7%
Massachusetts	33,732	3.4%	31,400	3.1%
Virginia	27,178	2.7%	25,500	2.5%
Pennsylvania	23,788	2.4%	31,200	3.1%
Wisconsin	23,010	2.3%	17,500	1.7%
New York	22,619	2.3%	35,400	3.5%
Florida	20,379	2.0%	12,200	1.2%
Total	1,001,054		1,001,000	

Census figures do not include Chinese born in SE Asia.

ORR estimates from U.S. Congress, 1992.

ORR figures are the cumulative for 1975 to 1991.

Source: U.S. Bureau of the Census, 1990 Census Report.

and previous professional work experience. In contrast, the second wave represented a wider range of socioeconomic backgrounds. Although still more representative of middle-class segments of their native populations than those who remained, this cohort was more likely than the first to include individuals with lower educational levels and rural, rather than professional work experience (Le, 1993; Bach and Carroll-Seguin, 1986). Refugees from this second wave were also more likely than previous groups to have spent lengthy periods in refugee camps.

Differences in the population characteristics of Southeast Asians by time of entry are reflected in the 1980 and 1990 Census data for California adults between the ages of 18 and 54.

To minimize the influence of time-dependent acculturation on observed outcomes, the characteristics of the 1975-80 cohort as reported in the 1980 Census are compared with the characteristics of the 1985-90 cohort as reported in the 1990 Census.[6] While 65 percent of the 1985-90 cohort had limited English language abilities (spoke English poorly or not at all), only 50 percent of the 1975-79 cohort fell into this category in 1980. Educational differences are even more substantial. According to the 1990 Census, 59 percent of the 1985-1990 refugees had less than a high school education, compared to only 38 percent of the 1975-1979 cohort.

Differences in population characteristics by time of entry are also reflected in differences across ethnic groups. In California, the percentage of prime-age adults (18 to 54) with limited

Table 3. Changes in Federal Refugee Funding
of Cash and Medical Assistance*

Date of Change	State share of AFDC/Medicaid/SSI	RCA/RMA	Gen. Asst. (inc. GA Med.)
Thru 03/31/81	No time limit	No time limit	No funding
04/01/81	36 months	36 months	No funding
04/01/82	36 months	18 months	Months 19-36
03/01/86	31 months	18 months	Months 19-31
02/01/88	24 months	18 months	Months 19-24
10/01/88	24 months	12 months	Months 13-24
01/01/90	4 months	12 months	No funding
10/01/90	No funding	12 months	No funding
10/01/91	No funding	8 months**	No funding
12/01/91	No funding	8 months***	No funding

*All time periods counted from refugee's date of arrival in U.S.

**For new applicants

***For persons receiving RCA/RMA as of September 30, 1991.

Source: Office of Refugee Resettlement, 1993, p. 20.

English language ability varies from a low of 30 percent for Vietnamese to a high of 83 percent for Southeast Asians of Chinese ancestry. The respective percentages for Cambodians, Hmong, and Laotians are 54 percent, 60 percent, and 55 percent. There are also parallel differences in educational attainment. While only 34 percent of the Vietnamese had less than a high school education, 81 percent of the Southeast Asians of Chinese ancestry did. The respective percentages for Cambodians, Hmongs, and Laotians are 59 percent, 67 percent and 63 percent. These variations by time of entry and ethnicity, as we will see below, have significant effects on welfare usage.

Southeast Asians and Welfare

Unlike other ethnic or racial groups, Southeast Asians have been channeled into welfare programs as part of a national strategy to facilitate their economic assimilation. Public assistance has been the cornerstone of U.S. refugee assistance programs. The Indochina Migration and Refugee Assistance Act of 1975 established the basic parameters of U.S. refugee resettlement policy, requiring states to provide the same social services to refugees as to non-refugees. Initially enacted for two years and set to expire in 1977, the Act provided assistance on the same basis as AFDC (Aid to Families with Dependent Children). Low-income refugees who did not qualify for AFDC were eligible for Social Security (SSI) or Refugee Cash Assistance (RCA).

While these basic services were extended beyond the initial 1977 expiration date, the federal government has slowly withdrawn its resources from refugee assistance programs. The time allotted for economic support has consistently declined over the years, as indicated by the figures in Table 3. Related to this trend has been an overall reduction in federal appropriations to Health and Human Services for refugee assistance; between 1986 and 1992, federal funding dropped from $421 million to a proposed $411 million. After adjusting for inflation, what seems like a modest drop in funding amounted to a 27 percent decline, a decline that cannot be explained by changes in the demand for refugee services. Moreover, when normalized by the number of newly admitted refugees, the level of federal

Table 4. Characteristics of Adults Receiving AFDC, California, 1989

	NH-White	Black	Latino	Southeast Asian
Sex				
% Female	79.7%	89.5%	81.8%	52.0%
Education				
No School	0.9%	0.7%	6.4%	34.0%
Less Than HS	31.3%	30.9%	61.6%	40.2%
HS Degree	30.5%	32.4%	18.0%	7.8%
Beyond HS	37.3%	36.0%	14.1%	18.0%
Marital Status				
Unmarried	56.9%	78.8%	60.4%	16.4%
Limited English Proficiency	4.9%	1.0%	28.6%	75.7%
Foreign-Born	10.7%	3.9%	49.7%	99.8%
Mean # Children	2.1	2.3	2.8	3.5
Mean Age	33.4	32.8	33.6	38.1

Sample includes heads of household or spouses between the ages of 18 and 54, with public assistance income in 1989 and at least one natural, adopted or step child.

Source: U.S. Bureau of the Census, as reported in Ong and Blumenberg, 1993

dollars per person dropped by 64 percent. Not surprisingly, dwindling federal dollars has shifted the financial burden from the federal government to the states.

The decline of federal assistance has not translated into a decline by refugees in the reliance on welfare. Instead, refugees have shifted to regular public aid programs. A 1992 survey shows that two-thirds of Southeast Asian households that entered the U.S. in 1985 still relied, wholly or partly, on public assistance (U.S. Department of Health and Human Services, Office of Refugee Resettlement, 1990, p. 58). This is roughly the same usage rate among refugees who arrived in the 1990s. Since most of these refugees did not qualify for federal grants, their payments came primarily from state-operated and funded programs. The only thing that the change in federal policy has accomplished is to shift the refugees into the welfare system more rapidly.

The direct incorporation of Southeast Asians into the welfare system has created a unique population on public assistance (see Table 4). The most salient difference among ethnic and racial groups on welfare is household structure. Southeast Asian welfare households are generally larger in size than other households on welfare. Close to 90 percent of all Southeast Asian AFDC households contain two parents, a sharp divergence from the customary image of the single welfare mother. In contrast, only 43 percent of non-Hispanic white, 21 percent of black, and 40 percent of Latino households contain two parents. Southeast Asian households also have higher fertility rates. In sum, the average family size for Southeast Asian households is close to five persons, while the average family size for other welfare households is approximately 3.5 persons.

Southeast Asian welfare households also differ significantly from other welfare households in terms of education and English language abilities. Educational levels among this group are bi-polar. Thirty percent of Southeast Asian refugees in AFDC households arrive in this country having had no formal education. Among all individuals in AFDC households only 7 percent have had no schooling. A large majority of Southeast Asians in AFDC households have limited facility with the English language, which is not surprising given that this population is largely comprised of immigrants.

Another unique characteristic of Southeast Asians on AFDC is high welfare persistency rates. According to data from the California Department of Social Services (1992), Laotians, Cambodians, and Vietnamese comprise three of the four top ethnic groups with the highest welfare persistency rates. From January 1992 to December 1992, 94 percent of Laotians, 93 percent of

Cambodians, and 89 percent of Vietnamese remained on welfare. The comparable statistics for blacks, Latinos and whites are 81 percent, 79 percent, and 74 percent (California Department of Social Services, 1992).

These percentages suggest that Southeast Asian welfare recipients have a more difficult time exiting from welfare than other recipients, but the statistics by themselves are not conclusive. Inter-racial variations may be due in part to differences in the mix of case loads (AFDC-U versus AFDC-FG) and differences in personal characteristics that influence employability. These issues are addressed systematically in the section on welfare-to-work programs.

Given the continued reliance on AFDC, it is not surprising that welfare usage among Southeast Asians is higher than any other ethnic/racial group. Over half of Southeast Asian adults live in households that receive AFDC. These figures vary across ethnic groups with welfare dependency at over 70 percent for Cambodian, Laotian, and Hmong households and 35 percent for Vietnamese households. And, as mentioned previously, welfare dependency rates among Southeast Asians in California are higher than they are in any other state in the country (Bach and Carroll-Seguin, 1986).

Determinants of Welfare Usage

The determinants of welfare usage among Southeast Asians are quite complex and vary among ethnic groups. In large part, usage is a (negative) function of economic assimilation, which is influenced by individual investments in education and training (human capital). However, while human capital investments (acquired through economic assimilation) are highly determinative of welfare usage, the impact of these factors is mediated by larger structural conditions such as the state of the U.S. economy, refugees' pre-migration experiences, and resources available in U.S. metropolitan areas.

Overall the literature on immigrants finds that educational attainment, English-language abilities, and levels of acculturation as proxied by years in the U.S. affect labor force participation rates as well as wage levels (see Borjas, 1990, for a summary of this literature). Studies on refugees, a subset of the broader literature on immigrants, show similar findings. Research indicates that the ability to speak English, as well as pre-migration professional and managerial work experience, positively influence labor force participation (Bach and Carroll-Sequin, 1986; Haines, 1987; Strand and Jones, 1985).[7]

Our findings concur with those of previous studies. The data suggest that economic assimilation as measured by the number of years refugees live in the U.S. is one of the strongest determinants of economic assimilation, reflecting both the acquisition of new skills as well as a growing familiarity with U.S. labor markets. Cross-sectional data from the 1990 Census show that the longer refugees live in the U.S. the higher their labor force participation. The labor force participation rate among Southeast Asians between the ages of 18 and 54 in California is 57 percent, significantly below that of all U.S. adults. The rate is particularly low for recent refugees; for example, only 37 percent of those living in the country three years or less participate in the workforce. However, after approximately 15 years in the U.S., the labor force participation of Southeast Asians begins to resemble that of all U.S. adults.

Based on the above research, we can assume that the same factors that influence economic assimilation also influence welfare usage. We start by examining each factor separately (a univariate analysis) based on a sample population extracted from the 1990 Public Use Microdata Sample; the sample contains all Southeast Asian males between the ages of 18 and 54 (see Ong and Blumenberg, 1993, for a description of the sampling procedure). The outcome, or dependent variable, is whether an individual resides in a household that receives AFDC assistance; in other words, the individual sampled may or may not receive welfare payments directly but may rely on the benefits received by other family or household members. For convenience, we use the term AFDC usage to signify individuals who live in AFDC households. Therefore, the AFDC usage rate is the proportion of adult males consisting of AFDC users.

As expected, the probability of being a member of an AFDC household varies directly with human capital — educational attainment, English language ability, and general acculturation as proxied by years in the U.S. Over three-quarters of those with little (one to eight years) or no education were in AFDC households compared to only one-third of those with college educations. Nine-tenths of those who did not speak English at all were in AFDC households, while only three-tenths of those who spoke English very well were. Variation in AFDC usage by years of residence in the U.S. is also significant. Only a quarter of those who had lived in this country for over a decade were in AFDC households, while three-quarters of those who had lived in this country for five years or less were in AFDC households.

Demographic factors are also related to AFDC usage. The number of children per household increases the probability of living in an AFDC household because larger families place heavier home-related burdens on parents.[8] Only a quarter of those in households with one child collected AFDC, while three-quarters of those with four or more children did. The influence of children is consistent with the literature on economic assimilation, which indicates that higher fertility rates decrease labor force participation (Bach and Carroll-Sequin, 1986; Rumbaut, 1989). Usage also varies by ethnicity, ranging from a low of 35 percent for Vietnamese to a high of 77 percent for Hmong, although this is partially caused by differences in skills and education, as we will see later.

Finally, there is considerable variation by geographic location. The metropolitan areas of Los Angeles, Orange County, San Diego, and Santa Clara had welfare usage rates lower than the state average (47 percent, 32 percent, 47 percent, and 35 percent for the four respective areas), while the Bay Area had a higher rate (56 percent). The highest welfare usage rate (70 percent) is found outside of Los Angeles, Orange County, San Diego, Santa Clara, and the San Francisco-Bay Area, reflecting the sizeable population of poor Southeast Asians located in California's agricultural communities in the Central Valley.

Separating Influences

The individual factors mentioned in the above sections are highly correlated with each other. For example, ethnic differences in AFDC usage is due, in part, to ethnic variations in human capital and other factors. However, the ethnic group with higher welfare dependency rates also has lower educational attainment, poorer command of the English language, and shorter residency in the United States. Moreover, as suggested earlier, ethnic groups are not identically distributed throughout California communities.

Table 5. AFDC Usage Rates among Southeast Asians – 1990

	Observed AFDC Usage Rates	Diff. from Reference Group	Adjusted Difference
Vietnamese*	0.351		
Cambodian	0.753	0.402	0.271
Hmong	0.770	0.419	0.129
Laotian	0.716	0.365	0.184
Chinese	0.493	0.142	0.072
Years in U.S.			
0-3*	0.737		
4-5	0.738	0.001	0.002
6-8	0.645	-0.092	-0.007
9-10	0.573	-0.164	-0.069
11-15	0.289	-0.448	-0.246
15+	0.230	-0.507	-0.313
English Proficiency			
Not At All*	0.902		
Not Well	0.705	-0.197	-0.201
Well	0.337	-0.565	-0.382
Very Well	0.290	-0.612	-0.447
Educational Attainment			
None*	0.783		
Less than 5 yrs	0.805	0.022	0.017
Less than 9 yrs	0.769	-0.014	0.017
Less than 12 yrs	0.568	-0.215	-0.062
High School	0.432	-0.351	-0.201
Beyond HS	0.334	-0.449	-0.199
Los Angeles	0.471	-0.224	-0.067
Bay Area	0.559	-0.136	0.001
Orange	0.320	-0.375	-0.104
San Diego	0.471	-0.224	-0.072
Santa Clara	0.348	-0.347	-0.052
Rest of State*	0.695		

* Indicates Reference Group

Source: Ong and Blumenberg, 1993

For example, the Central Valley, which exhibits a high AFDC usage rate, has relatively higher numbers of Hmong and Laotians than other areas of the state. One potential consequence of these correlations is that estimates of their effects on welfare usage may be biased when each factor is examined individually.

Standard statistical methods (logistic regressions) are used to estimate the independent effects of various factors on welfare usage. (Details of the model and estimates are reported in Ong and Blumenberg, 1993.) The results are consistent with the arguments presented above: ethnicity, years in the U.S., language proficiency, education, and geography all independently influence welfare usage. Table 5 provides a summary of these effects. The first column reports the observed usage rates by socio-demographic characteristics. The second column reports the variations between sub-populations, and the percentage is calculated as the difference between a given population and a reference population identified with an asterisk. For example, for education, the reference group is the population with no formal education; relative to the AFDC usage rate of this group, the usage rate of Southeast Asian males with a college education is 56 percentage points lower. These raw differences, however, overestimate the influence of additional years of education (or additional years in the U.S., etc.) on AFDC usage. The third column reports the adjusted differences, the group variation after accounting for other factors. In all cases, the adjusted differences remain important.[9]

As expected, usage is related to variations in human capital. English language ability, for example, has a strong effect on welfare usage. Those who speak English very well have a usage rate that is 40 percentage points lower than those who do not speak English at all. While the adjusted differences due to education are smaller than the unadjusted figures, education remains a crucial independent factor in explaining welfare usage. The adjusted usage rates between those with no education and those with some college education is 20 percentage points. However, educational attainment does not have a progressively linear effect. There is essentially no difference in AFDC usage between those with no education and those with one to eight years of education. The usage rate of those with some high school education but no degree is only 6 percentage points. Moreover, education seems to offer no additional decline in AFDC usage after the receipt of a high school degree; in other words, the usage rate of those with only a high school degree is the same as those with some college education.

Usage rates decrease by years in the U.S. with a particularly pronounced effect for those living in the U.S. over a decade. Compared to those residing in the country for less than four years, the usage rate among those living in the U.S. between 11 and 15 years is 24 percentage points lower. The results are consistent with findings by Rumbaut and Weeks (1986) who argue that time in the U.S. is the strongest predictor of welfare dependency. Fass (1986) replicates these findings using data from individual cohorts of refugees. He finds that among Southeast Asian refugees arriving in the U.S. in 1981, 80 percent initially received cash assistance. By 1982 the numbers receiving public assistance dropped to 75.2 percent and declined once again to 62.4 percent in 1983.

One interpretation of these figures is that time in the U.S. is a proxy for acculturation, which lessens reliance on public assistance. However, even if we accept this argument, the numbers indicate that a substantial proportion of Southeast Asians, perhaps well over a quarter, will remain on public assistance after living more than a decade in this country. But even this assessment may be too optimistic. Time of entry is also correlated with other events that are not readily observed in the data but nonetheless can affect AFDC usage. For example, differences in labor market conditions at the time of arrival in this country can affect welfare usage. For example, just as the arrival of refugees was at its peak during the early 1980s, the U.S. economy slipped into an economic recession; employment opportunities evaporated. Although economic adjustment among Southeast Asians continued throughout this recession, the point at which each new cohort of refugees begins to assimilate into the U.S. economy has deteriorated throughout the decade. This trend, Haines (1989) speculates, may be due to cyclical fluctuations in the unemployment rate. Initial difficulties can translate into a persistent "echo" that shows up as higher rates of AFDC usage in later years.

Differences in welfare usage by time of entry may also be tied to pre-immigration experiences. Southeast Asians are distinct from most groups because of their particular history as political exiles. Other studies show that refugees experience significantly greater psychological distress and dysfunction than other immigrants (Rumbaut, 1989). Refugees who arrived in the U.S. during the second wave of migration experienced very different conditions than those who arrived in the U.S. prior to 1980. Many second wave refugees were exposed to life under communist regimes, experienced protracted and dangerous escapes, and/or spent lengthy periods of time in refugee camps. Strand (1989) finds that "war memories," memories of violence and destruction, were one of the most serious problems inhibiting refugees' adaptation. This interpretation, that differences in usage by cohort is due in part to differences in pre-migration experience, is supported by Fass (1986) who finds that the reliance on cash assistance by each new cohort increased throughout the early 1980s.

The differences in pre-migration experiences are also correlated with ethnicity. Among the five Southeast Asian ethnic groups, Cambodians are most likely to be reliant on welfare, even after accounting for other factors. This is the ethnic group that is most likely to have underwent a traumatic pre-immigration experience in their escape from what is now popularly known as the "Killing Fields" and during protracted stays in refugee camps. Ethnic variations are also tied to differences in pre-immigration exposure to advanced capitalistic economies such as experiences with institutions and values that can influence one's ability to adapt to U.S. society.

And, finally, there is a persistent difference in welfare usage by geographic region. Residing in Orange County, Los Angeles, San Diego, and Santa Clara decreases the likelihood of welfare receipt, with the greatest effect occurring in Orange County. The higher cost of housing in some areas may lessen the purchasing power of AFDC benefits (which are uniform throughout the state), causing either selective migration of those more dependent on public assistance to regions with lower housing costs or greater economic incentives to work.[10] In addition to housing costs, the characteristics of the Southeast Asian communities in larger metropolitan areas may also influence welfare usage. Areas such as Los Angeles, Orange County, San Diego and Santa Clara have larger, institutionally more complete Southeast Asian communities, whose better developed sub-economies can provide more employment opportunities, particularly to those refugees who are less acculturated. However, these explanations, particularly the one based on housing costs, are not sufficient. The analysis also shows that the adjusted usage rate among those living in the Bay Area is essentially the same as those living in the "rest of the state" category.

Promoting the Transition to Work

Although the above analysis indicates a tendency for Southeast Asians to leave public assistance over time and with acquisition of skills appropriate to the U.S. economy, the federal government has long recognized that it should assist in this process. Unfortunately, the effects of government resettlement programs on welfare usage have not been consistent. Studies show that initial sponsorship, a commitment by organizations or individuals to assist with refugee resettlement, has had a significant effect on economic outcomes. Refugees assisted by American families and church congregations have a higher employment rate, thus a lower rate of welfare usage, than those assisted by their formerly resettled relatives (Bach and Carroll-Sequin, 1989).

In contrast, some refugee resettlement programs have had no apparent effect on economic adaptation, as indicated by an evaluation of Targeted Assistance Programs (TAP). The purpose of TAP is to provide job training services, English as a second language training, skills training, and other support services for refugees who are at or below the poverty level, with services targeted toward refugees who are currently receiving public assistance and who have been in the U.S. for less than 36 months. In a survey of Southeast Asian refugees in San Diego's demonstration project, Strand (1989) finds that data on job placement and job training utilization exhibit no relationship to employment status; refugees who used the services were employed at approximately the same level as those who did not. This finding is consistent with that found in Gordon (1989) who shows that despite intensified program efforts to reduce welfare dependency, the proportion of refugees living in households receiving assistance only declined by 5 percent, from 61 percent in 1983 to 56 percent in 1985.

Even for public assistance recipients who do find work, exit from public assistance is not guaranteed. Instead, there is a pattern of exit from and re-entry to welfare. Gordon (1989) finds that of the households receiving assistance in 1983, a little less than a third were no longer receiving assistance two years later; however, over a third of those not receiving welfare in 1983 were receiving it two years later. This bi-directional movement can also be seen in employment patterns. About a quarter of all adults who did not have jobs in 1983 were working in 1984, but a sixth of all adults who had held jobs in 1983 were not working in 1984.

Finding employment appears to be more difficult for Southeast Asian than other recipients. The 1990 Census data show that only 23 percent of Southeast Asian receiving AFDC worked during the previous year, a lower percentage than for blacks (27 percent),

Table 6. Estimated Two-Year Impact of GAIN by Ethnicity

	Southeast Asians	Non-Hispanic Whites	Latinos
Probability of Ever Worked			
GAIN	.563	.622	.570
Non-GAIN	.420	.544	.459
Raw difference	.143	.078	.111
Adj. difference	.128***	.052*	.054*
Months of AFDC			
GAIN	21.6	15.1	16.6
Non-GAIN	21.9	17.5	18.2
Raw difference	-0.3	-2.4	-1.6
Adj. difference	0.2	-1.6***	-1.0**

* p>.10; ** p>.05; *** p>.01

Source: Ong and Blumenberg, 1993

Latinos (35 percent) and non-Hispanic whites (41 percent). Moreover, among Southeast Asians living in households that received AFDC at some time during 1989, none worked more than nine hours the week prior to the Census.

The employment problem does not appear to be related to low motivation. In a small sample of participants in GAIN, California's work-incentive program, Hasenfeld (1991) found that 68 percent of Asian respondents had attempted to exit welfare compared to 53 percent of Hispanic, 38 percent of non-Hispanic white, and 28 percent of African American respondents. These figures indicate a very strong desire on the part of Asians to achieve economic self-sufficiency.[11] The social characteristics and economic conditions discussed earlier contribute to Southeast Asians' marginal attachment to work.

To further understand the effects of welfare-to-work programs, we examined the effects of GAIN on AFDC-U participants in San Diego and Los Angeles.[12] (A description of the data and analysis is contained in Ong and Blumenberg, 1993.) The results are summarized in Table 6. The data show that the probability of working at least some amount during the two years for which the data were collected is consistently lower for Southeast Asians than the corresponding probability for either non-Hispanic whites and Latinos, and for GAIN and non-GAIN recipients. Moreover, Southeast Asians collected more months of benefits that the other two ethnic groups.

The effect of GAIN, as measured by the difference between those participating and not participating in the program for non-Hispanic whites and Latinos, was to increase their probability of working and to decrease the number of months they required AFDC. In terms of work, GAIN had a larger impact on Southeast Asians than other racial and ethnic groups, increasing their work rate by nearly a third. Clearly, this group responded to the program by finding jobs. However, the increase in employment did not translate into less welfare usage. Unlike NH-whites and Latinos, GAIN had no detectable effect on lowering the months of benefits collected by Southeast Asians. In other words, Southeast Asians increased their participation in employment without leaving welfare. This finding remains when the analysis is conducted separately for Southeast Asians in each of the two metropolitan areas. In San Diego, the adjusted probability of ever working during the two-year period increased by 9.9 percentage points, but there was no change in months of benefits collected. In Los Angeles, the adjusted probability increased by 14.9 percentage points, with no change in months of benefits.

Although these outcomes appear contradictory, the underlying behavior is plausible given the regulations governing California's AFDC-U program. Households can remain qualified for AFDC-U so long as the principal wage earner works less than 100 hours per month. Consequently, the findings indicate that Southeast Asians responded to GAIN by working within the limits necessary to retain eligibility. This strategy, however, did not necessarily produce a net economic gain for recipients. With the exception of the first four months on aid, any earned income is deducted dollar-for-dollar from a recipient's grant, a deduction equivalent to a marginal tax rate of 100 percent.[13] If the program fails to compensate recipients for work-related costs such as child care and transportation, the reduction in benefits from working may actually result in even less total income. The loss of Medi-Cal benefits (California's Medicaid program for the poor) also appears to be another barrier. Based on qualitative interviews, Smith and Tarallo find the following:

> Many of California's new immigrants, particularly Southeast Asian refugees, facing the choice between work or health, have chosen to remain on AFDC or general assistance for extended periods primarily because it entitles them to Medi-Cal coverage. Although they are quite willing to work, and prefer work to welfare, they have been unable to find jobs that include employee health care benefits (1993, p. 160).

Concluding Remarks

The evidence indicates that Southeast Asians on AFDC constitute a population that is willing to work but that continues to rely on a strategy of combining employment and welfare to survive. One could argue that the source of the problem is the federal policy of using public assistance as the "safety net" for refugees. Given the multitude of problems ranging from the lack of English language ability to pre-immigration trauma, it is inevitable that a large percentage of refugees would rely on this "safety net." Once within the welfare system, many have a difficult time escaping. In part, this difficulty is due to a welfare program that is ill-equipped to handle the special needs of Southeast Asians. Continued poor employment prospects also contribute to the inability or reluctance of Southeast Asians to completely transition off of public assistance. With very limited marketable skills, the best they can expect are low-wage jobs with no medical or other benefits. Although a strategy of relying on welfare and only secondarily, if at all, on work may be rational, it is not desirable. It leaves many families in poverty and contributes to rising welfare dependency rates.

Our goal should be to help people be full and productive members of society, and, at the same time, ensure that they can live decent lives. This requires us to accept the reality that for some individuals, this goal will require regulations that allow for combining work with some form of public assistance, with an emphasis on promoting greater attachment to work and the labor market.

Some reforms such as changes in the maximum-work-hour rule and the effective "tax rate" on earnings can help (California Department of Social Services, 1993). An analysis of a sample of AFDC-U households in Merced County, California, shows that waiving the 100-hour work rule increased the number of working recipients by 29 percent. Lowering the rate of benefit deduction can also increase work effort. Instituting a "fill the gap" plan could increase work participation by California recipients by 50 percent.[14]

While these reforms can generate benefits, a much larger change in public policy is needed. Work should clearly be more desirable than welfare; however, as we have shown, the lack of employment security encourages welfare dependency. Fostering the transition from welfare to work requires access to health care, child care, and other needed services. Moreover, the income of the working poor should be augmented, not just through welfare, but through broader programs that ensure that if an individual works and plays by the rules, then that person and his or her family should not live in poverty.

Appendix — Welfare Programs

Aid to Families with Dependent Children (AFDC) has its roots in the 1935 Economic Security Act, which included a provision to provide Aid to Dependent Children. Today, AFDC is the country's largest welfare program. The federal government provides at least one-half of the program's funding, which is funneled through state governments. Benefit levels are set by the states and vary considerably in states with higher benefit levels contributing more funds to the program. *AFDC-FG* (Aid to Families with Dependent Children, Family Group) provides benefits to children when at least one parent is either absent, incapacitated, or deceased. The overwhelming majority of AFDC-FG cases consist of female-headed families. In California, 87 percent of all AFDC cases are AFDC-FG cases.

Aid to Families with Dependent Children, Unemployed Parent (AFDC-U) is for children who need financial assistance due to unemployment of a parent. Congress established AFDC-U in 1961 to aid two-parent households facing adverse economic circumstances, but this program was optional until October 1990. Prior to that time, approximately one-half of all states provided welfare support to two-parent households. The states that later added AFDC-U were given the option of imposing a limit on the number of months of benefits provided. To qualify, a parent must have been employed previously and be actively seeking work. The majority of AFDC-U cases consist of two-parent families in which the primary earner, generally the father, has lost his or her job. To remain on AFDC-U, the principal wage earner cannot work more than 100 hours during the month.

Greater Avenues for Independence (GAIN) is a California initiative designed to reduce welfare usage by improving the education and job skills of able-bodied recipients. GAIN originated in San Diego County and was subsequently expanded to the entire state in 1985, where each county has implemented the program according to local priorities, economic needs, employment opportunities, and composition of its welfare recipients. The program provides a broad range of educational, employment and support services, including basic education, job search, job clubs, vocational education and training, and long-term pre-employment preparation. These services are provided through tuition subsidies, transportation support, and child care. Training is provided by adult schools, community colleges, regional occupational centers, JTPA (Job Training Partnership Act) programs, and local CEDD (California Employment Development Department) offices.

Notes

1. This study is partially supported by a grant from the Ford Foundation to the LEAP Asian Pacific American Public Policy Institute, for the project on Asian Pacific Americans in the U.S. Economy. California's Department of Social Services provided invaluable assistance, particularly in the form of unpublished data. We want to thank Suzanne Hee for her work as a research assistant. We alone are responsible for the contents of this paper.

2. This figure includes numbers for the Chinese, Japanese, Filipino, Hawaiian and Korean population in the United States, excluding Alaska.

3. As a point of comparison, non-Hispanic whites comprised 32 percent, Latinos 36 percent, and African Americans 22 percent of individuals on AFDC in 1992 (California Department of Social Services, 1992).

4. The lower figure of 71 percent is based on data from California's Department of Social Services. Since aggregate figures do not allow us to determine how many of the Chinese AFDC recipients are Southeast Asian refugees, these figures likely underestimate the percentage of Asian AFDC recipients who are Southeast Asian. Our analysis of the 1990 Census data, which can be used to identify Southeast Asians who are Chinese, indicates that Southeast Asians comprised 87 percent of Asians on AFDC.

5. A part of this difference is due to California's less restrictive treatment of two-parent Southeast Asian households. Lower AFDC usage rates in other states can be due to several factors: until late 1990 about half of all states did not have an AFDC-U program, some states limited enrollment to a fixed period of time (e.g., six months within a 13 month period), and some states with AFDC-U programs made it difficult for refugees to claim employment prior to entering the country as employment that fulfills the requirement of prior paid work. California, however, does not have any of these features. These programmatic differences make the experience in California less comparable with the experiences in other states. However, programmatic differences are not a sufficient explanation because other states such as Massachusetts also have similar AFDC-U provisions but nonetheless have lower usage rates.

6. Ideally, we would categorize those who immigrated between 1975 and 1978 as "first wave" migrants, but the 1980 Census identifies only those refugees who entered between 1975 and April of 1980.

7. The evidence on the relationship between human capital acquisition and welfare is not entirely conclusive. Rumbaut (1989) finds that English proficiency is not significantly associated with welfare dependency. Moreover, some studies show that foreign education is mediated by other conditions and, therefore, is not a significant determinant of labor force participation while others find that pre-migration educational experiences are highly correlated with labor force participation (Strand, 1984; Bach and Carroll-Sequin, 1986; Rumbaut and Weeks, 1986).

8. One would expect an increase in the probability of receiving AFDC because larger families increase the size of benefits and the value of home production. With a given earnings potential, these two factors increase the attractiveness of public assistance relative to work. In the case of Southeast Asians, the earnings potential is extremely low given their limited human capital.

9. Two additional results not discussed in the text are the influences of household structure and size on welfare usage; single-parent households and the number of children increase the likelihood of welfare usage, *ceteris paribus*.

10. Although selective migration is partially captured by variations in human capital and other observed factors, geographic location is probably correlated with other unobserved factors that influence welfare usage.

11. This desire to work is also observed by Smith and Tarallo (1993).

12. Gueron and Pauly (1991) provides a summary of major evaluations of the effects of welfare reform on employment; however, the evaluations cited in their book do not examine racial or ethnic variations.

13. In California there is no difference between the need standard estimated for families and the maximum welfare grant. In contrast, other states such as Maine, provide a "fill-the-gap" financial incentive plan whereby recipients can retain 100 percent of their earnings up to the need standard with no reduction in AFDC grant levels.

14. At the time of this research, California was implementing a number of these reforms.

Chapter 7

Health Professionals

on the Front-Line

Paul Ong and Tania Azores

Asian Pacific Americans are disproportionately involved in the struggle to deliver decent health care to the poor in the urban inner-cities. While Asian Pacific Americans comprise only 3 percent of the total population, they represent nearly a quarter of the health care providers in the public hospitals in our largest metropolitan areas. For many, these health professions are the primary source of service in a fragile and under-financed system. As the first section of this chapter documents, an unacceptable number of our citizens do not have the personal resources to access services in a huge and sophisticated health industry. Unequal access to services is a part of the broader social and economic polarization afflicting this country, with income and race serving as strong determinants of people's ability to receive timely and effective treatment. The tragic consequences of this inequality are glaring in our metropolitan areas, which house large concentrations of the medically underserved. The herculean task of serving this population has fallen on public hospitals, which are discussed in the second section of this chapter. These front-line facilities are underfunded, understaffed, and overwhelmed, creating a system that is short on supplies, chaotic, and inefficient.

The third section of this chapter documents the factors that have made Asian Pacific Americans an increasingly important source of health care professionals for these facilities, and for the country as a whole. The key factors are high rates of graduation from American medical and nursing schools and high rates of immigration of foreign-trained practitioners. The latter factor plays a central role in the concentration of Asian Pacific medical personnel in the public hospitals of America's largest metropolitan areas. As the data in the fourth section of this chapter show, they constitute as much as a quarter of the physicians and nurses.

Stratified Health Care Privileges

America's health system is both one of the world's most advanced and most primitive. During the post-World War II period, per capita expenditure on medical services increased by six-fold in real dollars, from $371 in 1949 to $2,227 in 1992.[1] This expenditure places this nation well ahead of most other advanced economies.[2] It is estimated that this nation's health expenditures will reach one trillion dollars in 1994. As a percent of total expenditure, medical services grew from 5 percent to 14 percent. This has enabled Americans to afford cutting-edge technology and highly specialized health care providers and researchers. Many with once crippling or fatal diseases now enjoy an opportunity to live a better and longer life.

While many Americans enjoy unparalleled health care, others have, at best, limited access. America's health system is hierarchical with disparate sets of privileges. Some communities, particularly in the inner-cities, have less than a tenth of the resources available to their more affluent counterparts. The consequences are localized morbidity and mortality statistics closer to that of under-developed economies than of industrialized economies.[3]

The two groups that have benefitted greatly from growth of the health system are workers and their families who receive health insurance coverage through employment, and the elderly who are covered by Medicare. Employer-provided coverage grew rapidly throughout this period, stimulated at various times by wage control, favorable tax laws, and union demand. By the late 1980s and early 1990s, the majority of Americans received health insurance coverage from an employer-provided program.

The elderly are primarily covered by Medicare, a federally operated insurance program started in 1966 to provide hospitalization and other coverage. Today, Medicare accounts for over half of all federal health dollars, which includes direct benefits and research. Despite some flaws, this program has provided the elderly poor with far greater security than available to many others. This program, along with Social Security, has been one of this nation's major successes in the social policy area. By ensuring decent access to health care, Medicare has provided elderly access to a disproportionately large share of health services.[4]

In contrast, those not covered by private health insurance or Medicare are poorly served by the health system. This group can be divided into two populations. (See Table 1 for estimates of these populations.) The first group includes those on public assistance, particularly Aid to Families with Dependent Children, who are included in the federal-state Medicaid program.[5] This program, which also started in 1966, has had difficulties providing minimal basic health care to the poor. The eligibility requirements mean that Medicaid does not cover all poor people. Over the last decade, only half of those living in families below the federal poverty level were covered by Medicaid, and by the early 1990s, less than half were. Even participation in Medicaid does not guarantee adequate access to health care. Only a third of all physicians fully participate as providers.[6] This low rate is not surprising given that reimbursements for Medicaid patients are generally less than two-thirds of the rate that private insurance companies pay doctors for non-Medicaid patients (*U.S. News and World Report*, September 20, 1993). In major metropolitan areas such as New York City, the reimbursement rate for some basic services can be as low as a quarter of the cost of providing the care; consequently, in 1989, less than a sixth of the medical doctors billed Medicaid for services, with most of them working out of clinics and outpatient departments of hospitals, rather than private offices (Berliner, 1993, p. 30).

Finally, there is a large and growing population of the uninsured, who are only a serious illness away from becoming financially devastated. Nearly 17 percent of the population in 1991 below age 65 were uninsured,[7] and the uninsured rate among the poor was over twice as high as the non-poor. Six in ten of the uninsured live in households that have incomes less than twice the official poverty line.[8] This sizable uninsured population has no counterpart in other Western industrialized economies, where almost everyone enjoys some form of health insurance coverage. The majority of the 37 million uninsured Americans,

Table 1. Health Insurance Status, Non-Elderly Population

	Private Coverage	Other Coverage	Medicaid Only	Un-insured
All Persons	72%	3%	8%	17%
By Income Status*				
Poverty	21%	4%	42%	33%
Low Income	57%	5%	9%	29%
Others	88%	2%	1%	10%
By Race				
Non-Hispanic White	80%	3%	5%	13%
African American	50%	5%	21%	24%
Latino	47%	2%	16%	35%
Asian Pacific Islander	70%	3%	7%	20%
By Metropolitan Size**				
Large	67%	2%	11%	20%
Medium	75%	1%	7%	16%
Small	79%	2%	6%	12%

* Those classified as being in poverty lived in families with an income below the federal poverty line; low-income individuals lived in families with an income between 1 to 1.99 times the poverty line; all others lived in families with an income at least twice the poverty line.

** Large metropolitan areas include MSAs of at least three million persons; medium metropolitan areas include MSAs of at least one million to less than three million; and small metropolitan areas include all other MSAs.

Source: Tabulations by authors from March 1992 Current Population Survey.

perhaps as much as 86 percent, are workers and their families, and most can be classified as the working poor. They work for firms that do not or cannot afford to provide health benefits. This is a population that has grown dramatically in recent years as income polarization increased, and as more firms eliminate or reduce health insurance coverage as a part of their restructuring.

Not having insurance or being poor has a marked impact on usage rates and health care seeking. A 1986 survey revealed that despite their worse health conditions, the poor were less likely to receive health care, and that the uninsured were almost twice as likely to be without a regular source of care than the insured (Freeman et al., 1987; Weisfeld, 1987). An analysis of the 1989 National Health Interview Survey shows that the uninsured were less likely to receive health care than the insured, and this was especially true of the chronically ill.[9]

The lack of financial resources does not allow the poor and uninsured to practice preventive medicine or seek a regular source of primary or ambulatory care. They are crisis-oriented, using health care facilities sporadically and often inappropriately, such as hospital emergency departments for non-critical conditions (Hawkins and Higgins, 1989, p. 132). Although many of the poor pay at least some of their health related costs, there are millions who cannot pay. This medically indigent population, usually made up of low-income, uninsured persons, generates billions of dollars worth of uncompensated health care costs each year.

America's major cities have a large share of those on public assistance or the uninsured. According to estimates from Current Population Survey data, this medically underserved group comprise nearly a third of the population in metropolitan areas with at least three million persons, which is a substantially higher ratio than in small metropolitan areas. The problem in the largest metropolitan areas is even greater. In Chicago, 1.4 million persons in 1991, representing 25 percent of the non-elderly population, were either uninsured or had Medicaid only. New York City had 2.7 million persons, comprising 37 percent of the non-elderly population, who fell into this category. And Los Angeles had the highest uninsured/Medi-Cal rate among the major metropolitan areas, with 3.4 million comprising 40 percent of the total non-elderly population.

Within the large urban areas, those on Medicaid or uninsured are heavily concentrated in poor neighborhoods that have few health care providers. This is ironic because there is no shortage of providers in these metropolitan areas. These cities have a disproportionately large number of providers because of the presence of a sizable affluent population, medical schools, and hospitals that serve a national or even international clientele. Nonetheless, a physician surplus coexists with a physician shortage. In New York City, private physicians concentrate in primarily wealthy areas of the city, while low-income areas of the city are medically underserved because physicians are reluctant to set up practice there (Berliner, 1993, p. 30).

This pattern of avoidance by private providers can be found in every major city and has led to a great disparity, where the ratio of private practitioner to the population in an affluent neighborhood can be as high as 1:150, while that for the poor section of the city can be 1:15,000 (Ginzberg, Berliner, and Ostow, 1993, p. 7). Chicago is an example of this: it has an overall physician/population ratio of about 1:850 persons, but the ratio in the shortage areas may be as high as 1:16,000 or 17,000 (Salmon, 1993). Similar disparities can be found in Los Angeles, where the physician to population ratio in affluent Beverly Hills is ten times lower than in low-income Watts (Brown and Dallek, 1993, p. 122). Programs that subsidized the training of physicians or some of their operating costs in exchange for a promise of serving "underserved areas" have had limited success (Berliner, 1993, p. 31).

The problems facing the medically underserved have worsened over the last few years as the poor and uninsured have become victims of cost containment. Private insurance and federal spending raise demand so rapidly that the cost of providing medical care outpaces the overall rate of inflation. Between 1950 and 1991, overall prices (as measured by the Consumer Price Index for urban residents) increased by 465 percent, while medical care increased by 1,072 percent. This excessive inflation has seriously cut the purchasing power of the dollars spent on health care and partially accounts for the increasing burden of medical care on the whole economy. The threat of runaway health care spending has led to efforts to contain cost.

Public sector efforts to control prices have been limited to setting reimbursement rates for programs funded by the federal government and by the states.[10] The alternative has been to cut spending. While attacking Medicare has proven to be politically unfeasible, the same was not true for other health programs. Congress, under the Reagan Administration, reduced federal funding of Medicaid, shifting greater responsibility for program administration to the states. The net effect was the reduction of health coverage for the poor and near poor during the decade of the eighties. According to Ginzberg, Berliner, and Ostow (1993), over 60 percent of persons at or below federal poverty level were covered by Medicaid in the mid-1970s. By the early 1990s, this number had been reduced to 44 percent. The impact clearly showed up in the National Access Surveys of 1982 and 1986, which revealed a reduction in access to health care for the poor (Freemen et. al, 1987; Weisfeld, 1987).

State governments have also pursued cost cuts, partly by shifting or unloading responsibilities to local jurisdictions, as illustrated by the case in California (Brown and Cousineau, 1987). In a major effort to cut back health care programs, the state removed 250,000 people from Medi-Cal in the early 1980s, and transferred the responsibility for their care to the counties, which were also having fiscal difficulties. In return, the counties received only 70 percent of what the state would have spent for patient care under Medi-Cal. With declining public revenues, this shifting and whittling of responsibility among different levels of government has continued.

Public Hospitals

For many urban poor, locally funded hospitals serve as their primary source of medical care (King, 1989), and, in turn, these public facilities serve a disproportionate share of this population (Bindman et al., 1990). In California, for example, county hospitals served 44 percent of Medicaid patients and 66 percent of the uninsured in 1988. In neighborhoods suffering from a paucity of private practitioners, public hospitals are on the front-line of providing care to the economically disadvantaged. Unfortunately, this system is under fire, overwhelmed by large and growing numbers of patients and squeezed by limited and often declining funds.

The challenges facing Los Angeles County, which has six

hospitals and 45 health centers, illustrate the problems facing the local public health system. The County operates the second largest public health system in the nation, providing nearly one million inpatient days, three million outpatient visits, and 400,000 emergency room visits per year to its population (Los Angeles County, Department of Health Services, 1992). The County has three large inner-city hospitals — Martin Luther King-Drew, Harbor-UCLA, and County General-USC — located in low- or moderate-income neighborhoods that are predominantly black or Latino.

Patient care at these inner-city facilities is at best inadequate. They are so poorly funded and understaffed that they are unable to meet the legally required quality of medical care for the indigent (Dallek, 1987; Brown, Aneshensel, and Pollack, 1993). The problem is aggravated by the private sector which has over time been less willing to provide uncompensated health care. The consequence of this diversion of indigent patients to public hospitals, along with other factors, is "to create more pressures upon the public sector health services system" (County of Los Angeles, Department of Health Services, 1992, p. 62). With limited capacity and a large population in need, the county's hospitals typically operate at 90-100 percent occupancy.

Understaffing and limited resources directly translate into poor or inadequate service (Dallek, 1987). Care is often delayed or cut short. The average waiting time in the emergency rooms is more than six hours. At times, there are often two nurses for as many as 50 emergency room patients. These shortages force emergency-room physicians to perform nursing functions. Patients who need critical beds often wait as long as three days in the emergency room. Non-emergency care is also poor. Cardiology patients who should be seen every one to two weeks are scheduled at three to six month intervals because of patient load, and the wait for an appointment at the Gynecology and Internal Medicine Clinics can be up to three months. The quality of care at one facility was so poor in 1989 that it was in danger of losing its accreditation.[11] It had one of the worst mortality rates in the nation, particularly among newborns.

The conditions in Los Angeles are not unique. In New York City, the public hospitals, which are operated by the New York

City Health and Hospital Corporation, a quasi-public agency, provide services to the majority of patients who are uninsured poor or on Medicaid (Berliner, 1993, p. 34). This distribution is due in part to private hospitals shifting (dumping) uninsured patients to the public sector. Unfortunately, the public facilities "are understaffed, operate with obsolete or broken equipment, and do not function with a high level of competency" (Berliner, 1993, p. 25). Moreover, the number of these facilities has declined, down from 13 to 11, leading to a corresponding decrease of 1,000 acute-care beds. The quality of care faced by the poor in Chicago's public hospitals is no better than that in the other two metropolitan areas. Despite large sums of new funds for capital and other types of improvements, there has been no noticeable progress, in part because of bureaucratic inefficiency and waste (Salmon, 1993, pp. 53, 79) The services that are provided are often substandard (Salmon, 1993, p. 80).

As indicated above, the lack of adequate funding adversely affects staffing. Employment issues vary by professions. Public hospitals have less difficulties hiring physicians than nurses, but these hospitals face other problems with their medical staff. The New York City Health and Hospitals Corporation, for example, has found it easy to fill its staff positions because of two possible reasons: "a physician surplus or, alternatively, simply of the difficulties of starting a private practice" (Berliner, 1993, p. 32). However, the type of doctors that they can recruit is limited by the low pay and stress associated with working in an over-loaded system. The 1990 Census data for four metropolitan regions (Southern California, the greater San Francisco Bay area, Chicago, and New York) indicate that the typical physician in public hospitals earns only three-quarters of that of the typical physician in private hospitals, and less than two-fifths of the typical physician in the non-hospital in the private sector.[12]

A part of the discrepancy in earnings can be attributed to the greater use by public hospitals of younger or recently graduated doctors, many of whom are still in training, and to the hiring of foreign medical graduates, who have relatively fewer opportunities to practice elsewhere. While 36 percent of the physicians in private practice in four of the largest metropolitan regions are 40 years or older, only 28 percent of the physicians in public hospitals are.[13] Moreover, nearly half (47 percent) of the physicians in these facilities are immigrants. Consequently, in many poor communities, young and immigrant physicians in public hospitals are their sole source of medical service given the paucity of private physicians.

For the nursing staff, public hospitals have great difficulties recruiting personnel. This matter is not unique to these facilities. The United States has been plagued by recurrent nursing shortages since as early as 1915 (King, 1989; Flanagan, 1976; Carlson, Coward, and Speake, 1992). A review of the record shows that from the fifties to the eighties, the country experienced seven serious shortages (nursing vacancy rates of 10 percent or more in hospitals), each one lasting from one to three years (McKibbin, 1990). The most recent one continued to the end of the last decade, proving to be "the most persistent and prolonged" shortage in four decades. It has taken the severe and protracted recession of the early nineties to eliminate this shortage.

The shortages have occurred despite a phenomenal growth in the number of nurses from 600,000 in 1960 to over two million by the late 1980s. The shortage is partly due to the rapid growth in the health care industry, creating a dynamic shortage. There is also a cyclical component, with severe shortages during expansionary periods when demand for services is high. Government programs designed to increase the number through educational subsidies and reforming nursing education have helped but have proved insufficient. The shortage is due to the unattractiveness of the occupation. Wages have been held down by monopsony behavior by hospitals and by pervasive gender discrimination in our society. Moreover, working conditions are poor. Life on a hospital floor, where the vast majority work, is very stressful and nurses lack the autonomy that characterizes medical professionals because the medical system subordinates them to physicians. These factors have not only made the profession undesirable for many, but also have generated high turnovers and burnouts. Therefore, it is not surprising that there is a recurring shortage.

Within the nursing market and its recurring shortages, public hospitals are at a disadvantage, despite often offering prevailing wages. Given that working conditions in the public sector are less desirable, public hospitals must offer a compensating premium to stay competitive. Unfortunately, there is no real difference between those working in public and private hospitals.[14] Without a compensating differential, it is not surprising that public hospitals tend to have higher vacancy rates than their private counterparts, a problem that persists even when the shortage is abating in the private sector.

Asian Pacific American Health Care Providers

Over the last quarter century, Asian Pacific American health care professionals have emerged as a noticeable and growing labor force. While Asian Pacific Americans comprise 3 percent of the total population in 1990, they comprise 4.4 percent of the registered nurses and 10.8 percent of the nation's practicing physicians.[15] They are not only disproportionately overrepresented in these two medical fields, but their numbers grew at a phenomenal rate, by approximately seven-fold and five-fold, respectively, since 1970.[16] The Asian Pacific providers can be divided into two groups, those educated in the United States and those trained abroad.

Given that Asian Pacific Americans have extremely high rates of college and university attendance, as discussed in Chapter 3, it is not surprising that a large number have been graduating from U.S. health programs. Their share depends on the relative prestige of the degree and occupation. The percentage from all reporting registered nurse programs, which include those in community colleges and in hospitals, was 1.9 percent in 1989 and grew modestly to 2.5 percent in 1991. However, the percentage of Asian Pacific Americans graduating from baccalaureate nursing programs is both higher and growing more rapidly, from 2.3 percent in 1989 to 4 percent in 1991. The statistics for medical graduates are even more impressive. Between the late 1970s to the mid-1980s, the Asian Pacific share grew from 2 percent to 6 percent, and by 1991 the statistic stood at 11 percent.[17]

Despite the disproportionate numbers graduating from domestic medical and nursing programs, Asian Pacific American health providers who were educated in the U.S. comprise only a small part of the total Asian Pacific health care labor force. The significant presence of Asian Pacific Americans in U.S. medical and nursing schools is a recent phenomenon. With continuing high rates of graduation, U.S.-educated professionals will become an increasingly important source of providers in the future; however, they are in the minority today. Estimates based on the 1990 Census indicate that only roughly a third of the working Asian Pacific physicians were educated in this country, and approximately half of these were either born in the U.S. or were children when they immigrated to the United States.[18] The corresponding statistics for nurses are even lower, with approximately a quarter receiving a U.S. education and roughly half of these being either born in the U.S. or children when they immigrated to the United States.[19]

Despite the imprecision of the data, the estimates clearly reveal that immigration over the last quarter century has been the major source of today's Asian Pacific health care providers. This is not a new phenomenon, although there have been changes in the sending countries. Graduates of foreign medical and nursing schools have been an important part of the U.S. health care system since shortly after World War II. The passage of the Smith-Mundt Act of 1946 created the exchange visitor (J-1) visa category, which enabled health care professionals (and others) to enter this country on temporary basis for educational purposes, primarily to receive training as interns and residents. For some, this became an avenue for permanent immigration;[20] however, other regulations prevented Asians from taking extensive advantage of this provision, and Europeans comprised the bulk of the temporary visitors as well as the permanent immigrants. This racial bias was eliminated with the passage of the Immigration and Naturalization Act of 1965, which dropped the discriminatory national quotas and created preferential categories for certain occupations.

During the late 1960s and early 1970s, when there was a physician shortage in the country, medical graduates received preferential treatment in their application for immigration, temporary worker, or exchange visitor visas. The impact of this favorable treatment can be seen in the increase in numbers of foreign medical graduates (FMGs). Even before the 1965 Immigration Act, FMGs grew from 6 percent of the total numbers of physicians in 1959 to 10 percent in 1963 (Leibowitz, 1988, p. 2). By 1976, there were 85,456 FMGs, comprising 21 percent of the total numbers of physicians.[21]

When the shortage turned into a surplus, the favorable treatment accorded to foreign medical graduates (FMGs) disappeared. The Health Professions Educational Assistance Act of 1976 made it more difficult for FMGs, eliminating the blank labor-certification that had previously enabled them to receive an occupational visa based on their training, and adding an examination to screen potential exchange visitors and immigrants (U.S. Commission on Civil Rights, 1980). FMGs could continue to apply for an occupation-based immigrant visa, but only on a case-by-case basis, which required sponsors to prove that positions could not be filled by U.S. workers. In practice, this limited occu- pational immigrants to positions in geographic areas or specialties with shortages. The post-1976 restrictions slowed rather than stopped the flow of FMGs. By 1986, there were over 123,090, comprising 22 percent of all physicians. In 1986, after an analysis indicated that a majority of immigrants who had entered via occupational visas no longer practiced in a shortage area, the U.S. stopped granting immigration visas based on the shortage criterion. However, even with this decision, nearly 9,000 physi- cians were able to enter the country during the 1989, 1990, and 1991 fiscal years. The most recent figures show that FMGs still comprise 21 percent of all U.S. physicians (Roback et al., 1992), indicating that international flow of these professionals has roughly kept up with the expanding pool of physicians in the United States.

Asian nations have been one of the major sources of FMGs. Prior to the mid-1960s, most FMGs were from Europe, but with the end of the biased quota system, the flow from Asia grew. In the early seventies, as many as 5,000 Asian Pacific FMGs entered annually as immigrants (U.S. Commission on Civil Rights, 1975). In 1971, they comprised 77 percent of medical exchange visitors. Their share of newly-arriving immigrant physicians and surgeons was equally large, over two-thirds during the early 1970s. Between 1972 and 1985, 29,843 physicians from the major Asian Pacific sending countries (India, the Philippines, Korea and China, Hong Kong, and Taiwan) immigrated to the U.S. (Ong, Cheng, and Evans, 1992). By the early 1980s, Asian Pacific FMGs comprised nearly half of the total stock of the FMG population (Eiler and Loft, 1986). Even under the more stringent regulations after 1986, immigration has continued, as shown in Table 2. For the three fiscal years (1989,

1990, and 1991), 4,453 physicians from Asian Pacific countries became permanent immigrants, over half of all such immigrants. Only one in ten came through the occupational preference categories, while the vast majority came through family sponsorship.

The immigration of foreign-nurse graduates (FNGs) has followed a different pattern than that of FMGs. The policies governing the movements of FNGs have been shaped by recurring and endemic shortages of registered nurses described earlier. This labor shortage has contributed to a continuing preferential treatment for FNGs both as immigrants and as temporary workers. Unlike physicians, where the exchange-visitor is important for non-immigrants, the H-1 category, which gives persons the right to work in the United States on a short-term basis, has been important for FNGs. Nursing has not only continued to qualify

Table 2. Immigrant Health Care Providers
by Country of Birth
Fiscal Years 1989, 1990, 1991

	Physicians	Nurses	Other Health Occup.
Total, All Countries	8,798	18,888	10,901
Philippines	901	9,875	2,862
India	1,424	1,003	570
People's Republic of China	807	460	318
Korea	78	285	141
Taiwan	249	193	278
Hong Kong	95	201	175
Other Asian	899	324	585
Total Asian	4,453	12,341	4,929
All Others	4,345	6,547	5,972

Source: Tabulations by authors from INS Tapes

persons for H-1 sponsorship, but FNGs have received relatively more access to labor certification for the purpose of qualifying for permanent immigration than physicians in the post-1976 period. Moreover, the federal government responded to the shortage of nurses in the late 1970s and parts of the 1980s by allowing temporary workers to prolong their stay in the country for as long as six years. But even this proved to be insufficient in the late 1980s because of the potential losses from those whose visas would expire, even with the extensions. Congress acted by passing Immigration Nursing Relief Act of 1989 (INRA), which allows nurses who entered the U.S. with H-1 visas before September 1, 1989, and have worked in nursing for three years, to adjust to permanent status without regard to per country caps on immigration.

Despite the favorable treatment of FNGs, foreign-trained nurses make up only a fraction of the nursing work force, less than a tenth in 1990.[22] Where they are important is in selective hospitals suffering from severe shortages, such as the inner-city facilities in older metropolitan areas facing fiscal difficulties. These hospitals have actively recruited nurses from throughout the world, using their own recruiters and outside agencies based both in the United States and abroad. Although many hospitals favor FNGs from Western countries such as Great Britain and Canada, Asia has been the largest source of foreign nurses.

This trend is clearly evident among both the temporary and permanent immigrants. In the late 1960s, Asians comprised four out of every five nurses on J-1 visas, which was then the primary mode of entry for non-immigrant nurses. This pattern continued after H-1 visas (temporary work visas) replaced J-1 visas. In the late 1980s, Asians comprised over three-quarters of all H-1 nurses. There has also been an equally remarkable change among nurses who are permanent nurses. In 1966, 10 percent of immigrant nurses were from Asia, but by the late 1980s and early 1990s, three-quarters were. The immigration of Asian Pacific nurses first reached a high point in the seventies when their numbers doubled from 1,768 at the beginning of the decade, comprising 36 percent of all nurses entering under the professional category, to 34,576 in 1974 when they comprised 65 percent of all immigrating nurses. Altogether, roughly 37,000 registered nurses immigrated from just four Asian sending countries between 1972 and 1985 (Ong, Cheng, and Evans, 1992). As Table 2 shows, this high rate of immigration continued, with over 12,000 entering during the fiscal years of 1989, 1990, and 1991. Over a third were adjusters who took advantage of the 1989 Immigration Nurse Relief Act, and another quarter entered through the occupational quotas. The combination of temporary and permanent immigration has left its mark. By the late 1980s, over three-quarters of the foreign-trained nurses in the U.S. were Asian Pacific (1988 National Sample Survey of Registered Nurses).

Although there are FNGs from throughout the Asia Pacific region, the Philippines is the biggest supplier of nurses to the U.S. Nearly 25,000 Filipino nurses immigrated to the U.S. between 1966 and 1985. Almost 10,000 Filipino nurses immigrated between 1989 and 1991, comprising more than half of all nurse immigrants for that period. The dominance of Filipino nurses among those with temporary working visas is also great. Almost three-fourths of all H-1 nurses are from the Philippines (Interpreter Releases, 1989). In all, between two-thirds and three-quarters of the Asian Pacific FNGs are from the Philippines.[23]

Asian Pacific Americans on the Front-Line

Asian Pacific Americans are not only overrepresented at the national level in the medical and nursing professions, but they are especially overrepresented in the public hospitals of major metropolitan areas.[24] This pattern is due in part to self-selection by Asian Pacific Americans, both U.S.-and foreign-educated practitioners. Because of their professional standing and the values and lifestyle that accompany this education and economic position, many prefer to live and practice in cosmopolitan cities. Moreover, the large metropolitan areas offer a rich cultural life and large Asian Pacific communities that cater to ethnic-specific needs. However, this self-selection process is only one factor.

Immigration is a primary factor in producing the relatively high numbers in medical professions. As stated earlier, the immigration law provided, and in some cases still provides, preferential consideration to the highly-skilled. Hospitals in major metropolitan areas have been major sponsors of both temporary workers and permanent immigrants. During the seventies, many of these hospitals, particularly those not directly affiliated with U.S. medical schools, filled their positions for medical residents with foreign graduates (Salmon, 1993, p. 81). Many hospitals in New York and Chicago responded to the nursing shortage in the late 1980s by recruiting nurses from foreign countries (Berliner, 1993, p. 32; Salmon, 1993, p. 73). By the late 1980s, a quarter of registered nurses in New York City were foreign-trained, about half of them on temporary visas.[25]

The foreign-educated professionals in the metropolitan hospitals provide crucial services, particularly to the poor. In general, FMGs served a disproportionately larger share of disadvantaged patients and saw more Medicaid patients than other physicians (Studnicki et al., 1976; Swearinger and Perrin, 1977). This is due in part to their presence in FMG-dependent hospitals. Those facilities that have FMGs comprising at least a quarter of their medical staff tend to have a larger share of Medicaid patients (Leibowitz, 1988, p. 29).

FNGs also provide crucial services in the hospitals. According to the Vice President of Nursing at Beth Israel Medical Center in New York City,

> (H-1 nurses) tend to be concentrated in certain services and units . . . the areas where there is the most significant risk of stress and burnout in the profession are the intensive care units and the medical/surgical services. Therefore, while every individual nurse is valuable, those working in these areas are virtually irreplaceable and of critical importance to our health care system.[26]

These nurses are so crucial that "if New York were to lose 5 percent of its nursing complement, neglect and mortality would accelerate and place an unconscionable strain on already over-burdened U.S. nurses."[27] Their contributions are also indirect.

> Without foreign nurses, our already over-extended nurses would be unable to cope. Without the assistance that foreign nurses offer, many nurses would simply leave nursing for less stressful and less physically demanding jobs.[28]

The importance of H-1 is not limited to New York. In one Southern California Hospital, for example, half of 90 H-1 nurses were working on critical care units, where they had 80 open positions.[29]

Many of these foreign-educated professionals in the metropolitan hospitals are Asian Pacific. For example, according to data gathered by the Philippine Nurses Association of America, Filipinos comprise 85 percent of H-1 nurses in New York City and 92 percent in New Jersey. The consequence of recruitment and hiring of Asian Pacific FMGs can be seen in the geographic patterns of recent immigrants. INS data for the fiscal years of 1989, 1990, and 1991 show that 42 percent of the physicians and 59 percent of the nurses settled in just four metropolitan areas: New York/Newark, Chicago, San Francisco/Oakland, and Los Angeles.[30]

The impact of this trend can also be seen in 1991 EEOC data for all hospitals in the four areas.[31] Asia-educated professionals, along with U.S.-educated Asian Pacific Americans are highly visible among the professional ranks: 21 percent in New York, 28 percent in Los Angeles, 24 percent in the San Francisco Bay area, and 13 percent in Chicago.[32] They, more often than not, comprised more than half of the minority professionals employed in hospital settings. Although the statistics include all Asian Pacific professionals, a large majority are foreign-educated.[33]

Among metropolitan hospitals, the public hospitals are more likely to use Asian Pacific health care providers. As stated earlier, financial constraints and poor working conditions have forced these facilities to recruit and hire foreign-trained professionals. Los Angeles County's Martin Luther King Hospital, which serves a predominantly low-income black and Latino community, exemplifies the growing dependency on Asian Pacific medical and nursing professionals. The Asian Pacific share grew from 27 percent in 1983 to 34 percent in 1989,[34] with the majority being Asian-educated practitioners. While most other public hospitals in major metropolitan areas are not as dependent, there is no question that Asian Pacific Americans are tremendously overrepresented, as shown in Table 3. Within the four metropolitan areas, Asian Pacific health practitioners comprise about a quarter of all physicians and nurses employed in local public hospitals.

Table 3. Ethnic Distribution of Health Professionals in Four Metropolitan Areas

	Asian Pacific Americans	Non-Hispanic Whites	Others
Physicians			
All	18%	70%	12%
Hospitals	21%	66%	13%
Public Hospitals	24%	53%	23%
Registered Nurses			
All	16%	61%	23%
Hospitals	19%	59%	22%
Public Hospitals	24%	37%	39%

Note: Statistics apply to those employed during the enumeration week for the 1990 Census.

Source: Tabulations from U.S. Bureau of the Census, 5% Public Use Microdata Sample, 1990.

Concluding Remarks

As we have seen, Asian Pacific Americans have assumed a disproportionate share of the responsibilities to provide health care in the public hospitals, and in this country's health system in general, and by doing so have contributed to the well-being of this nation. These responsibilities should be accompanied by a set of opportunities, which would benefit both the practitioners and their patients.

Practitioners should have the opportunity to improve their skills and practice good medicine. For foreign-educated professionals, many public hospitals are not equipped to provide the additional training needed to improve and refine skills. In the case of FNGs, the training can be crucial in determining whether they can pass the RN licensing exam and continue to practice in their chosen profession. Training alone, however, is insufficient. Public hospitals are plagued by poor service, but the quality of service is not related to the use of foreign-educated practitioners. The quality of care appears to be affected by hospital characteristics rather than the presence of a FMG (Leibowitz, 1988). For nurses, a shortage of staff leads to a heavy workload, frustration and an inability to provide professional care (Spangler, 1991). The stress and understaffing found in many public hospitals may be contributing factors for the lower quality of service, as indicated by the earlier discussion on the facilities in Los Angeles.

Asian Pacific professionals should also have the opportunity to practice in a harmonious workplace. Unfortunately, cultural and language differences have created inter-group tensions on the job (Imahara, 1993). One study of nurses reveals that differences in language, interpersonal relations, and lifestyles create misunderstandings and conflicts between nurses educated in the Philippines and Anglo-American nurses (Spangler, 1991). Fortunately, acculturation on the part of Filipinos ameliorates these problems, but this is a slow process, one that can be helped along by more training. In general, there is a need for greater understanding and tolerance about different cultures, and more appreciation for the potentially unique contributions of those educated abroad.

Finally, Asian Pacific Americans should have a voice in the operations and decision-making of the public hospitals. While they comprise a disproportionate share of the medical and nursing staff in the public hospitals in the large metropolitan areas, they have not moved into supervisory and management positions in the same proportions. This discrepancy can be seen in detailed employment statistics for the three major public hospitals in Los Angeles. Asian Pacific Americans comprise 34 percent of the professionals (physicians and nurses), 28 percent of supervisory professionals (e.g., Supervising Clinic, Staff or Surgery Nurse, or Senior Physician), but only 12 percent of management positions (Chief Physicians, Directors of Nursing, or Nursing Directors). There is no simple explanation for this discrepancy, but nonetheless, the consequence is a lack of an Asian Pacific perspective in the development of policies, which, in turn, can adversely affect the effectiveness and appropriateness of health care in these facilities.

The Asian Pacific voice is particularly important as we undertake the debate over health care reform. Inadequate health care for the poor, along with rising costs, is at the heart of the current discussions on the President's proposal for reform. Although some changes will occur, it is likely that we will continue to see unequal access to health care. There will still be those who have less coverage, live in neighborhoods that have few medical resources, and rely on public facilities. There may be new incentives to increase the number of physicians and nurses working in the inner-cities, but it is unlikely that the maldistribution of private-sector professionals will be completely eliminated. Under these conditions, Asian Pacific Americans will continue to constitute a disproportionately large share of the providers on the front-line. Incorporating the concerns and insights of these individuals would help in the planning for whatever new health system emerges.

Notes

1. These and the following national statistics are based on data from the 1990 and 1993 *Economic Report of the President*. The dollar amounts are reported for 1992 dollars, and the 1992 figure is based on the third quarter.

2. Statistics on international comparisons are based on data from the Organization of Economic Cooperation and Development, Department of Health and Human Services, and the data on per capita expenditure and insurance coverage are cited in the White House Domestic Policy Council, 1993, p. 11. The data show that per capita expenditure in the U.S. is approximately twice that in the industrialized countries of Europe and over one-and-a-half times that in Canada.

3. These dismal statistics are the outcome of both larger social and behavioral problems that create health problems and the lack of adequate health care services.

4. The large medical bills of the elderly are not just the consequence of Medicare. The elderly have greater health needs given the illnesses associated with advanced age. Medicare, along with Medicaid for the medically indigent elderly, has allowed this population to secure medical treatment, much of which is very expensive.

5. This program also includes the elderly who are medically indigent, and thus cannot cover the co-payment for Medicare, and the non-elderly disabled. Although children and adults in families accounted for 72 percent of the enrollees in 1990, they received only 29 percent of the dollar benefits (Kaiser Commission on the Future of Medicaid, 1992).

6. This is according to data from the American Medical Association, which are cited by the Kaiser Commission on the Future of Medicaid, 1992.

7. Data on the uninsured is taken from the chapter on "The Economics of Health Care," in *Economic Report of the President*, 1993, and page 137 in particular, from the White House Domestic Policy Council's *Health Security, The President's Report to the American People* (1993), and from Employee Benefit Research Institute (1992). Additional data compiled from the 1992 Current Population Survey by the authors. There are differences in estimates, depending on how the insurance-status of children are determined. Professor E. Richard Brown of UCLA provided valuable comments on using the CPS data; however, we alone are responsible for the compiled statistics.

8. For a family of four, the poverty line in 1991 was $13,924. The poverty line varies by family size and composition.

9. This is based on Hafner-Eaton, 1993. This study also indicates that after controlling for numerous independent variables (e.g., insurance, health, and income status), utilization of health care by Asian Pacific Americans is considerably lower than other racial groups. This may be due to several factors, such as culturally determined health care behavior, and language and cultural barriers.

10. President Carter attempted to regulate hospital expenditures but his plan was rejected by Congress in favor of a voluntary program proposed by the American Hospital Association. The program was initially able to control rising hospital outlays, but it had no lasting effect (Ginzberg, 1993).

11. This facility was Martin Luther King-Drew, which houses the Drew Medical School (Brown, Aneshensel, and Pollack, 1993). Ironically, this hospital was established in response to findings from the McCone Commission's report on the causes of the 1965 Watts riots, which cited the gross inadequacy of health care in the areas affected by the riots. While having this facility in South Central, which includes Watts, represents some improvement, the inability of providing quality care shows a lack of long-term commitment.

12. This is based on median total earnings in 1989 as reported in the 1990 1% Public Use Microdata Sample, which include salaries and self-employment income. The median is used because a large number of physicians have earnings that fall in the top, open-ended income category, thus any estimate of the mean would be seriously biased downward. The estimated median annual earnings for physicians in the four metropolitan regions are $45,000 for those in public hospitals, $60,000 for those in private hospitals, and $121,000 for those in a private, non-hospital setting.

13. This group of four includes the following: New York, Nassau-Suffolk, and Newark Metropolitan Statistical Areas (MSAs); Chicago MSA; Los Angeles, Orange, San Bernardino, and Ventura Counties; and San Francisco, Oakland, and San Jose MSAs. These regions were selected because they contain large numbers of Asian Pacific American health care providers. The statistics are compiled from the 1990 Census 5% Public Use Microdata Sample.

14. Annual earnings and hourly wages are estimated from the 1990 5% Public Use Microdata Samples for the four metropolitan regions. The median annual earnings in 1989 for RNs in public hospitals was higher than that for RNs in private hospitals ($35,000 and $32,000, respectively), but the median hourly wage was slightly lower ($18.00 and $18.13, respectively). Those working in hospitals generally earn more than those working outside hospitals, a pay difference that is associated with the greater stress and poorer working conditions in hospitals.

15. These figures come from the CD-ROM version of the Equal Employment Opportunity (EEO) File compiled from the 1990 Census.

16. The 1970 numbers for Asian Pacific registered nurses and practicing physicians only include figures for the Chinese, Japanese and Filipino population. There were 1,242 Chinese, 2,524 Japanese, and 8,051 Filipino nurses. For practicing physicians, there were 2,632 Chinese, 1,654 Japanese and 5,701 Filipino.

17. *Minorities and Women in the Health Fields*, 1987 Edition, U.S. Department of Health and Human Services, Health Resources and Services Administration; Association of American Medical Colleges, *Minority Students in Medical Education: Facts and Figures*, Volume 6, December 1991.

18. The Public Use Microdata Sample for the 1990 Census does not contain information on place of education. In the case of U.S.-born, we assume that they received their education in this country. Because some may have gone abroad for their medical education, this assumption biases the estimates in favor of the number of U.S.-educated persons. For immigrants, we first calculate the number of U.S.-educated persons by first imputing the age of individuals at the time of entry into the United States, which is equal to age at the time of the Census minus years in the U.S. Because the time of entry into this country is reported as categorical data, we estimate the number of years in this country by taking the mid-point for each categorical period. If we assume the physicians typically complete their medical education by age 24 then we estimate that 36 percent are U.S.-educated. Twelve percent were U.S.-born and 5 percent are immigrants who were 12 years old or younger when they entered the U.S.

19. The method described in the previous footnote is also used to estimate the statistics on nurses. If we assume that nurses typically finish their education by age 21, then 25 percent are U.S.-educated. This is based on the 8 percent who are U.S.-born and 17 percent are immigrants who were 21-years old or younger when they entered the U.S. If we assume that nurses typically complete their education by age 20, then 21 percent are U.S.-educated. Data from the 1988 National Sample Survey of Nurses indicate that 73 percent of Asian nurses received their basic nursing education abroad.

20. During the 1950s, several legislative modifications to the act limited the use of these temporary visas and implemented restrictions on adjustments to permanent status.

21. The FMG numbers include 24,170 U.S. citizens who received their education abroad. However, this can also include naturalized citizens (Roback et al, 1986).

22. This is based on estimates from the Census. Data from the 1988 National Sample Survey of Nurses, by the PHS Division of Nursing, U.S. Department of Health and Human Services, indicate that only 3 percent of the RNs received their basic nursing education abroad. However, it appears that the number of Asian Pacific Americans RNs is undercounted. While 1990 Census data show that over 4 percent of all RNs are Asian Pacific Americans, the Survey of Nurses show that only 2.3 percent (based on the weighted sample) are Asian Pacific American. This discrepancy may be due to ethnic differences in the response rate to the Survey, or to a difference in definitions of RNs used by the Census and the Survey. The Census relies on self-reporting while the Survey relies on listing of those with licenses to practice.

23. In the 1988 National Sample Survey of Nurses, 72 percent of the Asian-educated respondents were from the Philippines.

24. The relative overrepresentation is not limited to the large metropolitan areas. This is due in part to the maldistribution of all doctors and nurses, which leaves both the inner-cities and small towns underserved. On the other hand, FMGs are more evenly distributed throughout the country (U.S. Department of Health and Human Services, 1983). One consequence is that foreign-medical graduates are relatively more likely to be found in non-metropolitan areas because some of these communities have turned to immigrant doctors. A recent study reports that an estimated 75 percent of physicians in rural Michigan are immigrants, and that about half of Illinois' 12,000 immigrant doctors have their practice outside the cities and suburbs (Johnson, 1993). In the small town of Dixon, Illinois, the hospital is staffed by doctors from China, Korea, and India.

25. Prepared statement of Stephen H. Cooper, VP, Hospital Association of New York State before the House of Representatives at the Hearing on H.R. 1507 and H.R. 2111, Immigration Nursing and Relief Act of 1989, on May 31, 1989.

26. Testimony of Irene McEachen, VP, Nursing, Beth Israel Medical Center in New York City before the House of Representatives at the Hearing on H.R. 1507 and H.R. 2111, Immigration Nursing and Relief Act of 1989, on May 31, 1989.

27. Testimony of Katherine Abelson, Exec. VP, Local 1199 Drug, Hospital and Health Care Employees Union/RWDSU/AFL-CIO before the House of Representatives at the Hearing on H.R. 1507 and H.R. 2111, Immigration Nursing and Relief Act of 1989, on May 31, 1989.

28. Prepared statement of Stephen H. Cooper, VP, Hospital Association of New York State before the House of Representatives at the Hearing on H.R. 1507 and H.R. 2111, Immigration Nursing and Relief Act of 1989, on May 31, 1989.

29. Prepared statement of Stephen H. Cooper, VP, Hospital Association of New York State before the House of Representatives at the Hearing on H.R. 1507 and H.R. 2111, Immigration Nursing and Relief Act of 1989, on May 31, 1989.

30. Place of intended residence is reported by zip code. We used the following three-digit codes to define our areas: 070 to 073 and 100 to 116 (New York/Newark); 600 to 606 (Chicago); 940 to 949 (San Francisco/Oakland); and 900 to 918 (Los Angeles).

31. The total is based on unpublished data provided by the Equal Employment Opportunity Commission. Percentages are for Los Angeles-Anaheim-Riverside CMSA, San Francisco-Oakland CMSA, New York, New Jersey and Connecticut CMSA, and the Chicago(IL)-Gary(IN)-Lake County(WI) CMSA. Unless otherwise noted, statistics included in this paragraph are drawn from this source.

32. As a comparison, the 1990 Census shows that Asian Pacific Americans comprised no more than 15 percent of the population in these four metro areas (9 percent in Los Angeles, 15 percent in San Francisco, 3 percent in Chicago, and 6 percent in New York).

33. Using the method described earlier, we estimate from the 1990 Census that 44 percent of the physicians and 21 percent of the nurses in the four metropolitan region are U.S.-educated.

34. The statistics are compiled from data provided by Professor Tom Larsen of California State University, Los Angeles.

Chapter 8

Scientists and Engineers

Paul Ong and Evelyn Blumenberg

From Silicon Valley to Route 128, from laboratories in major research universities to private think-tanks, Asian Pacific American scientists and engineers have made enormous contributions to the U.S. economy. A few have risen to the pinnacles of their professions as Nobel Prize winners, presidents of universities, and executives of "high-tech" corporations. Far more important are the hundreds of thousands who receive less public recognition but nonetheless perform invaluable services. While this infusion of Asian Pacific Americans has brought im-measurable benefits to this nation, their presence has raised numerous issues that must be resolved to maximize individual potential and the national interest.[1]

To understand the importance of this group of professionals, we start by first summarizing the role of technology, and scientists and engineers (S&Es) in the U.S. economy. Despite a sizeable expansion of the S&E labor force over the last two decades, the United States has failed to produce sufficient numbers during a time when technology has come to play a more important role in determining the competitiveness of nations in the global economy. The next section examines the phenomenal growth and characteristics of the Asian Pacific S&E labor force. Asian Pacific scientists and engineers have very high levels of educational attainment, are concentrated in research and development, and are overwhelmingly comprised of the foreign-born but U.S.-educated. The third section focuses on the supply of immigrants, which is governed by a complex process involving the "Westernization/Americanization" of higher education on a global scale and by immigration regulation. Together, these two factors have created an extremely educated labor pool of Asian

Pacific S&Es who fill critical positions in the U.S. economy. The final section examines how well these professionals are faring. The analysis indicates earnings parity, although immigrants are likely to earn less than non-immigrants. The major issue confronting Asian Pacific Americans in these fields is the "glass ceiling," specifically the barriers to upper management positions.

Scientists and Engineers

The economic well-being of the United States depends on its technological capacities (Porter, 1990; Grossman and Helpman, 1991; Nelson and Wright, 1992; Dollar and Wolff, 1993). Since World War II, investments in higher education and research and development (R&D), and the expansion of a highly-educated labor force have contributed to increasing productivity and a rising standard of living. More recently, technology has taken on importance in terms of international trade. One indication is the fact that America's exporting industries are more technologically intensive than America's manufacturing base as a whole; exporting industries employ a higher proportion of highly-educated workers than the rest of the economy (Abowd and Freeman, 1991, pp. 17-18). The industries where we have an advantage over other nations are those where we have a technological edge.

Scientists and engineers are crucial in determining this nation's technological capacity through their role in the creation of basic knowledge, the transformation of it to practical applications, and designing and operation of complex and sophisticated equipment. Scientists and engineers are central to the innovation of products and production processes. They are the critical personnel for such complex projects such as the Information Superhighway, the Joint International Space Station, the Human Genome Project, and SEMATECH, the joint public-private R&D venture in semiconductors. Their contributions are not limited to these high-profile endeavors. S&Es apply their talents to improving everyday electronic and mechanical equipment, drugs and chemical-based products, and thousands of other goods. As a group, S&Es comprise a significant part of the labor force in what Robert Reich calls the symbolic-analytic services (1992), which constitute the key sector of advanced economies.

While this nation's high-technology labor force has expanded, the growth is less than one might expect given the increasing importance of technology, both domestically and internationally. Between 1970 and 1990, the number of S&Es climbed from 1.8 million to 2.9 million, according to the U.S. Census.[2] Despite this increase, the growth of the S&E labor force (65 percent) only slightly outpaced the growth of the total labor force (51 percent). In other words, S&Es as a percentage of the total workforce increased only marginally (from 2.2 to 2.4 percent). Moreover, changes in the educational levels do not indicate an unambiguous upgrading. On the positive side is a decline in the proportion of S&Es with less than four years of college education, which decreased from 41 percent 1970 to 30 percent in 1990. On the other hand, the proportion with some graduate training has not increased. In 1970, 25 percent had five or more years of college education, while in 1990, 23 percent had post-bachelor's degrees. Other data reveal that the problem is particularly severe at the doctorate level. Total Ph.D. production in S&E increased rapidly after 1960, peaked in 1972, and then declined until the late 1970s; only in the 1980s has the number of science and engineering Ph.D.s increased, but much of this is tied to an increase in the number of foreign students (Atkinson, 1990).

The difficulty this nation faces in producing an adequate supply of S&Es at the right time and in the right place is rooted in the very nature of the labor market for these workers. This country has suffered from niche and cyclical shortages due to changes in public expenditures, rapid expansions or contractions of industries associated with product cycles and business cycles. For example, defense spending, long the single largest source of public expenditure on R&D and the production of high-technology goods, first built up the aerospace industry and then later decimated it, dislocating thousands of aerospace engineers (Ong and Lawerence, 1993). In contrast, the rapid growth in high-technology sectors in micro-electronics has heightened the demand for highly-educated scientific workers, even while this nation has lost production to off-shore and foreign operations (Ong and Mar, 1992).

The sudden fluctuation in demand throws the market into disequilibrium. In the short term, the supply of S&Es is unable to adjust quickly. This is caused in part by a limitation on the transferability of skills across fields; consequently, a shortage in one industry cannot be easily relieved by recruiting individuals working in other industries. Moreover, the number of new entrants cannot be rapidly expanded. The effective number of new entrants is determined by the number of students who entered higher education years earlier, when the relative attractiveness of the field could have been very different. In other words, response to changes in demand takes years, by which time the need could have reversed or shifted to other sectors.[3]

Producing S&Es with advanced training suffers from not only fluctuations in demand but also from a more basic market imperfection. Research and development, as a public good, generates social benefits that may not be captured as profits by private industry. One consequence is that investments in R&D can be lower than optimal from a societal perspective. This flaw has been the basis for government incentives to R&D, but despite these efforts R&D expenditures as a percentage of GND declined throughout much of the 1970s and 1980s.[4] The inability of private enterprise to completely internalize the benefits of R&D translates into lower salaries for highly-trained workers and dampens the demand for graduate degrees in technology fields. Northrup and Malin (1985) find that since the mid-1960s the starting salaries of Ph.D., master and bachelor graduates with engineering and technology degrees have converged; between 1966 and 1982, the relative difference between the monthly starting salary of a Ph.D. and master's and between master's and baccalaureate declined by more than one-half.

An analysis of 1990 Census data show that the returns to advanced degrees may not be sufficiently high to attract individuals to pursue graduate studies.[5] For both scientists and engineers, earning a master's degree increases hourly wages by 14 to 15 percent, which is considerably higher than working two additional years, generating a 3 to 4 percent increase annually.[6] These estimates are likely to be biased upward because the admissions process creams the most talented, so some of the increase should be attributed to the screening and not just to the education. There appears to be sufficient incentives despite the trends in starting salaries of S&Es with master's versus those with bachelors. For those who continue with their education, completing a doctorate would increase wages by about another 9 percent for scientists and 15 percent for engineers relative to those with a master's degree. Nonetheless, difficulties in completing the required course of study and uncertainty over employment opportunities make the venture risky and lead to a lower expected rate of return (Ehrenberg, 1992). It takes at least another four years after completion of a master's degree to complete a doctorate, time that can be used to acquire on-the-job experience that also increases wages. The adjusted net returns to a doctorate, then, do not appear to offer enough financial incentives for many to continue. Of course, factors other than financial reward contribute to the decisions of those who do pursue advanced studies, but at the aggregate level, they do not completely offset the shortcomings inherent in the labor market.

Characteristics of Asian Pacific
Engineers and Scientists

No other minority group has contributed more to the technological capacity of this nation than Asian Pacific Americans. Although the S&E labor force is still largely non-Hispanic white, Asian Pacific Americans have become an increasing presence. They accounted for less than 2 percent in 1970 but nearly 7 percent by 1990. This increase has been driven by an incredible growth of the Asian Pacific S&E labor force. During the two decades, the number jumped from about 21,000 to 150,000, an increase of 603 percent. Extrapolating from recent trends, it is likely that there are now over a quarter-million Asian Pacific scientists and engineers. Like the larger Asian Pacific population, the S&Es come from ethnically diverse groups.   Chinese comprise the largest ethnic group (34 percent), followed by Asian Indians (23 percent), Japanese (12 percent), and Filipinos (10 percent).

The presence of Asian Pacific Americans varies considerably by field and level of education, as well as by place of employment and activity. Table 1 summarizes estimates from the 1980 and 1990 Censuses.[7]   While Asian Pacific Americans are underrepresented among those without a bachelor's degree, they are extremely overrepresented among those with graduate degrees.[8] They comprise one-sixth of those with either a master's or professional degree. Their greatest presence is among engineers with a doctorate degree, comprising over one-fifth of this group. Moreover, Asian Pacific S&Es are highly concentrated at the centers of high-technology. For example, in Silicon Valley, America's premier site for the production of semi-conductors and other related electronics products, they comprise one-quarter of all scientists and engineers, and over one-third of those with advanced degrees.[9]

Along with higher levels of education, Asian Pacific Americans are more likely to participate in research and development. Table 2 summarizes the primary activities of white and Asian Pacific

Table 1. Racial Distribution of Engineering and Scientific Labor Force, 1980 and 1990			
	NH-White	Asian Pacific	Others
1980, All			
Total	90%	4%	6%
Less than BA	90%	2%	8%
BA	91%	4%	5%
MA/Prof.	87%	8%	5%
Ph.D.	83%	14%	3%
1990, All			
Total	85%	7%	8%
Less than BA	87%	3%	10%
BA	87%	6%	7%
MA/Prof.	81%	12%	7%
Ph.D.	81%	15%	4%
1990, Engineers			
Total	86%	7%	7%
Less than BA	89%	2%	8%
BA	87%	7%	6%
MA/Prof.	80%	14%	7%
Ph.D.	73%	22%	6%
1990, Scientists			
Total	85%	7%	9%
Less than BA	84%	3%	13%
BA	86%	6%	8%
MA/Prof.	83%	11%	6%
Ph.D.	84%	13%	4%

Estimated from U.S. Bureau of the Census, 1990 1% Public Use Microdata Sample.

The total may not equal 100 percent because of rounding.

S&Es with at least a bachelor's degree.[10] One distinctive difference is that Asian Pacific Americans have a lower probability of being in management positions; this phenomenon will be discussed later. The other important racial difference is the relatively high numbers whose primary activity is R&D, 34 percent compared to 24 percent for whites.   This is not unexpected given the educational characteristics of Asian Pacific Americans. Having an advanced degree increases the odds of participation in R&D (for all S&E, the figures are 18 percent for those with a bachelor's, 27 percent for those with a master's or professional degree, and 41 percent for those with a doctorate). Variations in educational composition, however, account for only about one-third of the racial difference.[11] Within degree categories, Asian Pacific Americans exhibit a higher probability of doing research and development, and the greatest difference is among those with a doctorate degree,

Table 2. Primary Activity of Those Employed as Scientists and Engineers

	R&D	R&D Management	Other Management	Other
1982, All				
White	24%	6%	13%	57%
Asian Pacific	34%	5%	8%	54%
1982, Bachelor's				
White	18%	5%	15%	61%
Asian Pacific	21%	3%	10%	66%
1982, Master/Prof.				
White	27%	8%	12%	53%
Asian Pacific	33%	6%	9%	52%
1982, Ph.D.				
White	40%	7%	4%	49%
Asian Pacific	54%	6%	1%	39%
1989, Ph.D.				
White	36%	8%	9%	47%
Asian Pacific	52%	8%	3%	37%

Source: U.S. Department of Commerce, Survey of Natural and Social Scientists and Engineers, 1989; National Science Foundation (1991a)

14 percentage points.

Another unique characteristic of the Asian Pacific S&E labor force is the prominence of immigrants. While 92 percent of non-Asian Pacific S&Es in 1990 were born in the U.S., only 17 percent of Asian Pacific S&Es were. Nearly half of the foreign-born (47 percent) arrived during the 1980s. The composition by nativity varies by degree level, with the percentage of U.S.-born falling with higher educational attainment. While 27 percent of those without a bachelor's degree were U.S.-born, only 6 percent of those with a doctorate were U.S.-born. Being an immigrant, however, does not imply being foreign-educated. In fact, the vast majority are educated in the United States, as documented by Table 3.[12] This is particularly true for those with advanced degrees.

The Supply of Immigrant S&Es

Given the dominance of immigrants among Asian Pacific S&Es, it is important to examine this particular supply more closely. INS (Immigration and Naturalization Service) data reveal the magnitude of the flows. Between 1972 and 1985, over 50,000 S&Es from the major Asian Pacific sending sources (India,

---

Table 3. Scientists and Engineers in 1982 by Nativity and Place of Education

	U.S.-Born	Foreign-Born U.S.-Educated	Foreign-Born Foreign-Educated
NH-White	94%	4%	2%
Asian Pacific	21%	63%	16%
Others	75%	19%	5%
Asian Pacific American by Education			
Bachelor's	36%	31%	33%
Master/Prof.	16%	78%	6%
Ph.D.	8%	83%	9%

Source: U.S. Department of Commerce, Survey of Natural and Social Scientists and Engineers, 1989

South Korea, the Philippines, Taiwan, Hong Kong, and China) became permanent immigrants (Ong, Cheng, and Evans, 1992, p. 545). More recent data show that another 17,000 became permanent immigrants between 1989 and 1991. Several factors contribute to the influx of Asian Pacific immigrant S&Es. A necessary condition is the "Westernization" of higher education in the technical fields, which creates an international labor pool, and the United States has played the key role in this process in recent decades (Ong, Cheng, and Evans, 1992). This is manifested in the adoption of Western and American curriculum in the technical fields by universities throughout Asia and other parts of the Third World. Frequently, the courses are taught by professors trained in the U.S.[13] This process has created an international class of workers receiving roughly the same basic education in the sciences and engineering. However, given the limitations of higher education in Asia, this applies primarily to undergraduate education.

The "Americanization" process works in another and even more important way. Given this country's preeminence in technology during much of the post-World War II period, the U.S. emerged as the most desirable place to study for students from developing nations.[14] Between the academic years of 1954-55 and 1990-91, the foreign-student population in the U.S. grew from 34,232 to 407,529. There are more foreign students studying in this country than the total for the next three leading host countries. Over one-half of the foreign students in the U.S. are from Asia, and another fifth are from other Third World nations. In engineering and science, the number of foreign students increased from 18,545 in 1959-60 to 145,740 in 1990-91, with the vast majority coming from the Third World.

Foreign students are particularly noticeable in graduate programs. For example, while foreign students comprised less than one-tenth of the engineering undergraduates in 1985, they made up over one-quarter of those in master's programs and over two-fifths in doctorate programs (Falk, 1988, p. 58). Although the figures in the sciences are less dramatic, foreign students nevertheless comprise a significant number of the graduate students in these fields as well. In the two fields taken together, the percentage of non-U.S. citizens receiving doctorates from U.S. universities more than doubled from 16 percent in 1960 to

34 percent in 1990. By 1990, 7,444 foreign-born earned doctorate degrees in science and engineering, up from only 3,295 in 1970 (National Science Foundation, 1991a). The increase has continued despite both the fluctuations in the total number of science and engineering doctorates granted during the 1970s and the improvement of educational institutions in developing countries.

Asians make up the largest contingent of foreign students studying in the U.S. The total number from Asia grew from less than 10,000 in the mid-1950s to 130,000 by 1989-90 (Zikopoulos, 1991, p. 14). For the latter year, nearly one-half were in engineering and scientific fields (46 percent), and among the Asians in these fields, over two-thirds were graduate students. With this heavy concentration, it is not surprising that Asians comprised a large majority of all foreign students in science and engineering — 63 percent of all foreign students and 74 percent of those in graduate studies.[15] Almost one-quarter (23 percent) of all science and engineering Ph.D.s conferred in 1990 were awarded to Asian-born students (National Science Foundation, 1991a).

The countries of origin among foreign-born Asian science and engineering doctorates have shifted over the years. In 1960, over half of the doctorates awarded to foreign-born Asian students went to individuals born in China and India (59 percent). Among the remaining Asian countries, Korea and Japan were the countries of origin for roughly 8 percent each. By 1990, an increasing number of students entered from Taiwan and Korea. Seventy-one percent of foreign-born Asian Pacific scientists and engineers in 1990 were from four countries — the People's Republic of China (20 percent), Taiwan (20 percent), Korea (19 percent), and India (14 percent).

While most came under the assumption that they would return and contribute to the development of their home country, many, perhaps a majority, stayed in this country after completing their education. This is particularly true for those with advanced degrees. A little more than one-third (35 percent) of all non-U.S.-citizens receiving doctorates in 1990 planned to seek employment or further training outside of the U.S.; the majority intended to remain in the U.S., perhaps largely in hopes of gaining permanent immigrant status (National Science Foundation, 1991a). Data on Taiwanese students indicates how extreme this no-return phenomenon can be. Between 1961 to 1981, only 15 percent of the

86,000 persons who went abroad to study returned, and the large majority of these emigrated to the United States (Liao and Hsieh, nd). Even among those who do return to their native countries, many eventually come back to the United States. The stayers, along with the returnees who re-migrate and emigrants trained in their native country constitute the total supply of Asian Pacific immigrant S&Es.

Several factors contribute to the flow of highly-educated Asian Pacific Americans. The first is that the sending countries are less attractive places for these students to pursue their career. These countries have not achieved a level of economic development that would generate the necessary demand for these types of workers, lack the technological infrastructure needed to support sophisticated research and development, and generally offer low salaries. Although these disadvantages slowly wane as development proceeds, the United States still offers far superior employment and career opportunities. Because the frame of reference that influenced educational and career choices is international, the low rate of return for advanced degrees within the U.S. labor market, which was discussed at the beginning of this chapter, is not a disincentive for Asian foreign students. Indeed, receiving such a degree can offer a high rate of return because it increases the probability of working in the U.S. for these individuals.

The odds of becoming a permanent resident are shaped by immigration regulations. After the enactment of the 1965 Immigration Law, Asian Pacific Americans have qualified for occupation-based visas, which have been made available to those who can fill positions where there is a labor shortage.[16] Given the shortages of the S&E labor market, the immigration law has created a major avenue for migration of those with college and university degrees in science and engineering, especially those with advanced degrees. Although the regulations were tightened in the mid-70s, there are still nonetheless large flows of Asian S&Es.

This can be seen in Table 4. Adjusters, those who had entered the country on temporary visas, comprised nearly half of all immigrants, and most received permanent residency through one of the occupational categories. Among the adjusters, 44 percent held F1 visas (student), and another 39

Table 4. Immigrant Scientists and Engineers, 1989-91

	Engineers	Math/ Computer Science	Scientists	Total
Total Asian Pacific	13,063	2,504	1,433	17,000
% of All Immigrants	46%	52%	38%	46%
Country of birth				
India	32%	26%	41%	32%
Taiwan	16%	31%	14%	18%
China	14%	14%	18%	15%
Hong Kong	6%	9%	4%	6%
Mode of Entry				
Adjusters, occup.	34%	61%	50%	40%
Non-adjusters, occup.	13%	12%	13%	12%
Other adjusters	8%	12%	13%	9%
Settlement by State				
California	37%	28%	21%	34%
New York	10%	16%	17%	11%
New Jersey	8%	20%	9%	10%
Illinois	6%	6%	5%	6%
Texas	5%	5%	7%	5%

Estimates from U.S. Immigration and Naturalization Service, Immigrant Public Use Tapes, 1989 to 1991 Fiscal Years.

percent held H1 visas (temporary worker). The presence of so many H1s indicate that many students underwent an intermediate step in becoming a permanent resident. The data also indicate that one-quarter of the non-adjusters entered through the occupational categories. Thus, over half of these new immigrants entered to fill positions in areas of labor shortages.

The flow of Asian Pacific immigrants has helped meet the demand for S&E workers in the U.S. Moreover, regulations help screen workers so that immigrants tend to help fill niches within shortage areas. These immigrants are not necessarily first in the hiring queue. U.S. employers prefer hiring permanent residents or citizens. The literature cites a number of reasons for this preference. First, the labor certification process, the process in which employers document that they have made a good-faith effort to hire U.S. citizens before hiring immigrants, may impose additional costs on employers in the form of tedious paperwork and delays, costs that could be avoided if employers hire permanent residents or U.S. citizens (Finn, 1988; Cannon, 1988). Second, many foreign graduates from U.S. universities have difficulties obtaining security clearances and may, therefore, be unsuitable candidates for employment in defense-related industries (National Research Council, 1988). And finally, a preference for U.S.-born workers may ultimately rest on racial or ethnic prejudices.

Despite the above factors, about half of U.S. firms that use S&Es hire foreign-born employees (National Science Foundation, 1986). Frequently, this hiring occurs when there are few or no other applicants in the labor queue for a position. This is particularly true when the opening is for those with graduate training. It is this latter factor that helps explain why the educational levels of Asian Pacific S&Es tend to be very high.

In some cases, the matching of jobs and immigrants can alleviate shortages at the aggregate level. Fields in which employers most frequently report shortages to the National Science Foundation tend to be the fields with high inflows of foreign nationals (Finn, 1988). For example, in 1980-81 employers reported few shortages of recently graduated Ph.D. students in the life and social sciences; consequently, the percentage of foreign nationals in these two fields was small, 8 percent and 6 percent respectively. However, within engineering, the relationship between immigration and areas of relative aggregate shortage is not so apparent because foreign nationals constituted between one-third and one-half of all new Ph.D.s entering the U.S. workforce regardless of the relative degree of shortage in a particular sub-field of engineering. In these areas, the matches are defined at the level of individual positions.[17]

Earnings and Glass Ceilings

How well Asian Pacific scientists and engineers fare can be measured by their earnings and their representation in management positions. Aggregate measures of earnings indicate a convergence of earnings between Asian Pacific Americans and NH-whites. For example, the median annual salary for Asian Pacific doctoral S&Es as a percentage of the median for whites grew from about 93 percent in the early 1970s to 100 percent in the later 1980s (National Science Foundation, 1991). The latter figure is consistent with an analysis of 1990 Census data, which yield an earnings ratio of 99 percent between Asian Pacific Americans and NH-whites. For scientists and engineers at all educational levels, the ratio is 97 percent. There is also rough parity when the data is analyzed by broad occupational categories (see Table 5).

The above comparisons, however, do not reveal if Asian Pacific Americans earn the same as NH-whites after accounting for factors such as education, occupation, and immigrant status that should influence wages. Data indicate that the two populations are not comparable because Asian Pacific Americans are more likely to hold advanced degrees, to work as engineers, and to be immigrants. When the 1990 data is disaggregated by degree and broad occupational groupings, the results show that Asian Pacific Americans generally earn less than their NH-white counterparts, in some cases about one-tenth less. Several factors, such as type of activity, age and years of professional experience, gender, nativity, place of education, and place of employment can account for observed differences. Moreover, discrimination also affects earnings.[18]

Analyzing "pure" racial difference is best done by examining U.S.-born scientists and engineers because any discrepancy in pay for immigrants may be due to cultural and linguistic factors rather than racial differences. Our analysis indicates that U.S.-born Asian Pacific scientists earned more than their NH-white counterparts after controlling for observable factors, but finds no inter-group difference among engineers.[19] The higher earnings of Asian Pacific scientists may be due to differences in the quality of education since they are more likely to have attended elite universities. In other words, there may be some bias against this group that is not detected due to our inability to control for quality of education. Although we do not know of any study of engineering which controls for this factor, one study of recent college graduates in all fields that controls for the quality of

Table 5. Median Annual Earnings, 1989 (x1,000)

| | Engineers | | Scientists | |
	Non-Hispanic Whites	Asian Pacific	Non-Hispanic Whites	Asian Pacific
All Ed. Level	$40.5	$40.8	$35.0	$34.6
Less Than Bachelor's	$36.5	$36.0	$30.6	$26.0
Bachelor's	$40.8	$37.0	$34.9	$32.0
Master's/Prof	$49.6	$45.0	$40.0	$40.0
Ph.D.	$57.2	$54.0	$48.0	$44.0

Estimates from U.S. Bureau of Census, 1990 1% Public Use Microdata Sample.

education finds lower earnings for Asians, *ceritis paribus* (Weinberger, 1993).

Among Asian Pacific Americans, there are significant differences of wages by nativity, time of entry into this country, and place of education. An analysis of 1990 data indicates that recent Asian Pacific immigrants (in the country for five years or less) in the sciences earn about one-fifth to one-quarter less in hourly wages than their U.S.-born counterparts, and that recent immigrants in engineering earn about one-third less than their U.S.-born counterparts.[20] The gap declines with additional time in the U.S., and disappears after 20 to 25 years. The wage differences are even greater in terms of annual earnings, indicating recent immigrants not only receive a lower wage but also work fewer hours. Moreover, wage differences may be due to the increase in the number of Asian Pacific scientists and engineers who enter the U.S. without an American education; thus, the lower earnings of recent immigrants may reflect unobserved differences in the quality and type of education among immigrant cohorts. An analysis of the 1989 Survey of Natural and Social Scientists and Engineers, which contains information on place of education, indicates that those with a foreign education earn about 10 percent less than those with a U.S. education, and that there are no differences in the wages between the U.S.-born and foreign-born employees with a U.S. education after controlling for other factors.[21]

Immigration regulations may contribute to the low wages of new immigrants. In order to hire an alien, employers must prove that no U.S. worker is qualified and available for that position and that the job offer meets prevailing wages. The positions that are least likely to be filled are those where the offering wage fails to attract domestic applicants.[22] Foreign scientists and engineers may be willing to accept lower salaries in order to obtain full-time employment in the U.S., a prerequisite for permanent residency (Gruenwald and Gordon, 1984).[23] For example, Asian Pacific doctoral scientists and engineers who are temporary residents earn only 82 percent of the median annual salaries of those with permanent residency (National Science Foundation, 1991). However, the low salaries can only be a short-run phenomenon because when residency is established, the worker is no longer bound to their first place of employment. As they operate more freely in the labor market, their wages would begin to converge with their U.S.-born counterparts.

Despite the improvement in earnings of immigrants with length of residence in the U.S., Asian Pacific Americans continue to confront a "glass ceiling" that denies them entry into top managerial positions. The statistics in Table 2 clearly show that they have a substantially lower probability of being in management; and this finding remains true within degree levels. When they do enter management positions, they do so within the area of Research and Development. Few rise to executive positions in this area of employment. For example, in 1992 there was not a single Asian Pacific executive in the large computer and semi-conductor firms in Silicon Valley, despite the fact that Asian Pacific Americans comprised the largest minority group in the high-technology industries of that region (Pollack, 1992). The glass ceiling also exists within academia. According to a 1985 survey by the National Research Council, less than 9 percent of Asian Pacific American faculty at four-year institutions listed administration as their primary work activity, compared with 17 percent of the entire faculty (Miller, 1992). Asian Pacific Americans have been noticeably absent, at least until very recently, from leadership positions as deans, institute heads, and advisory board members.

This lack of upward mobility is not due to a lack of economic incentives or interest. In both the sciences and engineering, S&Es whose primary activity is managerial earn about one-fifth more than S&Es with other duties.[24] Moreover, a majority of Asian Pacific S&Es express a desire to move up to administrative positions (Wong and Nagasawa, 1991). Even those who state that they do not want administrative positions may be discouraged by the poor prospects facing Asian Pacific Americans; thus they have adjusted their expectations accordingly. If the explanation is based on neither economic nor individual motivation, then what is the cause?

One clue comes from our analysis of the 1989 Survey of Natural and Social Scientists and Engineers, which indicates that the difference in composition by nativity plays a major role in the racial gap. The first column in Table 6 reports the unadjusted Asian Pacific-to-NH-white odds ratios of being in management. The value of .67 means that Asian Pacific Americans are only two-thirds as likely to be in a management position as NH-whites. Given the earlier discussion, it is not surprising that the odds are better for R&D management but worse for other managerial positions. The second column reports the odds ratios after adjusting for a number of independent factors, including immigrant status and whether one is educated in the U.S.[25] With these controls, the odds ratios increase significantly, and when past managerial experience is included, the ratios indicate parity. The results reveal that immigrants were considerably less likely to hold non-R&D management positions. Compared to U.S.-born, immigrants with U.S. educations are one-fifth less likely to hold R&D management positions, and immigrants with foreign education are one-half less likely to hold these positions. Since Asian Pacific Americans are more likely to be immigrants, this has contributed to their lower representation in management positions.

One interpretation for why immigrants face poorer prospects centers on cultural and language differences (Miller, 1992; Hoy, 1993). Despite a functional command of English, many may lack key verbal and communication skills. Moreover, many may lack assertiveness skills that are deemed necessary for leadership positions. Whether or not they actually lack these attributes, the characterizations are widely held by employers and senior executives. In one survey of industry leaders, "language difficulties were repeatedly mentioned as factors" in lowering the prospects of foreign engineers moving into upper management (Cannon, 1988, p. 110). However, foreign engineers have an excellent chance of gaining access to management positions in R&D organizations, where access to technical management is based on professional criteria (Cannon, 1988, p. 113). In other words, Asian Pacific Americans are viewed as good technicians but not managers (Park, 1992).

Table 6. Asian Pacific-to-NH-White Odds Ratios of Being in Management

	Unadjusted	Adjusted by current characteristics	Adjustment including prior management experience
Management	.67	.91	1.00
R&D Management	.84	.96	1.09
Other Management	.58	.90	.97

See text for explanation of estimates.
Source: 1989 Survey of Natural and Social Scientists and Engineers.

It is not clear how much cultural and language differences really adversely affect managerial ability and how much the perception is used to rationalize decisions based on other biases.[26] Moreover, there is a danger that these perceptions form the basis for racial stereotypes that create "statistical" discrimination, a form of discrimination where individual Asian Pacific Americans are judged on the basis of the "group mean" rather than on their own merits. Such racial stereotypes can potentially harm not just immigrants but also U.S.-born.

The glass ceiling has two consequences. One, it forces some Asian Pacific Americans to pursue the entrepreneurial path. This has been true in several cases in Silicon Valley (Park, 1992). While this may be a factor in some individual cases, it is not clear that the glass ceiling has had a significant impact on entrepreneurial activity at the aggregate level.[27] Data from the 1989 Survey of Natural and Social Scientists and Engineers show that the self-employment rates of Asian Pacific Americans and NH-whites are both 6 percent. Of course, the Asian Pacific rate might have been lower in the absence of the glass ceiling, but nonetheless, actual entrepreneurship is not a major phenomenon among Asian Pacific scientists and engineers.

The second consequence of the glass ceiling is reverse migration.[28] Ong and Hee (1993) argue the following:

> Several factors contribute to the reverse migration. The newly industrialized economies now have the resources to pay globally competitive salaries, and have the scientific and technical infrastructure that allows the highly educated to continue their career. At the same time, there is a sense that the United States is not the land of the unlimited opportunity. Certainly the existence of the glass ceiling is causing some Asian Pacific Americans to reconsider the pursuit of their career goals in the U.S. (p. 150).

While reverse migration is still a minor flow and its role in the transfer of technology across international boundaries is limited, the phenomenon is indicative of the potential and far-reaching consequences of the unequal opportunities facing Asian Pacific American scientists and engineers.

Concluding Remarks

The evidence clearly shows that Asian Pacific scientists and engineers, particularly those with advanced degrees, have helped this nation fill a crucial labor need. Without the growth of Asian Pacific S&Es, particularly the immigrant component, the shortages of highly-educated labor in the technical fields, and the corresponding losses to the economy, would have been enormous. Future developments will create a need for an even larger Asian Pacific S&E labor force.

As other nations have developed their technological infrastructure, increased their R&D expenditure, and benefitted from the international flow of knowledge, we have entered into an era of worldwide technological competition. During the last two decades we have seen that capturing or maintaining technological leadership is a pivotal factor in defining a nation's comparative advantage and the competitiveness of firms. In the new global economic order, trade is increasingly based on nations specializing in selective technology-based industries. Although the United States still holds or shares the lead in several fields, it is no longer preeminent in all areas.

In order to remain competitive, this nation must accelerate the growth in its technological workforce and improve the quality of this workforce as well. Those with highly specialized graduate training are essential for research and development, which is in turn necessary to expand the frontiers of technology. The advantage that this nation had enjoyed in this area has waned. Compared to several industrialized nations (Japan, Germany and France), this nation in the 1960s had a substantially higher ratio of scientists and engineers in R&D to the total labor force, and although the U.S. has maintained this ratio over time, the other countries have been closing the gap (Nelson and Wright, 1992). Whether this nation can stop or even reverse this relative decline will depend on its ability to produce a larger supply of S&E workers and to upgrade their education and training.

Unfortunately, the growth patterns described in the beginning of this chapter do not portend a sanguine future. Ensuring a new supply of highly-educated S&Es will be more problematic in the near future. The supply of scientists and engineers at the baccalaureate level will decline over the coming decade due to a drop in the college-age population (Atkinson, 1990). The size of the 22-year-old cohort in the U.S. peaked at about 4.3 million in 1991 and will decline to approximately 3.2 million by 1996. The one hope is that the decline in the college-age population could be offset by an increase in the proportion of students receiving bachelor's degrees in science and engineering.

Asian Pacific Americans have the potential of being a major source to fill this critical need. The supply based on those who are either U.S.-born or U.S.-raised will increase dramatically because their numbers have grown with the overall Asian Pacific population, because they are more likely to attend college, and because they are more likely to major in the sciences and engineering. However, this future "domestic" supply is smaller than the supply of S&E immigrants that prevailed in the 1970s and 1980s.

Unfortunately, there is no guarantee that the flow of S&Es from Asia will remain high. The increased number of slots for occupational immigrants under the 1990 Immigration Act will make it possible for Asian S&E immigrants to migrate. At the same time, other forces are working against this. With increased economic development, Asian countries will become better able to educate their students at home, to create professional opportunities for their graduates, and to pay internationally competitive salaries. The impact can already be seen, for example, in the increase during the 1980s in the rate of return of Asian students who studied in the United States. Several countries are making the transition from being "exporters" of S&E talent to being "re-importers" of highly-educated and highly-experienced personnel. They have established programs that actively recruit Asian Pacific scientists and engineers with work experience, and this bilateral internationalization of the S&E labor market will undoubtedly increase the size of reverse migration. While developments in the sending countries will be important, they by themselves are not likely to decrease the flow of immigrants significantly.

A potentially far more important force that threatens the supply of Asian Pacific S&Es is the current anti-immigrant sentiment. The central but unanswered question is whether this xenophobic political movement will produce new restrictions on immigration from the Third World, which will not only affect scientists and engineers, but all Asian Pacific Americans.

Notes

1. The wording of this sentence is borrowed from a report by the National Research Council entitled *Foreign and Foreign-Born Engineers in the United States — Infusing Talent, Raising Issues* (1988).

2. The 1970 statistics are calculated from Bureau of the Census, 1973. The 1990 statistics are estimated from the 1% Public Use Microdata Sample. There are differences in the definition of educational attainment. The 1970 data are reported by the number of years of education completed for the experienced civilian labor force, while 1990 data are reported by degree received for the total experienced work force.

3. The fluctuations in demand generate disequilibrium between supply and demand, and a "cobweb" effect (Freeman, 1971). Given that short-run supply is inelastic, increased demand translates into higher wages. The initial shortage can lead to a surplus in the future because the current generation of new students respond to the increases in wages by majoring in the field where there is a shortage. If this cohort graduates at a time when the demand for their services has waned, the influx of students can eventually flood the market inducing yet another cycle of falling wages and reduced enrollments.

4. The decline in R&D expenditures is, in part, due to the fact that the problem of public goods is internationalized in a global economy.

5. This is based on standard wage regressions where the log of annual earnings and the log of estimated hourly wages are the dependent variables. The sample was drawn from the 1990 1% Public Use Microdata Sample and contained only U.S.-born respondents in a scientific or engineering occupation who had earned at least $1,000 in 1989. To reduce the ambiguity of what a professional degree means, the sample was restricted to those with either a bachelor's, master's, or doctorate degree. Our model includes independent variables for gender, race, years of experience, educational degree, geographic region, and consolidated metropolitan areas. Separate regressions were estimated for scientists and for engineers.

6. The effects are roughly the same in terms of annual earnings.

7. The estimates are based on those who were in the labor force (employed, or unemployed but looking for work) and were classified in a S&E occupation or taught in a S&E field at the college/university level. The 1990 Census provides educational information by degree, but the 1980 Census does not. We assumed that those with four or five years of college had a bachelor's degree, while those with eight or more years of college, the top reported category, had a doctorate. Those with more than five years but less than eight years of college were classified as having master's or professional degrees. We tested the sensitivity of our definition of those with a bachelor's degree. Using only four years of college led to an unrealistically high estimate of the number with a master's or professional degree. The limitation of the 1980 data probably led to the inclusion of persons without a Ph.D. in the doctorate category.

8. In 1990, 33 percent of the Asian Pacific S&Es had a master's or professional degree, and another 12 percent had a doctorate degree. For all other S&Es, the respective statistics are 17 percent and 5 percent.

9. These estimates are based on the 1990 5% PUMS. Asian Pacific Americans are also overrepresented among production workers (Park, 1992).

10. The 1982 estimates are based on respondents who worked in a scientific or engineer occupation. We use whites rather than non-Hispanic whites in this analysis because the published 1989 report does not provide statistics for the latter group. Because an overwhelming majority of white S&Es are not Hispanic, there is very little difference in the 1982 statistics for NH-whites and whites.

11. This is based on calculating the proportion of Asian Pacific S&Es that would be in R&D if they experienced the white participation rate by each of three degree levels — those with a bachelor's degree, those with a master's or professional degree, and those with a doctorate times the proportion of Asian Pacific Americans with a doctorate degree. This hypothetical rate is 27 percent, which is 3 percentage points higher than that for all white S&Es but still 7 percentage points lower than the observed rates for all Asian Pacific S&Es.

12. The statistics are based on respondents with at least a bachelor's degree and who classified themselves as a scientist or engineer by profession (education and experience).

13. For example, in 1988 over two-thirds of the S&E faculty at Seoul National University, South Korea's premier institution, had a foreign doctorate, and nearly three-quarters of this group received their training in the United States (Seoul National University, 1988).

14. The statistics on foreign students come from Zikopoulos, 1991b.

15. The concentration of Asians is not new, but the data show that their relative share has increased over the last few decades. Students from Asian countries received 42 percent of all non-U.S. science and engineering doctorates awarded in 1960-64 and 68 percent in 1990 (NSF, 1991).

16. Prior to 1965, U.S. laws favored highly-skilled individuals; but racial bias in the immigration law prevented large numbers of Asians from taking advantage of these quotas.

17. The immigrant supply also helps address cyclical shortages due to periodic fluctuations in the demand for scientists and engineers.

18. See Harberfeld and Shenhav (1990) for an analysis of salary discrimination of women and black scientists.

19. This is based on the regressions outlined in footnote 2. The results indicate that annual earnings and hourly wages of Asian Pacific scientists were 10 percent higher than for NH-whites. The estimated parameters were significant at only the $p<.10$ level, but this may be due to the small number of U.S.-born Asian Pacific Americans in the sample. The results indicate no statistically significant differences between Asian Pacific and NH-white engineers. The results also show that women and blacks earned less than men and NH-whites, which is consistent with the literature.

20. This is based on standard wage regressions where the log of annual earnings and the log of estimated hourly wages are the dependent variables. The sample was drawn from the 1990 1% Public Use Microdata Sample and contained Asian Pacific respondents in a scientific or engineering occupation who had earned at least $1,000 in 1989. To reduce the ambiguity of what a professional degree means, the sample was restricted to those with either a bachelor's, master's, or doctorate degree. Our model includes independent variables for gender, race, years of experience, educational degree, geographic region, consolidated metropolitan areas, year of entry, and English language ability. Separate regressions were estimated for scientists and for engineers.

21. The earnings regressions include as independent variables gender, race, years of professional experience, age, educational degree, geographic region, year of entry, managerial activity, part-time work, and place of education. Although there is no control for English language ability, the analysis of the 1990 Census data for Asian Pacific scientists and engineers indicate that excluding this variable does not bias the included variable. This is not surprising since Asian Pacific Americans in these fields tend to have at least a fair command of English; thus the estimated parameter for this variable is often insignificant. The sample includes respondents working in a S&E occupation who had at least $1,000 in earnings. Separate regressions are estimated for scientists and for engineers. The sample for scientists is small (n=337) and did not produce robust estimates. The results discussed in the text are based on the analysis of engineers.

22. This individual aspect of the wage-induced shortage of S&Es with advanced degrees is discussed in section one, where there is an adverse effect on the decision to pursue advanced studies.

23. This explanation, however, cannot account for the fact that in 1989 U.S.-born Asian Pacific doctoral scientists and engineers earned only 92 percent of that of white doctoral scientists and engineers (NSF, 1991).

24. This is based on an analysis of the 1989 Survey of Natural and Social Scientists and Engineers. The annual earnings regressions includes as independent variables gender, race, years of professional experience, age, educational degree, the sector of employment, geographic region, year of entry, managerial activity and part-time work. The sample included U.S.-born respondents working in a S&E occupation and had at least $1,000 in earnings.

25. The estimates are based on a sample of only paid workers with income in the U.S., between the ages of 30 and 64, and excludes those working in hospitals, the military, and international agencies. Scientists and engineers are defined by experience and education, which includes individuals who were working outside a scientific or engineering occupation. The analysis uses logit regression, and the list of independent variables also includes gender, degree, marital status, presence of children, age, years of experience in the profession,

geographic region of employment, type of employment organization (public, etc.), and occupational categories.

26. Certainly, the economic advancement made by Asian countries based on a different leadership styles would suggest that behaviors rooted in Asian Pacific culture are not inherently bad for effective management. Partial acceptance of this has come as American corporations adopt some Japanese practices. Of course, managerial styles cannot be completely transplanted given differences rooted in history and larger institutions.

27. Because high-tech industries have been rapidly expanding and changing, they offer Asian Pacific Americans, and others, the opportunity to "get in at the ground level" and build a fortune. Many of the largest Asian Pacific companies are in this sector, including Wang Laboratories, Computer Associates, AST Research, Everex Systems, and Advanced Logic Research (Pollack, 1992).

28. The fascination with "returning" as a solution to the frustration felt by Asian Pacific Americans who are blocked from moving up was captured by the 1986 movie *The Great Wall*, directed by Peter Wang. The movie begins with the protagonist, a Chinese American engineer, being passed over for a management position that he believed he should have received. His response was to return to China for a visit, with a possibility of staying. In the end, however, he realizes that he and his family belong in the U.S.

Part III

Policy Essays

Chapter 9

Urban Revitalization

Dennis G. Arguelles, Chanchanit Hirunpidok, and Erich Nakano

After years of federal neglect and inaction, the Clinton administration can be credited with bringing renewed attention to the nation's inner-cities. Corporate restructuring, capital flight and a deteriorating urban infrastructure have led to declining economic opportunities and increasing poverty, homelessness and blight in urban America. Home to primarily low-income and minority populations, inner-cities face formidable economic challenges. Only a comprehensive national urban economic development strategy can begin to meet these challenges, a task made more complex by urban demographic and economic changes in the last 20 years.

One of the most significant of these changes is increased immigration from Asia and the Pacific, bringing with it a bifurcated population of low-skilled and poorly educated workers as well as professionals and entrepreneurs with capital and other resources. This phenomenon creates new problems, but can also be a contributing factor to urban revitalization. Thus, it is imperative that Asian Pacific American communities are partners in any efforts to revitalize the nation's inner-cities.

This chapter is divided into four parts: First, it documents the needs and conditions of low-income Asian and Pacific Islander Americans in the inner-city, with particular focus on the ethnic enclave economy. Second, it discusses past urban policies and their impact on Asian communities. Third, it examines current initiatives aimed at revitalizing urban communities. Finally, it provides policy recommendations specific to the needs of low-income Asian American communities.

Our policy recommendations cover a range of issues from

small business assistance programs for Asian entrepreneurs to job training and protection for low-income workers. However, our primary emphasis is on the need to include Asian Americans in the development, and as beneficiaries, of federal urban revitalization policies. We argue this point for two reasons. First, many Asian Americans live in poverty and face tremendous economic obstacles. Despite this, the overall community is stereotyped as the "model minority," or economically secure and successful. This often results in the exclusion of Asians from economic development and anti-poverty programs. Second, recent immigrants to the United States have been scapegoated for the nation's economic problems. Contrary to this rhetoric, most immigrants contribute more to the economy and society than they receive, are not dependent on public assistance and bring with them an industrious and entrepreneurial spirit. The focus of public policy should not be to restrict immigration or deny benefits to immigrants, but to create economic opportunities that raise the standard of living for all residents. This requires the involvement of all communities, which is the key to a revitalized economy and is in keeping with this nation's commitment to being a pluralistic society.

Economic Profile of Low-Income Asian Communities

Chapter 5 by Ong and Umemoto provides a picture of life for inner-city Asian Pacific Americans. We summarize the key points that help frame our policy discussion. Most Asian Americans living in poverty are recent immigrants and part of the growing ranks of the working poor. They have part- or even full-time employment, yet bring home incomes below or just above the poverty line. They are locked into these low-wage jobs because of a combination of a lack of job skills and major structural changes in the national economy.

For these immigrants, the primary job skill they lack is English proficiency. In addition, many immigrants who arrive via family reunification preferences are from rural or low socioeconomic backgrounds. Consequently, they lack marketable job skills that can help them access better opportunities and higher wages in the labor market. Southeast Asian refugees in particular are often welfare-dependent and face high levels of unemployment. They encounter the problems faced by other recent immigrants as well as the additional effects of the trauma they suffered in the civil strife and harrowing escapes from their homelands.

Most poor Asian Pacific immigrants are concentrated in inner-city communities. Except for a handful of Chinatown core areas across the nation, Asians are not the majority in most of these communities. Poor immigrants often live in ethnically diverse areas where there is more of an income mix than the classic inner-city "slum" area. Affordable housing stock is very limited in these areas and families will often double or triple up in apartments in order to afford rent, leading to severe overcrowding.

These areas are often anchored by a vibrant ethnic enclave economy, or a network of enterprises owned and operated by Asian Americans. These economies provide vital, culturally-specific products and services in the ethnic language. Most of the enterprises that make up these economies are small, "mom and pop" retail or service businesses. They operate on the margins of profitability and face high levels of instability. These immigrant entrepreneurs are often channeled, through informal networks in the communities, into ethnic market niches — Cambodians in donut shops, Vietnamese in nail and beauty salons, Thais in restaurants — which quickly become hyper-competitive and unstable. This pattern limits business viability, employment opportunities and the potential for expansion.

Entrepreneurs are also channeled by economic factors into retail operations throughout the inner-city, often in poor African American or Latino neighborhoods. Asian immigrants fill the vacuum in the inner-cities left by the flight of larger retail chains, corporate disinvestment and bank and insurance redlining practices. The proliferation of Asian-owned businesses in these neighborhoods has inevitably led to resentment and high levels of racial tension and conflict.

Many of these small businesses rely on unpaid family labor, but some serve as a source of major employment for recent immigrant workers. Many light manufacturers, such as the garment and furniture makers, and service industries, such as contract janitorial and housekeeping services and restaurants, rely on low-skilled labor. Without these Asian-owned businesses, many Asian workers would have difficulty finding employment. However, because these workers are usually poorly educated and not organized, they are highly dependent on their employers. A paternal relationship develops between employers and their workers, often depoliticizing the work environment and leading to exploitative conditions. These factors have contributed to the return of sweatshop conditions, sub-minimum wages and even child labor in many urban communities.

One common misconception is that poverty and low-wage employment are just temporary conditions faced by most immigrants. With time, it is believed, immigrants are able to adjust and eventually access better economic opportunities. While this is true for some, there is a growing segment of newer immigrants and low-income workers who are at risk of being trapped in poverty indefinitely. They face this future because public services, such as education, job training, ESL classes, child care and other services which helped past immigrants adapt and advance have been devastated by federal and local budget cuts.

Another reason so many will be stuck in poverty is the current restructuring of the global and national economy, which, over the past 20 years, has resulted in a sharpening polarization of the labor market. Some local job growth has occurred in high-wage occupations associated with business services and high technology, but this employment is only accessible to those with very high levels of graduate and professional education. At the same time, a large growth of low-wage jobs in the service and retail sectors, and the elimination of millions of jobs in the middle has occurred. Asian Pacific immigrants with few skills and little education are finding fewer jobs available to them other than those in the low-wage sector.

As U.S. corporations seek cheaper locations to operate their production facilities, heavy manufacturing jobs will continue to be lost to other countries. These jobs were once the staple of urban workforces because they offered high wages and stability to blue-collar workers, particularly minorities. This trend and the need to create quality, high-paying jobs accessible to inner-city residents and newer immigrants are the greatest challenges facing urban revitalization efforts.

Impact of Past Urban Policies and Programs

One of the first major federal urban programs was "Urban Renewal" in the late 1940s. With the war over, America experiencing unprecedented economic growth, and a rise in suburbanization, repairing the nation's decaying and dilapidated cities became a priority of the Truman administration. However, urban renewal often resulted in the bulldozing of whole communities in favor of sterile office buildings. It was heavily criticized for being "top down" in its planning, and for leaving out the input of local communities.

The Civil Rights Movement ushered in a new era. In response to a growing demand to address inner-city poverty, the federal government enacted several programs, especially the "Model Cities" program of the Lyndon B. Johnson administration. The approach of model cities was to provide federal resources to assist local communities in planning and directing their own redevelopment. Once this process had occurred, the federal government would then fund and implement these plans. Unfortunately, Model Cities never accomplished its grand goals. Instead, it became embroiled in political turmoil, where outside vested interests and internal fighting paralyzed the program. The death of the Model Cities marked an end to efforts to concentrate funds in the most marginalized neighborhoods. Subsequent urban programs allowed local officials to dispense limited funds to other areas.

A common characteristic of both the Urban Renewal and Model Cities programs was their attempt to "redevelop" the physical environment of specific geographic areas, often with little regard for the needs of the area's residents. Both programs channelled resources into the rehabilitation and development of housing, commercial space and infrastructure. It was assumed that these activities would attract business, encourage private investment and create jobs. Later programs, such as the Urban Development Action Grant (UDAG) and the current Community Development Block Grant (CDBG),[1] also operated under this assumption. However, UDAG and CDBG gave local jurisdictions much more authority over how these funds were utilized and reduced the federal government's role in the implementation of local revitalization strategies.

All of these programs had limited success. Part of this can be attributed to the impact of corporate and economic restructuring, the magnitude of which few could anticipate. However, since Model Cities, critics have raised the issue of "people focused" urban policies rather than geographically-targeted redevelopment programs. This approach advocates for programs that improve an individual's mobility, giving them the option of leaving the inner-city to access better jobs and housing in the suburbs or wherever opportunities exist. Such programs include better education and job training, child care and access to suburban housing markets for low-income individuals.

While both approaches had their merits, the issue became a moot point under the Reagan and Bush administrations. In urban policy, the Republican administrations considered policies of targeting aid to distressed places a squandering of resources and counter to market forces. Although CDBG, UDAG and the Economic Development Administration (EDA)[2] survived the Reagan administration's efforts to eliminate them, the Reagan perspective was fully sympathetic to an unimpeded market. The administration felt the role of the federal government was to accommodate rather than resist the market forces that distribute people and industry across the land and to help declining communities adjust to their new, diminished circumstances (Harrison and Bluestone, 1988, p. 67).

The economic policies of the Reagan/Bush era hurt America's inner-city poor across racial and ethnic lines. The 1980s was a decade which saw the general withdrawal of federal support for programs to address the needs of those on the bottom of the economic ladder, and a widening gap between the rich and poor. The stark rise in homelessness and the housing crisis in urban areas can be at least partially attributed to the 70 percent decline in federal funds for housing and urban development during this era. For example, the Department of Housing and Urban Development's (HUD) budget, which peaked in 1980 at $55.7 billion, was reduced to $15 billion by

1987 (Goldsmith and Blakely, 1992, p. 47).

The conservative approach to monetary policy resulted in enormous casualties. In 1982, four-and-one-half million more workers were unemployed than in 1979, and entire cities were brought to the brink of bankruptcy, including Youngstown, Detroit, Buffalo, and Akron (Goldsmith and Blakely, 1992, p. 91). As federal aid decreased, states and cities became increasingly dependent on their own resources. By 1985, the nation's mayors began to rely on a strategy based on partnerships with the private sector in order to fill the resource gap left by dismantled federal programs.

However, this strategy often manifested in attempts to revitalize downtown business districts by subsidizing corporate development. Oftentimes, city governments gave tax breaks to projects with little regard for social purpose or need. Transforming the urban environment into a space amenable to corporate needs left a good share of the resident population out of the process, creating and increasing the gap between the haves and have-nots. Moreover, the process raised property values that had once been stagnant, driving up speculation and rents, and causing gentrification. The explosion in real-estate prices would only drive the middle class out of the city and into more affordable suburbs, isolating the cities even more.

The History of Neglect of Asian Pacific Americans

Economic hardship among Asian Pacific immigrants in the inner-cities and the needs arising from them were usually neglected by past urban policies, particularly in the Reagan/ Bush era. For instance, to the extent that the federal government generally withdrew large-scale support for urban economic aid, the 1980s saw a growth of neighborhood-based community economic development strategies and organizations. Community Development Block Grants and private foundation sources were often geared towards these community-based efforts at commercial revitalization, business development and affordable housing production. Typically, these efforts followed the traditional model of targeting abandoned urban areas hit hard by disinvestment and the flight of manufacturing facilities.

However, as discussed earlier, the relatively greater geographic dispersal of low-income Asian Pacific Americans does not lend itself to this geographic approach. Even where there are concentrations of low-income residents, most of these communities do not fit the model — most poor Asian Pacific Americans are part of the working poor, not chronically unemployed; instead of a lack of business activity, there is typically an ethnic enclave economy that is vibrant though marginal; Asian Pacific Americans do not typically concentrate in declining manufacturing areas associated with plant closings. As a result, most Asian Pacific communities continue to be overlooked by urban policy.

One major policy trend that developed under the Reagan/ Bush era was the emphasis on small business development as the "engines" of economic and job growth in the inner-cities. During the latter 1980s, an entire industry of small business assistance programs developed to provide capital and technical assistance to small businesses.

In some cases, Asian Pacific small businesses were able to take advantage of programs such as the Small Business Administration's (SBA) loan program, primarily in communities where there existed Asian banks that handled SBA loans. However, small business programs tended to underserve Asian Pacific small businesses and the ethnic economy. First, Asian Pacific small businesses and entrepreneurs in greatest need are usually run by immigrants, and few small business assistance programs have the language capacity and cultural understanding to work with these entrepreneurs. Second, many small business assistance programs geared towards the inner-cities emphasize startups and increased minority (primarily African American and Latino) entrepreneurship. As mentioned earlier, many Asian Pacific communities already have vibrant ethnic economies, thus the particular need is not increasing entrepreneurship, but assistance in diversification, expansion, increasing the viability of existing businesses and helping them move into growth markets.

Current Federal Initiatives

The Clinton administration's urban strategy is a combination of different approaches and initiatives which represent an effort to develop a comprehensive urban policy. The strategy makes use of both geographically targeted and increased mobility approaches to urban assistance, recognizing that each has its merits. It attempts to balance Republican-supported supply-side policies with directly funded programs and through the creation of non-market institutions. Finally, it attempts to do all of these things at a time of very limited resources and enormous federal debt. The result is a series of modest initiatives, driven as much by political feasibility as economic need.

These initiatives are described by HUD Secretary Henry Cisneros as having the goal of "maximum opportunity." That is, some of the programs attempt to improve conditions in the inner-city and make these areas more livable for those who cannot or choose not to move out. This is accomplished by directly targeting federal monies and providing incentives to encourage private investment into these areas. Other initiatives attempt to give inner-city residents the tools to improve their mobility, in some cases, directly subsidizing their incomes. While promising, each of these initiatives requires careful examination and scrutiny, particularly in terms of their impact on low-income Asian communities.

The cornerstones of the urban revitalization strategy are "Empowerment Zones" and "Enterprise Communities," which passed as a part of the budget bill in August of 1993. These programs represent the administration's attempts to target resources to distressed geographic areas. They differ only in that Empowerment Zones receive far more benefits. A derivation of past Republican "enterprise zone" proposals, these zones attempt to use tax incentives to encourage business development and expansion in targeted areas. In Empowerment Zones, employers can take a 20 percent credit on the first $15,000 in wages paid to an employee that is a resident of the zone. They can also increase expensing to the lesser of $20,000 or the cost of the qualified zone property placed in service during the year. This is a special incentive to manufacturers, who often purchase large amounts of machinery and equipment. By combining these tax credits with local incentives such as less regulation, it is believed that previously hindered free-market forces in the inner-cities will take over, new capital and private investment will be attracted to the areas, jobs will be created for local residents and blight will be replaced by new development.

However, the program is not solely based on faith in the free-market. It includes one billion dollars in Title XX (Social Service Block Grant) monies to local jurisdictions receiving Empowerment Zone or Enterprise Community designation; $720 million of this money will go to nine Empowerment Zones (six urban, two rural and one Indian reservation) and the remaining $280 million to 95 Enterprise Communities. Local jurisdictions with either Empowerment Zones or Enterprise Communities can also issue up to three million dollars in tax exempt bonds for use in economic development activities. In addition, all federal departments and agencies are directed to channel resources to these areas. This could mean as much as seven billion dollars in additional benefits. Other stipulations in the program include tax credits to businesses donating funds to Community Development Corporations located in the zones.

Whether this strategy will be effective is unknown. Many states and local jurisdictions have developed en-terprise zone programs offering various local incentives. Such programs have met with mixed results and little quantitative data exists to validate their effectiveness. Thus, policymakers, academics and advocates have divergent views about their success. A 1986 HUD report claimed that 80,000 jobs had been created or saved and over three billion dollars in investments generated by state-sponsored zones nationwide. However, many zones show no tangible improvement. Poverty and unemployment rates in Los Angeles' Greater Watts Enterprise Zone are higher now than they were when the program started in 1986. Even in zones where growth and investment did occur, Dick Cowden, executive director of the American Association of Enterprise Zones, admitted "causation was sketchy at best."

At the heart of the enterprise zone debate is whether they actually create *new* jobs and investment, or whether, as many unions claim, they simply cause the *relocation* of existing businesses, resulting in no net gains. While the Clinton plan includes stipulations to discourage relocation, most existing inner-city businesses are small enterprises, operating on the margins of profitability and with little tax liabilities. Tax breaks do little to help them expand, create jobs or improve their long-term viability, reasons the National Federation of Independent

Businessmen (NFIB) placed tax credits well behind other factors in determining where to locate. Access to capital, affordable insurance premiums, skilled workers and public safety play more significant roles.

In addition to the Empowerment Zones and Enterprise Communities, the Clinton administration hopes to help the inner-city by making more capital available to impoverished communities through a combination of leveraging federal funds with local monies to create community development lending institutions and a crackdown on discriminatory lending practices by commercial banks. These initiatives represent a cross between geographically targeted and increased mobility approaches. Specifically, the Clinton initiatives include a Community Development Financial Institution proposal, a National Community Development Initiative and other programs.

The administration is proposing funds be allocated for Community Development Financial Institutions — community development banks, community credit unions, or community development corporations with loan funds. These institutions can provide financing for physical development projects such as youth centers or affordable housing, as well as provide loans and credit for small businesses. These funds will help boost these financial institutions and provide much needed capital for projects that have difficulty obtaining financing from traditional banks and lending institutions. They tend to target specific geographic areas in their lending activities.

As long as banks continue *de facto* redlining practices (where they designate economically depressed and minority communities as areas where they will not provide loans), and resist providing capital for affordable housing and small businesses development, community development lenders will fill a critical gap. Such institutions can provide capital for physical development projects and small business expansion and diversification to meet specific needs of inner-city communities. However, the Clinton plan also includes improved enforcement of the Community Reinvestment Act (CRA) and a directive to the Federal Reserve and Department of Justice to crackdown on discriminatory lending practices, redlining and other practices by commercial lenders that deny capital to low-income and minority communities. A stronger CRA can potentially provide home loans and small business capital that greatly increases mobility of inner-city residents.

HUD and the Clinton administration have put emphasis, at least in words, on the importance of community-based organizations and nonprofits in their urban revitalization efforts. Specifically, they intend to build the capacity of local communities to carry out housing and economic development work. One such effort is the National Community Development Initiative (NCDI). The NCDI will leverage $25 million in HUD monies with another $75 million from private foundations to create a fund to support community economic development (CED) projects around the country. This fund could bring tremendous benefits to low-income communities, which need affordable housing, economic development and job training programs as well as the community-based institutions with the capacity to carry out such work. The NCDI will be administrated by two nonprofit intermediary organizations, the Enterprise Foundation and the Local Initiative Support Corporation (LISC).

Community-based organizations will also be strengthened through the National Community Economic Partnership Act, an initiative that is now a part of Congress' anti-crime legislation. The act will provide between $40 and $165 million in funds to support business development in economically distressed communities. Part of the monies will go to established, nonprofit community development corporations (CDCs) who must match the funds with non-federal monies. A smaller amount will go to newly developing CDCs or community development banks who must generate a match of 25 percent. These monies can go toward developing revolving loan funds, micro-loans or other investments deemed worthy by these community-based institutions. A smaller portion of the funds will go to new or emerging CDCs to assist with strategic planning and to help them build their capacities to carry out lending and other economic development activities in their communities.

As of February 1994, the House version of the bill, sponsored by Congressman Marty Martinez, authorized $165 million in funding. However, a similar Senate version authorized only $40 million. A joint committee will eventually determine the actual amount, which, given the significant need for such funds in the inner-cities, will hopefully be closer to the House version. This capital can potentially bring new economic activity to severely distressed areas, as well as be used for the expansion and conversion/diversification of existing businesses. In either case, it can contribute to the creation of jobs and opportunities in inner-city areas and make them more livable for residents.

Other urban initiatives that can be considered part of the Clinton plan to provide "maximum opportunity" include a permanent extension of the Low Income Housing Tax Credit, which provides incentives to individuals and corporations to contribute to affordable housing developments. HUD is currently working with the AFL-CIO and other organizations with pension funds to channel monies toward community development. This could mean another one billion dollars in capital flowing into the inner-cities. The administration is also taking steps to fight discrimination in housing markets to ensure that inner-city residents and minorities have access to better housing opportunities.

Clinton's FY 1995 budget calls for an overall increase in HUD's budget to $29.5 billion, up from last year's $27.5 billion. The new budget calls for a special $500 million set aside in CDBG funds for Empowerment Zones and Enterprise Communities, a $150 million Economic Revitalization Grants program and, as discussed earlier, a substantial increase in funding to assist the homeless. However, programs facing cuts include public and elderly housing.

All of these proposals go hand-in-hand with health care reform, job training, school-to-work programs and other initiatives. Community-based economic development strategies that have blossomed over the past two decades have proven to be effective and meaningful. Community organizations, many of whom organize and seek to empower low-income residents and workers, have built affordable housing, served as lending institutions, built child care centers, spurred commercial development and provided job training. Such organizations have, in many cases, provided a voice for low-income residents in shaping broader local and regional economic development policy. It is a positive sign that urban policy under the Clinton administration seeks to place emphasis on relying upon and empowering such community-based activity as driving forces for economic change on the local level. While this urban strategy in its entirety sounds comprehensive and promising, many of the initiatives exist only as bills and have yet to be passed by Congress. Many appear to be positive steps, but may be too under-funded to have significant impacts. Of course, only time will reveal the effectiveness of the various programs.

Recommendations for Future Urban Policy and Asian Pacific Americans

The themes struck by the Clinton administration and their nascent policy initiatives present new opportunities for urban economic development that can truly make a difference for low-income and minority inner-city communities in general, and for Asian Pacific Americans in particular. In order for this promise to be realized, however, the process of policy development and implementation must be inclusive and it must be based on a diversity of models of distressed communities in need. As this takes place, existing economic development policies can be correctly adjusted to best address the critical needs, and new and innovative initiatives can be created where existing policy is inadequate. For low-income Asian Pacific communities, four key needs stand out: building the capacity of Asian Pacific community-based organizations to carry out community economic development strategies; promoting diversification and expansion of small businesses in Asian Pacific communities; empowering immigrant workers; and addressing the economic sources of inner-city racial conflict.

Inclusion must be the starting point of making federal urban policy more responsive to Asian Pacific Americans. Traditionally, urban economic development policy has generally ignored or neglected Asian Pacific Americans. In the past, this could have been attributed to the relatively small number of Asian Pacific Americans. Also, Asian Pacific communities have largely been concentrated in greater numbers on the West Coast while urban policy has historically been shaped by models from the East Coast and Midwest urban centers. But over the past two decades, Asian Pacific Americans have been the fastest growing minority in the U.S., and in urban centers across the country, they now undeniably represent a significant population. Despite this, policymakers have been slow to recognize these communities, let alone understand them. Without a doubt, this has much to do with prevalent stereotypical perceptions of Asians as economically successful and without problems.

Urban policy cannot be successful without an understanding of Asian Pacific communities and how various ethnic groups interact in the inner-city. Older models of urban poverty and economic distress based upon Midwest cities of previous decades — abandoned urban areas suffering from plant closures, high unemployment, an absolute decline in economic activity and disinvestment — no longer exclusively reflect the diversity of economic distress faced in the inner-cities. Policymakers must reach out to Asian Pacific communities and others and educate themselves about the new realities of the cities today if they are to shape effective policy.

For instance, the Empowerment Zone/Enterprise Community initiative seems generally targeted towards the traditional model of abandoned, distressed urban areas. Tax incentives are geared toward bringing large-scale, outside manufacturing or commercial developments. While it is unclear whether this strategy will be effective, even in traditional abandoned urban areas, it is clear that they are unlikely to help small, "mom and pop" enterprises that are the majority of firms in Asian Pacific enclave economies. Tax benefits are of little benefit to businesses that have few paid employees and have little tax liability.

Despite these overall weaknesses, the Empowerment Zone/ Enterprise Community (EZ/EC) strategy is clearly one of the cornerstones of the Clinton policy. As such, tremendous resources will be spent to make it successful. The additional $100 million in Title XX funds per urban Empowerment Zone, the promise to expedite waivers and a reshaping of federal regulations and programs in the EZ/EC's based on local input all hold the promise of a greater impact than the tax incentives alone. It is critical that federal policymakers recognize that urban distress is reflected in a diversity of "models," and that Asian Pacific communities be included as part of the designations nationally.

BUILDING CAPACITY IN COMMUNITY-BASED ORGANIZATIONS

Because many Asian Pacific communities are relatively new, and because policymakers hold "model minority" perceptions of Asians, the capacity for Asian Pacific community economic development work lags far behind that of other communities. Although there are long-standing and sophisticated Asian Pacific community development organizations in the San Francisco Bay Area, there are generally few if any Asian Pacific community organizations in most cities that can carry out CED work. To address this problem, special attention must be given to providing support, operating funds, training and technical assistance to emerging community development institutions. This is an investment in community "infrastructure" that can pay off in the long run because it can empower low-income communities to help themselves.

Secretary Cisneros met with Asian Pacific community leaders in Los Angeles in 1992, and promised to provide HUD assistance to help emerging community development organizations get off the ground. While HUD has yet to deliver funds for this effort, these initiatives offer the potential for training, and other resources to take up community-based economic development.

Typically, such capacity-building efforts have been, during the 1980s, carried out by private, nonprofit groups in the emerging community development "industry." The National Community Development Initiative (NCDI), of which HUD is a partner, reflects such efforts. Over the past two decades, various "intermediary" organizations have developed which solicit and channel private foundation and corporate dollars into community-based housing and economic development projects. These intermediaries include the Local Initiative Support Corporation (LISC), the Enterprise Foundation and others. Private foundations and corporations, usually out of touch with community-based activities, feel more comfortable giving money to these large intermediaries and letting them decide how to distribute the funds. For example, the funders of NCDI, which include the Ford and Rockefeller Foundations, will have LISC and the Enterprise Foundation decide which cities and which organizations will receive NCDI funding.

While LISC and other intermediaries have successfully leveraged millions of private dollars into community development, many are critical of their lack of attention to emerging communities, such as Latino and Asian Pacific communities. Because of their access to funds, these intermediaries wield tremendous power in determining the future course of community development. Yet, as private, nonprofit organizations, it is not clear how communities in need can hold them accountable and ensure their responsiveness.

As these and other capacity-building initiatives are shaped by the federal government, Asian Pacific communities will need to ensure that they are included and that programs are responsive to a broad range of distressed communities. This requires policies that address the unique position of Asian Pacific Americans.

BUSINESS DEVELOPMENT PROGRAMS

As noted in the previous section, the vast majority of Asian Pacific-owned businesses are very small and operate on the margins. They function on long hours of hard work and tremendous dedication. They are also of critical importance because they are a major source, and often the only option, for employment for recent immigrant workers. Operating under marginal conditions, these businesses can only offer unstable, low-wage work with few benefits. If given the opportunity, assistance and direction, these businesses could become more viable, providing better employment and playing a significant role in revitalizing the overall economy.

The new Community Development Lending initiative offers an important opportunity for such assistance. Once again, it will be important that these monies not solely target the traditional model of distressed urban areas, but also include Asian Pacific Americans and their needs. These funds provide an opportunity to build institutions for community development lending and small business assistance, perhaps using federal monies to leverage contributions from Asian-owned banks and other private sector sources. Such institutions could provide capital and small business loans that otherwise would be very difficult to secure from regular banks. This capital could be provided where the need is most critical — in helping marginal businesses diversify and move into new, more viable ventures or markets; and helping existing small businesses expand their operations and markets and create jobs.

But capital alone is not enough. Many immigrant entrepreneurs need other assistance, which can best be provided by community-based institutions with the language and cultural capability to work with them effectively. These entrepreneurs need help in identifying and learning about new growth industries, markets and other business opportunities, as well as technical assistance to help them run their businesses more efficiently and to access financing, job training and other business development programs.

Asian Pacific businesses must be brought to the table in large-scale public-private economic development projects such as transportation and defense conversion. The huge infusion of public monies into transportation, for example, represents tremendous opportunities in many cities for not only construction and transit-related development, but innovative local industries such as electric vehicles or advanced mass transit manufacturing. Asian Pacific Americans, along with other low-income and minority communities, must receive their fair share of procurement and contract opportunities created by such projects. Asian Pacific communities must also insure that the benefits from such minority set-asides and contracts actually translate into better jobs and increased opportunities for workers, not just professionals and business owners.

EMPLOYMENT PROGRAMS

Traditionally, economic development policy has purported to be primarily concerned with helping working people or the unemployed. However, it has focused on the "supply" side of the economic development equation — on the businesses — in the hopes of creating jobs and providing advancement opportunities. After a decade of wholescale economic and social policies focused almost exclusively on the supply-side, it is clear that such an approach does little to help poor and working people directly.

Most low-income Asian Pacific Americans are part of the working poor — they cannot find stable, full-time work, or they work full-time but cannot make a decent wage. Because of their lack of job and educational skills and the structure of the job market, many are locked into low-paying jobs. Southeast Asian refugees, who face high rates of unemployment and welfare dependency, face even more severe obstacles to economic security. Efforts to improve the conditions of these workers cannot solely rely on assisting the businesses where they work or on attempting to generate more jobs through economic stimulus policies. Too many of these businesses create jobs that pay below-poverty wages, offer few, if any, benefits, exploit immigrant workers and impose harsh working conditions. There must also be a focus on directly providing low-income workers the means to improve their conditions and opportunities. While the Clinton administration has taken some steps in the right direction, this continues to be a major gap in its urban and economic policies.

The Earned Income Tax Credit program is the key initiative that targets direct assistance to the working poor. It is an ambitious attempt to, in the words of HUD Secretary Cisneros, "entirely eliminate the category of the working poor," by channeling tax subsidies to low-wage workers and helping to lift them out of poverty status. In order for such a program to be truly effective, resources must be allocated to community-based education to ensure that immigrant workers understand and take advantage of this benefit.

Job training continues to be a critical means by which workers can improve their skills and escape low-wage, dead-end jobs. Existing job training programs, such as the Job Training Partnership Act, must be improved to better serve immigrant workers. More emphasis must be placed on bilingual services, the paperwork burden must be streamlined and the program must be reformed to reduce the incentive to "cream" — to focus only on trainees with the best chance of success in order to meet performance requirements.

But job skill improvement efforts must not just be limited to JTPA programs — the goal should be to upgrade skills levels of entire sectors of the workforce, thus generating "demand" for more higher-skilled, higher-paying jobs. This means that urban economic policy is inextricably linked to educational reform, increasing and stabilizing the funding base for schools, youth and community college programs and other efforts directed toward developing a competitive workforce.

But what about the majority of workers who do not have the opportunity to enroll in college or in a job training program? Ultimately, policy must empower workers to improve their conditions *where they are*. New organizing efforts among these workers combined with a new set of economic development policies that encourage and support such efforts must take place. Whether through existing unions, new unions or community-based efforts, immigrant workers must themselves be empowered through organizing campaigns and education about their rights. Community-based groups can play a critical role, particularly with limited English-speaking immigrant workers. Such organizing involves complex cultural issues, special employer-employee relationships and a sensitivity to the precarious position of Asian enclave employers.

Concluding Remarks

One of the most critical issues facing Asian Pacific communities overall is racial violence and interethnic conflict. While cultural differences and other social dynamics play an important role in such conflicts, the underlying source of much of the tension is economic in nature. This includes resentment toward immigrant workers by the unemployed or by those who fear losing their jobs as well as resentment toward employers who hire immigrants.

A key source of this tension is related to the proliferation of Asian Pacific-owned retail businesses in poor, African American or Latino neighborhoods. These entrepreneurs began these businesses because with little capital and startup resources, they had few other options. These entrepreneurs often fill a vacuum created by the flight of retail chains and corporate disinvestment, but they become targets of anger and frustration of residents. Moreover, their presence in depressed neighborhoods also focuses attention on the discriminatory barriers to African American entrepreneurship.

After years of escalating tensions and tragically violent consequences, no answers or quick-fixes are available. But communities and policymakers must understand the sources of tension and work together pro-actively before they explode into violence.

These conflicts demonstrate how Asian Pacific Americans, whether residents, workers or entrepreneurs, are intricately bound to the conditions of others in the inner-city. It demonstrates why Asian Pacific Americans must be brought to the table, together with other poor communities, to address the economic crisis of the inner-cities. For Asian Pacific communities, the heightening ethnic conflict will hopefully spark a realization that they must play an integral role in uplifting the urban economy overall. This means Asian banks must be pressured to improve their lending practices, Asian businesses must improve their hiring and service practices, and Asian community groups must actively seek collaboration with other ethnic groups.

At the same time, the scapegoating of immigrants and Asian Pacific Americans must be fought by all communities as well. Anti-immigrant and anti-Asian bashing is growing and there is widespread ignorance about the backbreaking conditions and marginal returns suffered by the majority of Asian Pacific workers and small business owners.

All of this ultimately means inner-cities need a larger "pie"; all communities must be brought to the table with government and the private sector to squarely address the question of how to develop a larger, more diverse local and regional economy with better jobs and more ladders of opportunity. Otherwise, urban policy can too easily become a zero-sum game: either businesses or workers gain, either Asian Pacific Americans or African Americans gain. In his successful campaign for the Presidency, Bill Clinton emphasized investment in physical, economic and human infrastructure to build a stronger economy and society. He and Congress must follow through on this fundamental promise to the American people. By investing today in disenfranchised communities and in programs for poor and working people to help themselves, the returns of an improved quality of life and opportunities for social advancement will be immeasurable.

Notes

1. The Community Development Block Grants were established under Richard Nixon's administration as part of an effort to consolidate categorical grants-in-aid as entitlements to distressed urban areas.

The Urban Development Action Grant Program was enacted in 1977 under Jimmy Carter's administration to encourage localities to attract private investment in the restoration of deteriorated or abandoned housing stock and to solve other problems resulting from economic decline. The critical feature of the UDAG program was its requirement for private-sector financial commitment to be legally binding before UDAG funds may be released.

2. The Economic Development Administration was established in 1965 by the Public Works and Economic Development Act. The EDA administers four main programs, including a public works program, business loan and loan guarantee program, technical assistance grants program, and a special assistance program for sudden economic crises.

Chapter 10

Welfare and Work Policies

for Southeast Asians

Joel F. Handler and Paul Ong

We are once again in the midst of an intense period of welfare reform. Whether the Clinton administration's proposals, if enacted, will help Southeast Asian Americans become fuller members of our society or add to their problems is unclear. This population has suffered a series of tragedies starting with the protracted and devastating war in their former home countries. Most have suffered enormous personal and familial losses. Many have experienced the horrors of refugee camps where lives are suspended for months and years. The fortunate ones have been admitted as refugees to the United States, but for about half of this population, the resettlement program has failed to achieve its goal of assisting individuals to attain economic self-sufficiency. The unfortunate reality is that the refugee program has not had adequate resources to help most make the difficult adjustment to American life.

Far too many have been abandoned to a welfare system that stigmatizes its participants and that has done too little to move individuals into the economic mainstream. One can rightfully argue that the problem is rooted in a failed resettlement policy, but the current reality is that the fate of Southeast Asian communities will be tied to how we reform the welfare system. The original promise of promoting self-sufficiency can only be achieved by fundamentally changing our welfare policy and, more broadly, by our commitment as a society to ensuring economic dignity to those who are now marginalized.

Southeast Asians share a common interest in restructuring

welfare with others on public assistance, but also have unique issues that are historically and culturally defined. The welfare system that has trapped an extraordinary proportion of Southeast Asians in poverty is one that has also reinforced welfare dependency for far too many others. Consequently, efforts to improve the lives of refugees must be embedded in the broader campaign to make welfare work. As the same time, they have unique needs and, as documented in Chapter 6, programs designed for the typical welfare recipient can be inappropriate and ineffective in reaching this group. Unfortunately, proposals under consideration do not directly address these concerns. Because the reform proposals concentrate almost exclusively on teen parents and young adults, the special needs of Southeast Asians will either be ignored or suffer from a diversion of resources. The concerns of Southeast Asians should not be lost in the debate over welfare reform.

The President's stated goal of "ending welfare as we now know it" raises a serious dilemma for our society. It is difficult to disagree with the notion that public assistance should be a transitional program to employment for able-bodied adults. This notion is as much the product of our collective norm regarding the social and economic obligation to work as it is the product of a growing political frustration with a welfare system perceived as being ineffective, undesirable, open to abuse, and a drain on scarce resources. Even for those receiving benefits, the system has failed by focusing more on administering a program than helping individuals find employment. Our goal should be to enable these individuals to be productive members of society. There is truth in the notion that employment can provide people with a sense of purpose, a positive identity, and personal dignity. However, this is not easily achieved in our economy by those with limited skills, where the prevailing wage is not enough to lift families out of poverty. To be successful, welfare reform must be viewed as a policy that helps the working poor.

The problem of low wages is particularly relevant to that part of the welfare system that most affects Southeast Asian Americans, Aid to Families with Dependent Children-Unemployed Parents (AFDC-U), a relatively small program for two-parent families. Because the vast majority of Southeast Asians on public assistance live in such households, proposals to preserve and promote such family units are less relevant to this population. The central problem is that AFDC-U does not function as a transitional program helping the families become independent, thus leaving many unable to escape the "welfare trap." This is an undesirable outcome both for the families who are desperate to become self-sufficient and for society. The question is why is AFDC-U failing these families?

There are two reasons, which are related. First, the AFDC-U program is inappropriate, not only for these families, but also for other families on welfare who are capable of entering the paid labor force. Second, because of major structural changes in labor markets, it is obsolete to think of work versus welfare. In short, we have to rethink the structure and relationship of both paid labor and income-maintenance programs.

The rest of this chapter is organized into four parts. Part one reviews the historical restrictions on most two-parent households from receiving public assistance. Part two examines AFDC-U and recent related work programs for recipients of public assistance from this source. Part three argues that for most of these parents, the labor market can offer only wages that would leave the family in or near poverty. The last part presents some options for welfare reform.

A Legacy of Narrow Eligibility

Welfare has been primarily a program that has excluded most two-parent households no matter how poor. The reluctance to include these families lies in the history and organization of the American welfare system.

The American welfare system, reflecting the English influence, started at the local level. Towns and counties provided general relief to the worthy poor. The guiding principle was to prevent the spread of pauperism, which was considered a moral failing. Relief to the able-bodied was restrictive and deliberately stigmatic so that the able-bodied would always prefer paid labor to relief. There were tough work requirements. The work ethic would not be compromised. This principle has remained constant throughout our welfare history.

In the late 19th century, various exceptions began to be made for the "deserving poor" — those who were excused from the paid labor force. These included the deaf, the blind, the insane, Civil War orphans, and impoverished Civil War veterans. In 1911, Illinois enacted the first Aid to Dependent Children (ADC) program.[1] This was the result of a campaign by the Progressive Child Savers to exempt another category from the paid labor force — mothers who were deprived of the support of their husbands. Prior to this time, no separate distinction was made for poor mothers or their children; all were considered part of the paid labor force. The idea spread rapidly and within a decade, most states enacted programs. The statutes were broadly framed, but in practice, only certain categories of mothers and children were let into the programs. Nationwide, the program was primarily composed of white widows. Excluded were mothers who were divorced, deserted, and never married, and virtually all African Americans.

There are some important lessons to draw from this early ADC experience. At the time that ADC was enacted, and up until the last couple of decades, the program mainly consisted of mothers who were not working. Under traditional patriarchic norms, which began about 1830, "proper" mothers stayed home and took care of their families. Women who worked were suspect, and professional women often forfeited marriage. In addition, the type of work that women did mattered; genteel work, for single young women, was preferred over manual labor. Of course, poor women, whether single or mothers, had to work. There were no welfare programs for them. But they were condemned for working and regarded as morally suspect. Immigrants and African Americans, who worked at the lowest jobs, were all but outcasts. Virtue — in this case, the proper mother — was defined by the deviant.

It was in this context that the initial ADC programs were bitterly contested by many prominent social reformers. They felt that giving aid to single mothers would not only weaken family responsibility but give aid to families that were morally suspect. This was also the period of child saving — where slum children were to be "saved" by sending them to reformatories, farms in the Midwest, or state industrial schools pursuant to juvenile court jurisdiction. The solution to the conflict was to delegate the programs to the county level where local judges with the aid of the professional social workers would select only the "worthy" mothers — the white widows. The rest were still "undeserving," that is, forced to remain in the paid labor force.

Thus, it is in this early example that we see the three major influences at work: the preservation of labor markets by requiring the bulk of poor mothers and their children to keep working; the enforcement of patriarchy — only "proper" women assumed traditional family roles; and race and ethnicity. The primary function of the early ADC programs, then, was symbolic. Through the use of myth and ceremony, they affirmed the patriarchic myth of the "proper mother" — the programs were called "Mothers Pensions" — by condemning those who were excluded. The ceremony was the small number of white widows who were supported.

Other income-maintenance programs that started before the New Deal continued the same pattern. Old Age Assistance (OAA) was to help the poor elderly. Yet, OAA bristled with conditions designed to weed out the "unworthy" aged — those who had been paupers or had criminal records or gave away their property to qualify for aid. In those days — the 1920s — there was no agreed upon retirement age and adult children were considered to be responsible for their parents. On the other hand, except for financial eligibility, Aid to the Blind (AB) was virtually condition-free. The blind were not part of the labor force.

In many respects, the Social Security Act (1935) continued this basic pattern. The three basic state programs — ADC, OAA, and AB — were funded as grants-in-aid. The federal government assumed half the costs, imposed some conditions, but the programs basically remained in the control of the states. The states continued to exclude the vast majority of mothers — those who were morally suspect because of marital status or race.

On the other hand, the pressure of the Depression led to a reconsideration of the aged. A retirement age was agreed upon, and available paid work was to be reserved for younger males. To the extent that states had any money, restrictions on OAA were eased, and there was strong political pressure to include the dependent aged in the proposed Social Security retirement program, Old Age and Survivors Insurance (OASI). However, the Roosevelt administration drew the line. The centerpiece of the Social Security Act was the establishment of a pension, insurance-like program for the deserving worker — those who worked steadily, paid their premiums, and then retired at age 65. This was the myth of insurance. The administration stoutly resisted blanketing the dependent aged for fear that the insurance-like aspects of OASI would be compromised and the program stigmatized as welfare.

There was another important aspect of OASI. At this time, and for about the next 30 years, the Democratic Party in the South had veto power in the Congress. These Southerners were not about to let federal income-maintenance programs disturb existing race relations as they feared pensions to black families would do. Accordingly, OASI excluded agricultural, domestic, and other marginal workers — in other words, virtually all aged blacks in the South and many elsewhere.[2] As a result, OASI remained relatively small until the early 1960s, when it was expanded to blanket the dependent aged. Social Security became a strong redistribution program, and poverty among the aged was substantially reduced. Thus, from the time of its inception, OASI was designed to provide benefits to the paradigmatic "deserving poor" — the steady worker, primarily a white male who was temporarily outside the labor market.

Unemployment and Welfare

The major political fight during the debates on the Social Security legislation involved the unemployed. Despite the massive numbers of unemployed, after the initial threats of social disorder subsided, the desire to preserve local labor markets and race discrimination crippled administration efforts. First, the generous and relatively successful work relief programs were sharply curtailed. Second, local business interests and the southerners were able to insist that the administration of unemployment insurance be located at the state level. Unemployment Insurance today remains locally administered. It is for the "deserving" worker, that is, those who have worked steadily in covered employment, and who are unemployed through "no fault" of their own. A claimant is disqualified if he or she is fired, quits, is on strike, is not currently looking for work, or unavailable to take a job if offered. In deference to the South, the program for many years did not cover many marginal jobs. Finally, benefits, except in serious times, were short-term and failed to cover most of the unemployed.[3]

For those who are left — childless adults and most two-parent families who are neither aged nor disabled — the situation is indeed bleak. They are the historic "undeserving poor," thus are not readily included in the welfare system.

Instead of meeting the problem of unemployment head-on, and confronting what was at best probably a small part of the rise in welfare rolls — namely, the trend toward separation of families to qualify for AFDC — the country engaged in the usual compromise of myth, ceremony, and the diffusion of conflict through delegation. States were given permission but not required to provide relief for the two-parent family — not in UI — but as part of the program identified with helping the female-headed household.[4] Moreover, this was a program already in deep trouble — stigmatized, subject to racist attack, and increasingly unpopular. The halting, grudging history of AFDC-U reflects its contradictory origins.

AFDC-U was initially enacted on a temporary, year-to-year basis (Law, 1983). The states were given substantial discretion in defining basic eligibility. The unemployed parent had to have worked a certain number of quarters. "Unemployment" had to be either completely out of work or working less than 100 hours per month (Handler and Hasenfeld, 1991, p. 168). Unemployment remained high, and in 1968, AFDC-U was made permanent, but still optional with the states. Congress restricted the program to fathers, but that provision was declared unconstitutional.[5] The program applies to the "principal wage earner" — the parent who earned the most during the past two years. Another important change in 1968 was the addition of Community Work and Training (CWT) which provided both training and job opportunities.

AFDC-U continued to remain the stepchild. Only about half the states adopted the program, and enrollments always remained small. Those who qualified were mandated to register for the federal Work Incentive Program (WIN), with periodic re-registration. Under CWT, states were authorized to count payments for work as AFDC-U expenditures. In practice, funds for CWT were very meager and their use quite restricted.

Only 13 states opted for such programs. The program quickly turned into low-wage jobs in the public sector. Thus, most of the costs per enrollee went for relief. The jobs, as expected, were for unskilled labor, and few meaningful training or educational opportunities were provided. Unemployed parents were more likely to be forced into the labor market and into low-wage jobs once they worked more than 100 hours per month, regardless of their level of earnings. Attrition rates were high, with 75 percent leaving without completing their assignments, and with half of the trainees who left the program continuing on public assistance. The program contributed little to economic self-sufficiency (Levitan and Mangum, 1969).

During the Reagan administration, the states were given permission to conduct demonstration projects called Community Work Experience Program (CWEP). West Virginia, having one of the highest unemployment rates, emphasized straight work-for-relief whereby recipients of AFDC and AFDC-U were required to work in unpaid jobs as long as they were on the rolls. Approximately 70 percent of all AFDC-U recipients were enrolled. CWEP assignments were often lengthy, but participation was neither full-time nor continuous. CWEP had no short-term impact on the employability or earnings of the participants (both men and women), there was only a small reduction in welfare receipt, and few participants acquired new skills. CWEP cost the government more than it saved, unless one included the value of the services; then, the net benefit to the government was $734 per recipient per year (Handler and Hasenfeld, 1991, p. 179).

The results from other state CWEP projects show similar results. Thus, in San Diego — which influenced California's GAIN (Greater Avenues for Independence) program and later the Family Support Act — the results for AFDC-U showed no consistent increase in employment or earnings, although there were significant reductions in welfare payments, mostly because of the reductions of the AFDC-U grants as a result of earnings and the application of sanctions. In other words, the government was better off, but not the recipients. San Diego AFDC-U recipients lost $91 in job search and $400 in CWEP by year's end. In subsequent San Diego experiments, AFDC-U participants still came out about the same — poverty status did not improve. In a survey of all the state demonstration projects, MDRC (Manpower Development Research Corporation) reported that the employability of the participants increased by only 5 percent to 7 percent over control groups, that most jobs were in entry-level, low-wage occupations with a median wage of $4.14 per hour and almost half of the participants who obtained the jobs still stayed on welfare.

Despite its modest results, the San Diego demonstration projects influenced the adoption of California's GAIN program. Almost immediately, GAIN began to suffer budget reductions. Familiar patterns of participation emerged. Only about a third of those who registered actually attended an initial program component (e.g., basic education, job search); almost two-thirds were deregistered or deferred. Initial assessment revealed that much higher than expected proportions of registrants have basic literacy deficiencies, in effect changing GAIN from a job program to a massive compensatory education program which prolongs the stay of participants in the program, increases the costs, and increases the pressure to move registrants into job search rather than remedial education.

Not surprisingly, shortly after GAIN was enacted, the (then) governor stated that: "GAIN should be transformed into a true 'workfare' program, where immediate priority is to remove people from the welfare rolls and put them on payrolls as quickly as possible." The governor especially objected to the extensive emphasis on education. After pointing to some rare misuses of education funds (e.g., graduate education), he proposed that participants be required to look for jobs before being diverted into education or training. As he put it, "Let the job marketplace, not caseworkers, determine who is employable" (Handler and Hasenfeld, 1991, p. 196).

The Family Support Act (FSA) of 1988 requires that every state establish a Job Opportunities and Basic Skills (JOBS) program that will be fully operational by 1992. Rather than providing detailed guidance, however, the FSA is, in fact, only a broad outline. A great many crucial decisions are left to the states in fashioning their own programs. FSA requires that all states adopt AFDC-U; however, those states that do not have the program (about half) can elect to terminate benefits after 6 months.

It is hard to know what is going on under the FSA because of the major problems in data reporting (Greenberg, 1992). Nevertheless, the evidence so far does not look promising. There is not only great variation among the states but also great ambiguity in the reporting categories. Overall, about 13 percent of recipients are "assisted by JOBS" but this could range from mere registration to actual participation in a program component. The best estimate is that only about 10 percent of adult AFDC recipients are in a program component, but again, there is great variation. In 24 states, less than 10 percent of families are in a JOBS component activity; in 41 states, less than 20 percent of families.

There are no national data on outcomes — whether participation has led to employment, the average entry wages, retention rates, benefits, the gains, if any, from education, or even the use of sanctions. According to Mark Greenberg (1992), some states are reporting bits of data — for example, average entry wages vary from about $6.75 per hour to $4.44, but most do not report hours worked. Retention rates vary. Because of the lack of uniform reporting requirements, it is very difficult to generalize, but it looks like many lose their jobs within a few months and many of the jobs still leave the families in poverty. Nine states reported entry level wage data. The range of reported entry level wages are $4.44 to $6.57. Assuming a 35-hour week, this translates into monthly wages of $668 to $989. Thus, in only one state would a family escape poverty ($964/month).

The gap between the rhetoric accompanying the Family Support Act and the performance to date is unsurprising. Given the states' economies and fiscal problems and the level of current funding, it is not reasonable to expect JOBS to do much of anything for the vast majority of welfare recipients. At present, the states are spending only about 60 percent of the allocated federal funds and serving at most 10 percent of the AFDC families. Even if the states spent 100 percent of federal funding, JOBS would probably not reach a quarter of AFDC families — past experience indicates that programs become more expensive per participant the larger the number served.[6] The problem of low participation is not the need for more authority to require participation; it is for more resources to operate programs.

The Economic Limits of Work and Welfare

When we place the experience of the welfare work programs in the context of present-day labor markets, we see that welfare recipients cannot even come close to supporting themselves by earnings alone. In view of their education and skill levels, their labor market consists of low-wage, low-skilled, and most probably, part-time jobs with no benefits. While there have been few studies of the employment experience of Southeast Asians, they are, particularly the "second wave," disadvantaged in the labor market. Despite the fact that many are skilled, they face at the minimum, severe language barriers. They are, for the present, less-skilled, low-wage workers.

However, the problem of low-wage work is not limited to low human capital. Structural changes play a key role. Several studies of the growing inequality of earnings have reached a very similar conclusion, namely, that the real earnings of the less skilled, less educated workers have declined substantially since 1973. Moreover, this decline occurred during a period of economic expansion (Blackburn, McKinley, Bloom and Freeman, 1990; Blank, 1992; Mishel and Frankel, 1991). Employed men, ages 18-65, with less than 12 years of education, earned 13 percent per week less in 1989 than they did ten years earlier. The decline was especially pronounced for prime-aged adults, 24-35, with a high school diploma or less. White male dropouts experienced a 19 percent decline as compared to a 14 percent decline for white females. Furthermore, this decline was not because of the shift in jobs from manufacturing to service; real wages declined in both sectors. The earnings of less skilled women have remained flat. However, women still earn substantially less than men (Blank, 1992, p. 6).

Not only did earnings decline, but so did employment for the less skilled worker. It is this combination — declining real earnings and rising unemployment — that has resulted in increasing poverty among families. They simply cannot work their way out of poverty. In 1989, 22 percent of poor working adults worked full-time, year-round, while 43 percent worked at least 50 weeks. It is not surprising that over the last two decades, there has been a steady decline in work among men in families in the bottom fifth of the income distribution (earning less than $12,497 in 1989).

The future does not look good for the less skilled worker. First, there have been the sectoral shifts in employment, namely, the declining manufacturing opportunities for this group. Wages in the service sector are lower but skill levels are higher. Second, unemployment rates have been rising, disproportionately affecting the disadvantaged worker. Third, while the impact of immigration varies, there has been a large increase in less educated immigrants and this has contributed to the decline in labor market participation for less skilled workers.

There has been a significant decline in the minimum wage, in terms of purchasing power. At $4.25 per hour (the current rate) for a full-time worker in a family of four, earnings are still only two-thirds of the poverty line. Between 1979 and 1987, the proportion of workers who earned poverty level wages increased from 26 percent of the workforce to 32 percent. Women are much more likely to earn low wages than men: in 1987, 40 percent of women workers were still below the poverty line. While the expansion of low-wage (below poverty level) jobs affected all workers, it was greatest for minorities.

On the supply side, it is often argued that the decline in basic reading and math skills accounts for the decreased earnings of the less educated. However, earnings for blacks fell while test scores and academic achievement rose, and earnings of less educated cohorts fell as they aged. The more likely explanation is that academic skills have not kept pace with job requirements.

Not only is there the spread of low-wage jobs, but the nature of employment is also shifting from full-time work for a single employer to various forms of "contingent" work (U.S. Government Accounting Office, 1991). Many workers are employed in part-time, temporary, contract, or other types of flexible work arrangements. According to the General Accounting Office, it is estimated that as of 1988 there were 32 million contingent workers, accounting for almost a quarter of the workforce. The contingent workforce grew rapidly in the 1980s, and is expected to increase again since new jobs are expected to be almost entirely in the service sector, where part-time employment is most likely to occur. According to the Bureau of Labor Statistics (BLS), almost two-thirds of the new entrants into the labor force by the year 2000 will be women, and they are more likely to hold part-time and temporary jobs. More than a quarter of women work part-time, making them 1.5 times more likely to be so employed than the average worker. Although most part-time workers are women, men now account for a significant fraction (Blank, 1990). It is estimated that by the turn of the century 40 percent of jobs could be part-time.[7]

Part-time jobs are more likely to be dead-end. Part-time workers keep their jobs for shorter periods than full-time workers. The average job tenure for a part-time worker is 3.4 years, as compared to 5.7 for full-time working women and 8.1 years for full-time working men. Part-time workers not only often lack health and pension benefits, they also receive a lower hourly wage. Controlling for education, gender, and age, part-time workers receive about 40 percent less per hour than full-time workers in the same jobs. Part-time workers are disproportionately in the low-wage distribution. Part-time workers constitute 65 percent of all people working at or below minimum wage (Tilly, 1990, p. 9). As a result, families headed by part-time workers are four times more likely to be below the poverty line as compared to families headed by full-time workers. A fifth of families headed by part-time workers were in poverty, and 12 percent also received welfare as compared to 2 percent of families headed by full-time workers (U.S. General Accounting Office, 1991, pp. 5-6). The significant portion of employees in part-time work, and the expected proportional growth of this form of employment, indicate that under-employment is going to be a continuing concern.

This, then, is the labor market for the population that we are concerned with. The Southeast Asian family on welfare is a two-parent family. Yet, in many of these families, only one parent has a full-time, low-wage job, or, if both work, the combined earners are less than two full-time jobs.

It is easy to see now why past and present welfare-work programs sort out the way they have. Despite all the publicity, the fact remains that very few participants are better off economically. The Riverside, California, program is now being touted as a success, but the average earnings increase for the participants is only $961 more per year than the controls. The "modest" effects of these programs are not surprising. The ones that have proved to be cost-effective are low-cost job searches pushing people into low-skilled, low-wage jobs, and low-cost, short-term programs are not likely to produce higher earnings.

The vast majority of welfare recipients have education and skill deficits, and much of JOBS is devoted to education and training. However, education and training is far more costly than job search. In addition to schooling costs, the participants are still on welfare. To date, there have been no evaluations of the cost effectiveness of this approach, but if past experience is any guide, there will be increasing pressure to scale back. WIN II replaced the education and training of WIN with immediate placement in low-skilled jobs when welfare rolls and costs continued to rise. Massachusetts abandoned its generous Employment and Training program when its economy soured. Also, we should recall the previously-mentioned California governor's statement about letting the job market, not the caseworker, determine who is employable.

Finally, we must not forget that industries employing relatively low-skilled workers are facing increasing competition from abroad, and these downward pressures on wages will continue into the foreseeable future, thus further diminishing the earnings prospects for the less skilled worker.

It is clear that requiring welfare recipients to work for their relief does little to improve their economic well-being. It is also clear that for the majority of AFDC recipients, even when they work, periodic dependency on welfare benefits is unavoidable. Thus the dominant cultural norm of viewing welfare as the antithesis of work contradicts the social reality, in which work and welfare must complement each other. As long as this dependence is not recognized, work programs will continue to serve their symbolic function while being mostly marginal to the social reality of poverty and welfare. At the same time, society will collectively believe that it is "ending welfare as we know it." But if history is any guide, life will go on for the overwhelming majority of welfare recipients.

Solutions

While much of the debate over welfare reform is driven by the concerns over single-female households, the plan being discussed by the Clinton administration could either open or diminish opportunities for Southeast Asians. According to the National Council of La Raza (1994), the administration's proposal consists of five main objectives:

• Promote parental responsibility through such efforts as allowing noncustodial fathers to live with their families, requiring teenage mothers to live with their parents, and preventing teen pregnancy.

• Making work pay by expanding childcare, facilitating receipt of tax credits for the working poor (the Earned Income Tax Credit), and encouraging new support programs for the working heads of two-parent families.

• Promote full-time participation in the labor force by providing access to education and training, limiting eligibility duration for cash assistance, and requiring able-bodied adults to work after the end of the time limit.

• Strengthen child support enforcement so that noncustodial parents contribute financial support to their children.

• Reinvent assistance programs to reduce administrative bureaucracy, combat fraud and abuse, and give states flexibility to experiment with work-related programs.

The above objectives could represent a major step forward.

At the policy level, we believe that it is crucial that the focus be on employment, not welfare.[8] Two-parent families, especially families such as Southeast Asians, primarily lack earned income. Here, two approaches should be used. First, there is a great need for education and training, a point we share with the Clinton proposal. The poor will not be able to escape poverty and welfare unless they improve their employment skills. For some Southeast Asians, there was a clear difference in employment between those who were able to obtain English language training and those who were not. For others, though, additional employment skills will be needed. However, one of the dangers of the current proposals is that they are focused on teen parents and young adults. The pressure, then, will be to concentrate education and training resources on these groups, which may lead to a diversion of resources from other adults on welfare. This is another reason why education and training should not be tied to the AFDC program. Rather, these programs should be separately organized — for all at-risk workers — and should include employer-based training and apprentice programs, as well as publicly sponsored education and training.

Second, in view of the continuation of low-wage, low-benefit jobs, large numbers of families with employed parents will still be in poverty. Here, a two-fold approach is needed. First, continuing efforts have to be made to improve the earnings and benefits from regular jobs. Second, earnings from work should be regarded as supplemental income. The expansion of the Earned Income Tax Credit by the Clinton administration is a major reform, and when fully funded, can increase family income significantly.[9] Food Stamps should be continued, and housing and child care subsidies increased. In addition, the Clinton health care proposals promise to be a significant reform. At the present time, the lack of health benefits discourages people from leaving welfare or from seeking jobs. With these kinds of supplements, substantial numbers of working families will be relieved of the burdens of AFDC.

Strategies to promote self-sufficiency should go beyond targeting individual behavior to tapping collective resources — beyond jobs to other forms of economic activities. Southeast Asian neighborhoods, like many other low-income areas, have numerous community-based institutions and agencies that can help individuals struggling to move off public assistance. The support should not be limited to employment and training services, but should include moral support and group encouragement. Jobs constitute an important but not the sole avenue to economic independence. Programs based on the ethnic economy, collective ventures, extended families and self-employment should be accepted and funded. These alternative strategies do not replace but, instead, complement existing ones. When appropriately used, the broader approach can greatly improve the chances of Southeast Asians to end welfare dependency.

The path we choose to end the current welfare system will say much about us as a society. It is far easier for us to demand that individuals assume responsibility of leaving welfare than for us to accept the obligation of ensuring that working individuals and their families live a decent life. There is no question that "ending welfare as we know it" is costly, at least in the short run. The cost, however, is not limited to the additional fiscal burden. There is a larger cost if our goal is to provide a reasonable minimal standard of living for all. Forcing welfare recipients into the labor market, even with a feasible amount of employment training, will not eliminate poverty, for market forces will continue to create a class of working poor. Our willingness to rectify this gross inequality is a measure of our character as a caring and just nation.

Notes

1. The program was called Aid to Dependent Children (ADC) until 1967 when it was changed to AFDC. For a history of the Aid to Dependent Children program, see Handler and Hasenfeld (1991).

2. Another important reason for the disproportionate absence of African Americans in OASI was the shorter life expectancy.

3. Despite its name, Unemployment Insurance today covers less than a third of the unemployed who receive benefits. The rest have either exhausted their benefits, or failed to qualify.

4. Unemployed adults qualify for Food Stamps, but the only income-maintenance program for most is General Assistance, which is administered at the state and local level. It is the most mean-spirited of all the programs. While there is great variation from locality to locality, benefits are very low and often short-term. There are severe restrictions and work obligations. Although precise estimates are hard to come by, most potentially eligible adults and families are not included.

5. *Califano v. Wescott*, 443 U.S. 76 (1979)

6. The cost of purchasing new services may be more than existing services, and states may have creamed in the initial stages — in terms of employability, trainability, and lesser child care costs.

7. Professor David Lewin, Director, UCLA Institute of Industrial Relations, *Time*, February 1, 1993, p.53.

8. This position applies not only to Southeast Asians but for most two-parent households on public assistance — for people who have work histories, are employable, and need only short-term assistance (Lynn, 1993).

9. EITC, when fully funded, with food stamps, would ensure that if a family of four (or less) had a full-time minimum wage worker, it would be lifted to the poverty line. This assumes that the minimum wage will be indexed to inflation, as proposed by the administration (Center on Budget and Policy Priorities, 1993).

Chapter 11

Health Care Reform

Geraldine V. Padilla and Bonnie Faherty

The proposed Health Security Act of 1993, referred to as the Clinton Plan, has reenergized the health care reform movement. It challenges federal and state legislators, insurance companies, businesses, health care providers, scientists and private citizens to examine health care delivery in this country and invent a better system. As law-makers and interest groups debate the Clinton Plan's strengths and weaknesses and compromise on alternatives, Asian Pacific Americans must confront four major issues that affect them: access to and utilization of health care services, cost of care, quality of care, and culturally sensitive care.

In addressing the impact of health care reform on Asian Pacific Americans, this chapter provides a historical perspective for the present environment of reform; describes the extent of popular support for reform; delineates general reform issues and advocated strategies; examines specific Asian Pacific American health care needs and reform issues; and outlines recommended Asian Pacific American positions in relation to health care reform.

Historical Perspective

Movements to reform the health care system are neither new nor limited to governmental initiatives. During the late 19th centuries, the public, not the health profession, saw the need for professional training to optimize care (Starr, 1982, p. 155). For example, three schools for nurses opened in New York, New Haven, and Boston during this era. These outsiders who drove the reformation of health care during this time were upper-class women. Beginning in the 1880s, the precursor of today's Mayo

Clinics served citizens near Rochester, Minnesota. The high standards and impressive success rate of their services helped change the negative perception of hospitals as places of death to a more positive image. Hospitals improved with better communication (the telephone), better transportation (the automobile), and technical advances in medicine such as better sanitation, pharmacological interventions, and surgical strategies (Starr, 1982; Litman and Robins, 1984).

Table 1. Key Dates in the History of Guaranteed Health Coverage

Date	Event
1929	First HMO, Ross Loos, established in Los Angeles.
1935	Social Security Act with medical benefits for elderly signed by President F.D. Roosevelt.
1945	President Truman unsuccessfully asks Congress to provide health care security for all Americans.
1956	Disability insurance added to social security.
1965	Medicare (federal health insurance for all ≥ 65 years) and Medicaid (health care for the poor) bills signed by President Johnson.
1973	HMO Act establishes more HMOs signed by President Nixon.
1979	National health insurance plan unsuccessfully proposed by President Carter.
1981	Restrictions on federal health expenditures and greater responsibility on states per President Reagan.
1985	Employers required to continue health coverage for 18 months at employee's expense for retired/terminated (Comprehensive Ommnibus Budget Reconciliation Act).
1988-89	Medicare protection of elderly for catastrophic illness passed and repealed.
1993	Health Security Act guaranteeing health coverage for all Americans proposed by President Clinton.

Based on *Los Angeles Times*, September 19, 1993, pp. A20-A21.

The turn of the century brought with it additional progress in the quality of health care. From the early 1900s to the present day, increasing government regulation and professional standards have promoted the quality of health care and the competence of care providers. State boards of nursing, medicine, pharmacy, etc,. issue licenses to health care providers. Hospitals and other institutions are monitored by state and national organizations and regulated by state laws. Government also became more involved in increasing access and controlling costs.

Congress passed the Pure Food and Drug Act in 1906 in response to Upton Sinclair's book, *The Jungle*. This work exposed improprieties in the meat packing industry, giving rise to federal regulation of drugs. This Act, amended many times, controls advertising, research, and unsubstantiated claims of effectiveness. State workers compensation laws began to appear around 1910, on the heels of the industrial revolution. The Flexner report, released in 1910, outlined specific recommendations designed to raise the standards of medical education. This report is frequently cited as the impetus for the professionalization and scientific basis of medical practice (Flexner, 1910). The influence of hospital associations extended to the financial structure of health care delivery. For example, they required second opinions for surgery and reviewed the length of hospital stays, restricted medical fees, and refused payment when charges were excessive (Starr, 1982, p. 205).

In the 1920s, government intervention into the health care system came through the passage of the Sheppard-Towner Act which encouraged the creation of centers for prenatal and child health by providing matching funds to states. In this decade, the Committee on the Costs of Medical Care (CCMC) began the work of examining the costs and environment of medical care delivery (Committee on the Costs of Medical Care, 1932). Unfortunately, the medical community reacted adversely to the CCMC health care reform recom-mendations.

The pain and desperation of the Great Depression of the 1930s softened the resistance to social reforms, including health. While many leaders desired health insurance in some form, most recognized that securing such a radical change in government policies was not politically feasible (Starr, 1982).

The House of Delegates of the American Medical Association would only venture to support voluntary health insurance plans. The Social Security Act of the mid-1930s did not include coverage for health care (Litman and Robins, 1984). Nonetheless, it was an important step in laying the groundwork for continued concern about the need for health care and later attempts at federal involvement in the provision of medical services.

The 1940s witnessed the passage of the Hospital Survey and Construction Act of 1946. More popularly known as the Hill-Burton Act, it encouraged hospital construction (Litman and Robins, 1984). The Veterans Administration expanded its health services to veterans after World War II. Free or low-cost services to deserving individuals emerged quietly and incrementally.

Arguably, the most significant event in the history of American health care reform was the passage of the Medicare and Medicaid bills with President Johnson's signature on July 30, 1965 (Litman and Robins, 1984). The various provisions in these amendments to the Social Security Act were designed to neutralize the opposition of various special interest groups, particularly the hospital industry and medical professionals. Its one glaring flaw was that it lacked cost controls.

In the 1970s, President Nixon began a movement that continues today and is reflected in much of President Clinton's proposal for reform. He announced a new policy designed to encourage the development of Health Maintenance Organizations (HMOs).

In the 1980s, President Reagan further supported the growth in HMOs. Like Nixon, he encouraged development of the proprietary sector in health care delivery. Senator Edward Kennedy broke with the Democratic President, Jimmy Carter, and others by proposing a plan placed strikingly in the private, not public, sector. His legislation would have included a health insurance card much like President Clinton now proposes.

No mention of the 1980s can neglect to consider the influence of Diagnosis Related Groups (DRGs) on health care delivery. These reimbursement categories were designed to control escalating costs of health care. DRGs totally changed the financial incentives for acute hospitals. While DRGs addressed reimbursement schedules for the Medicare population only, private insurers quickly followed suit. Suddenly, patients were being discharged "quicker and sicker" and a domino effect began that continues to reverberate throughout all of health care. While access issues were major concerns leading up to DRGs, they quickly faded into the background (Starr, 1982, p. 406). Current research is exploring methods comparable to the DRG mechanism for reimbursement of services delivered in other settings such as nursing homes and home health care.

The decade of the '80s is sprinkled with failed attempts to address cost concerns. Some examples include certificates of need, utilization review, price controls, professional standards review organizations, and health systems agencies (Litman and Robins, 1984).

The 1990s are characterized by a growing skepticism about the value of more medical care and high technology. Many believe that much of health care is devoted to alleviating the sequelae of social problems.[1] There is concern over the amount of health dollars consumed by problems resulting from individual behavior. Policymakers and opinion makers are returning to discussions concerning individual "responsibility" for health and "sin" taxes for the use of products detrimental to health. Employers are funding wellness-oriented benefits with the hope of decreasing health care costs and increasing productivity.

Current attitudes toward previously neglected groups are changing, influenced, no doubt, by the civil rights and women's movements and by the onset of AIDS. Health issues unique to women, racial/ethnic groups, the elderly, the disabled, and homosexuals are gaining attention, legitimacy and research support.

The Current Debate

The myriad of problems characteristic of our current system provided the impetus for the present climate of health care reform. The first issue is the lack of accessible health care and presence of utilization barriers for a growing number of recipients. Second is the explosive cost of health care. These costs are fueled by the inordinate complexity of the payment and reimbursement systems, the profit orientation of health service insurers, providers, institutions, drug companies, and other health-related businesses, the inadequate control of fraud and abuse, and the unwieldy growth of medical malpractice. Third is the quality of care, including the technical and professional competence of health care providers. Fourth is the lack of culturally sensitive care of racially, ethnically, and socioeconomically diverse clients by a similarly diverse pool of providers (General Accounting Office, 1992; General Accounting Office/Office of Controller General, 1992; Millman, 1993).

Proponents of health care reform believe that universal health insurance guarantees access to health services. Comprehensive benefits apply regardless of employment status, retirement status, economic level or health status. This may be true in areas with an adequate supply of health care providers and efficient transportation systems. However, other problems may contribute to the lack of access to care. A major barrier to care is the inadequate supply of primary care providers. One strategy advocated by the Clinton Plan is the use of advanced practice nurses such as nurse practitioners and certified nurse midwives to deliver care.

According to the Council on Graduate Medical Education (1993), it may take until 2040 to educate an adequate supply of primary care physicians. "If we expand care to the 37 million uninsured and restructure the delivery system to focus on primary care, it will be impossible to adequately provide primary health care through physicians alone. Nurse practitioners can lead the way here" (Trotter-Betts, 1993, p. 7). According to the American Nurses Association (1993, p. 3) nursing can educate 127,000-143,000 advanced practice nurses to deliver primary care by the year 2000. Such a number should meet 70 percent of the nation's primary care needs in seven years at a cost of $15 billion less than the cost of educating the same number of physicians.

A Gallup Poll of 1,000 adults over 18 years of age (Gallup Poll, July 12-30, 1993, cited by American Nurses Association, September 7, 1993) found that 86 percent of the respondents were willing to see an advanced practice nurse for basic, primary health care in place of a doctor. Another pollster, Peter Hart (May 1990, cited by American Nurses Association (1993), found that 70 percent of those polled respected nurses more than any other health care provider.

Accessibility can be further promoted as in the Clinton Plan through incentives for providing health care to rural and inner-city communities; federal support for nursing education; emphasis on health promotion and disease prevention which is less expensive than diagnostic and curative procedures; and support for home and community-based care which are less expensive than hospital care.

In addition to the socioeconomic barriers to care, there are recognized racial/ethnic barriers. Lack of adequate translation services, cultural differences that inhibit understanding between providers and receivers of care, and the lack of minority health care providers who can provide culturally sensitive care, all contribute to suboptimal care. As an example, the Clinton Plan offers training and practice incentives for providers to care for the underserved. And the increased choice of plans may make it possible for the culturally underserved to find appropriate health plans.

Along with the question of greater access, the current debate has focused on the cost of health care. There is no doubt in anyone's mind that health care costs are out of hand. For example, the United States, by the year 2000, is likely to spend 18 percent of its gross domestic product on health care. This is far greater than the amount spent by any other industrialized country (General Accounting Office, Office of the Controller General, 1992). Such a steep rise in health care blunts growth in other sectors such as business profits, individual incomes, and federal and state programs. The General Accounting Office predicts that unchecked growth in health care costs will make it impossible to control Medicare/Medicaid costs and balance the federal budget (1990). Despite the large amounts of money spent on health care, this nation has about 34 million with poor access to health care because they are uninsured. Many millions more are in jeopardy of losing access to health care because they are underinsured, may develop a serious illness, or may lose or change jobs (General Accounting Office, 1992).

Proponents of health care reform recommend managed competition among insurers and providers of care to control costs. "Managed competition [is] a system in which insurance companies and health maintenance organizations (HMOs) bid for business, and consumers pick from among competing health plans" (*Los Angeles Times*, 1993, p. Q6). Managed competition can hold down costs while maintaining quality: a) if it's true that the health care market could stand a more competitive milieu; b) if the American public can yield on the "try-everything-before-giving-up" attitude; c) if providers don't sacrifice necessary care to hold down costs whether or not the government imposes a ceiling on spending; and d) if an efficient watch-dog agency can handle individual complaints and suppress unethical monopolies.

A second cost-control strategy, managed care, means that specific health problems are subject to diagnostic and treatment protocols that provide necessary procedures while avoiding technological frills. Managed care also means that other medical services are closely monitored, a pre-admission approval is required for a hospital stay, doctors agree to a reimbursement schedule for specific services as in a preferred provider organization (PPO) or they are salaried as in an HMO.

A third cost-control strategy is the simplification of payment and reimbursement systems. For example, the Clinton Plan calls for a single claims form to reduce paperwork, simplify record keeping and regulations for insurers and providers of care. The plan offers a comprehensive benefits package that applies to all insured persons making it easier for providers to know what is covered, and for receivers of care to know what their premiums will buy. Simplification may also be acheived through national standards for automation of insurance transactions to promote easier communication between payers, insurers, and providers. Standards of automation should make it easier to control and track fraud and abuse.

A fourth strategy for reducing costs calls for insurance reform. *Newsweek* magazine (Samuelson, 1993, p. 31) explained the cause of the health care spending explosion as, "...the volatile mix of generous insurance and high-tech medicine." As medicine becomes more expensive, people clamor for more insurance protection against the rising cost of care. Greater insurance, in turn, makes it easier for health providers and hospitals to use more expensive technology knowing they will be paid. Insurance reform advocates believe that it's possible to control the profit motive that has led to escalating premiums if:

a) all customers are charged the same for the same comprehensive insurance package; b) insurance companies are required to insure all who apply and guarantee renewal; and c) insurance premium caps are enforced.

A fifth cost-control strategy is to control fraud, abuse and medical malpractice. For example, the Clinton Plan mandates stiff criminal penalties for those who would abuse the health care system. These penalties include seizure of assets derived from fraud, exclusion or fines for guilty providers, reinvestment of fines into anti-fraud efforts, coordination of efforts at the local, state, and national level including sharing data on offenders, and restriction on kickbacks and self-referrals. Advocates of malpractice reform urge caps on awards, penalties for trivial suits, and arbitration.

Costs can also be controlled through the use of less expensive health care providers. From literature reviewed, Safriet (1992) concluded that the costs of training physicians are four to five times greater than the costs of educating nurse practitioners and certified nurse midwives. Furthermore, the salaries of physicians are significantly higher than salaries of nurses (U.S. Congress, 1986). From a meta analysis of studies concerning nurses in primary care roles, Brown and Grimes (1993) found that nurse practitioner utilization costs are lower in general as compared to costs for physician visits. For example, nurses spent more minutes per patient, but the average cost per visit was less. The number of visits per patient was similar for nurse practitioners and physicians. Nurse practitioner patients experienced fewer hospitalizations, and had lower laboratory costs. Lower utilization costs were achieved with comparable or better clinical outcomes than those obtained under physician care (Brown and Grimes, 1993).

Containing cost, however, does not override other concerns. Most acknowledge that the quality of care, based on the competence and professionalism of practitioners as well as the scientific basis of health care, should be maintained. Appropriate training of primary care physicians and nurses is crucial to the mandate of quality health care for all. The support of outcomes research is critical to the development of valid practice guidelines based on scientific data about what works and what doesn't. In addition, public access to performance records of health care providers and agencies, and patient satisfaction data can serve to promote quality of care.

Support for Health Care Reform

No attempt at health care reform can succeed without a considerable base of support across the country. Princeton Survey Research Associates, on behalf of *Newsweek*, interviewed 751 adults on September 23-24, 1993 (cited in Morganthau and Hager, 1993). Data from this national sample revealed both support and skepticism about the Clinton Plan. On the positive side, the respondents said the plan meant more security concerning the availability of health care whatever a person's medical or financial problems (61 percent) and the same or better quality health care (55 percent). On the negative side, respondents felt that the Clinton Plan meant no real health-cost savings (47 percent), and more taxes (73 percent). To the extent that a reform program supports Medicare, it will receive the endorsement of the elderly. The American Association of Retired Persons praised the Clinton Plan for inclusion of prescription drugs and long-term care benefits (American Health Association, 1993c).

The *Los Angeles Times* (Brownstein, 1993) conducted a nationwide, telephone poll using random digit dialing to interview 1,491 persons in English and Spanish. The poll represented the views of the elderly, Anglos, blacks, Latinos, the uninsured, those insured through their employer or union, those who buy their own coverage, Democrats, Republicans and Independents. Asian Pacific Americans were not categorized, therefore, their specific response to the reform package was not described. This lack of public information concerning Asian Pacific American beliefs, opinions, and needs, is typical of the health care arena. Results were similar to the *Newsweek* poll. Respondents expressed broad but tentative support for the Clinton Health Plan because it provides universal health coverage. The majority did not believe their health care would improve and half of those polled expected to pay more for health care coverage.

A difficult issue in any health care reform proposal is the treatment of undocumented aliens. Any attempt to include illegals as part of the millions of uninsured Americans and legal residents would raise opposition from all quarters. Yet, to expressly deny all care to illegals would polarize all minority groups including Asian and Pacific Islander Americans.

The actions and positions of special interest groups are also factors that will shape health care reform. The American Nurses Association (ANA) supports health care reform that provides universal access to care, mandated comprehensive benefits, insurance reforms, and recognition of advanced practice nurses and registered professional nurses who can provide quality care for a variety of health care services. The ANA believes that health care reform needs to address the needs of children, the underserved and the elderly (Trotter-Betts, 1993).

Hospital associations, like the American Hospital Association (AHA), are in favor of health care reform that supports universal coverage and develops systems that are not difficult to administer and enforce, impose price controls, impose limits on private health expenditures, or go against deeply held religious beliefs ("American Health Association, 1993c). The AHA and 19 other organizations oppose reforms that reduce Medicare and Medicaid spending (Gearon and Kostreski, 1993). HMOs generally support health care reform since they are already in the forefront of cost control through managed care (Sponselli, McGurk, and Bronson-Gray, 1993).

While the American Medical Association (AMA) strongly supports the notion of universal access to health care, it opposes government regulation, unrealistic evaluation strategies like quality report cards proposed by the Clinton Plan, and insufficient action concerning malpractice reform (American Health Association, 1993a and 1993d). Despite opposition to government regulation to limit health care costs, it is unlikely that cost savings will occur without such regulation. It is also unlikely that providers will self-impose limits on costs without some form of government mandate.

The AMA also opposes health care reform programs that set quotas for training of primary care physicians (American Health Association, 1993a and 1993d). Yet, the Council on Graduate Medical Education, a congressional advisory committee, stated that 50 percent of physicians should be in primary care. At present only one-third of MDs are in primary care practices

(Council on Graduate Medical Education, 1993).

Finally, it is important to consider the position of the health insurance industry (e.g., Group Health Association of America, Blue Cross and Blue Shield Association, Health Insurance Association of America). The industry generally supports health care reform, as exemplified in the Clinton Plan. Understandably, the industry opposes the creation of structures that would replace them and government control of premium increases (American Health Association, 1993b).

Health Care Needs of Asian Pacific Americans

Understanding population growth, demographic patterns, and morbidity and mortality trends in Asian Pacific American people is basic to forming meaningful public policy. While specific projections may differ, there is consensus that Asian Pacific Americans are the fastest growing minority. The Asian Pacific population is projected to reach between 17.9 million and 20.2 million by the year 2020 (Ong and Hee, 1993). The U.S. Bureau of Census (1992) expects Asian Pacific Americans to reach 10.7 percent of the U.S. population by the year 2050.

A major problem in evaluating the impact of any health reform program on Asian Pacific Americans is the lack of information concerning this population. Neither the *Healthy People 2000* policy guidelines (U.S. Department of Health and Human Services, 1990), nor the *Health Status of Minorities and Low-Income Groups* report (U.S. Department of Health and Human Services, 1993) provide satisfactory data on Asian Pacific American health issues. For a health reform program to adequately address the physical and mental health care needs of Asian Pacific Americans, it is necessary to know the extent of potential or real health problems of these groups (Guillermo, 1993; Sue, 1993).

Special health problems of Asian Pacific Americans are summarized by Lin-Fu (1993) whose report is based on a number of published studies. Important genetic problems concern alpha and beta thalassemia and hemoglobin E. According to Choi and Necheles, about 5 percent of Chinese Americans in Boston are carriers of alpha and beta thalassemia. Another study found in the Crocker report stated that 28 percent of Laotians and 26 percent of Cambodians are carriers of hemoglobin E. Rowley, Loader, Sutera and colleagues found that 14 percent of Southeast Asians in Rochester, New York, are carriers of hemoglobinopathy. Lactase deficiency is common among Asian Pacific Americans. Genetic screening and counseling would be important services to offer Asian Pacific Americans under any health reform pro-gram. Providers are not always aware of these problems.

Lin-Fu (1993) further reports that two infectious diseases are of grave importance in Asian Pacific Americans: hepatitis B and tuberculosis. Hepatitis B is of particular concern in new immigrants from Southeast Asia where the problem is widespread. Infants born to infected mothers have a high risk of acquiring HBV infection and of remaining chronically infected. Chronic infection with HBV contributes to primary hepatoma and cirrhosis. For this reason, preventive prenatal care and post-delivery care of the infant are critical in controlling the spread of HBV. Tuberculosis, the other prevalent disease, also occurs with greater frequency in Southeast Asian refugees. Unfortunately, many Asian Pacific Americans are infected with drug resistant strains of the disease. Diagnosis and treatment for tuberculosis and other problems such as intestinal parasites should also be covered under any health reform plan.

The Lin-Fu report (1993) also describes the seriousness of the cancer problem among native Hawaiians who have the highest incidence of cancer of the stomach, breast, corpus uteri, and ovaries; and second highest incidence of lung cancer. Stomach cancer is also high among Japanese, while liver cancer is high among Chinese. Prevention services, if covered by a health reform plan, may decrease the incidence of some cancers. However, culturally targeted education programs would be needed to promote cancer prevention and detection practices among Asian Pacific Americans. Other notable health problems are nocturnal death in seemingly healthy young people, particularly Hmong and Laotians (Lin-Fu, 1987); cardiovascular disease (Chen, 1993a); and smoking (Centers for Disease Control, 1992).

Despite the myriad of health problems, the *Healthy People 2000* position paper includes only eight objectives for Asian Pacific Americans. Chen (1993b) summarized the U.S. Office of Disease Prevention and Health Promotion's 1992 publication, *Progress Reports on Healthy People 2000 Objectives*. He found that only one out of the eight objectives, the reduction of viral hepatitis B in children of Asian Pacific Americans, was on target. The following three objectives were not on target for Asian Pacific Americans: a) appropriate reduction in growth retardation in children, b) reduction in tuberculosis, and c) at least a 50 percent increase in recommended screening, immunization, and counseling services appropriate for age and gender. Three other objectives could not be adequately evaluated due to insufficient data for Asian Pacific Americans: a) reduction of cigarette smoking to no more than 15 percent among those 20 years or older; b) increase to at least 50 percent the proportion of counties that have established culturally and linguistically appropriate community health promotion programs; and c) development and implementation of a national process to identify significant gaps in the nation's disease prevention and health promotion data, including information for racial and ethnic minorities. One objective was inappropriate as an objective targeted to Asian Pacific Americans: the implementation at the state level of periodic analysis and publication of data regarding progress toward objectives.

For many, access to health care is hindered by the lack of insurance coverage. Asian Pacific Americans, like the rest of the U.S. population, are burdened with the increasing weight of health care costs. They undergo the same hardships as the rest of the nation: stymied growth in wages, increased costs of conducting business and producing goods, and larger deductibles and co-payments. Uninsured Asian Pacific Americans, like other uninsured Americans, can be further impoverished by a costly illness, and only seek care for acute and serious illnesses from overcrowded public hospital emergency rooms.

Financial and cultural barriers contribute to underutilization. Underutilization of mental health services is common among Asian Pacific Americans (Matsuoka, 1990). This underutilization need not represent less severe conditions. Asian Pacific Americans have been found to have greater disturbance levels (Sue and Sue, 1974). Factors that influence utilization of mental health services include location, availability, and cultural and linguistic appropriateness of services (Sue, 1993; Sue and Morishima, 1982; Tracey, Leong and Glidden, 1986). When there are few accessible services, then utilization is low.

This problem is also present in health services. Hafner-Eaton (1993) shows that Asians have considerably less access to the American health care system than other racial groups. The study controlled for insurance, health and income status. Ong and Azores in Chapter 7 speculate that less access may be due to culturally determined behavior, language and other barriers. Income and education are other determinants to access for Asian Pacific Americans. While fee-for-service plans may offer the best service, the expensive price can be a major barrier for those with limited financial means.

There exists a misconception shared by the public and legislators that Asian Pacific Americans already have an adequate number of health care providers to serve their community. The problem of access is further limited by a lack of providers in many communities. This misperception is compounded by the increase in Asian Americans admitted to medical schools, currently 15.9 percent of entering students in the U.S. (Guang et al., 1993). While some Asian Pacific American groups are well represented, others are not. For example, there is an inadequate supply of Vietnamese, Cambodian, and Laotian health care providers. Misperceptions stem from aggregating data for all Asian Pacific groups. The majority of Asian Pacific physicians practice in the northeast and northcentral states, while the majority of Asian Pacific Americans reside in the West. While Asian Americans are being accepted into U.S. medical schools in greater numbers than ever before, they elect specialty fields rather than primary care.

Given the myriad of health care problems, Asian Pacific Americans have a large stake in the current debate over reforming the health care system. The outcomes will determine whether many Asian Pacific Americans will have a healthy future or a future with poor and limited services.

Recommendations

Health care reform challenges Asian Pacific Americans to take a proactive stance in controlling the health care system that will affect them. To this end, Asian Pacific Americans have spoken out in support of health care reform as exemplified by the Clinton Plan, but do so with reservation. This section discusses recommendations from the caucus of Asian American Health Care Workers of the American Public Health Association; the Asian Pacific Health Care Venture, Inc., a community-based health organization that coordinates health care services for low-income Asian Pacific Americans; and the Asian and Pacific Islander American Health Forum, a national, nonprofit health advocacy organization.

Asian Pacific American groups urge universal access to health care for American citizens, legal residents, undocumented workers, and illegal aliens (Asian Pacific Health Care Venture, Inc., 1993; Guillermo, 1994; Shibata, 1994). This recommendation is based on the belief that coverage of undocumented and illegal persons is beneficial in the long term. For example, illnesses are likely to be treated at earlier stages when they cost less; prenatal care and immunization will protect everyone and cost less; agencies that provide care to undocumented and illegal persons can be reimbursed and will not be overburdened with costs; and some states will not be disadvantaged because of the large numbers of undocumented and illegal persons who use their public hospitals. Further, Medicaid recipients should be treated like all others to insure better care for these persons.

Unless health care programs/systems are adequately explained to Asian Pacific Americans who face cultural, linguistic or educational barriers to information, Asian Pacific Americans may make uninformed, poor choices. Despite health care reform efforts to provide comprehensive benefits, race and ethnicity will continue to be strong determinants of ability to receive timely, effective treatment.

The movement to provide more universal health care coverage, however, should not place undue financial burdens on Asian Pacific small business (Shibata, 1994). Many Asian Pacific small businesses operate at small profit margins. Requiring them to pay for insurance coverage for owners and employees would effectively put many out of business. Therefore, caps on premium payments by these small businesses should be low. Taxes on tobacco, alcohol, firearems and payroll (with protection for low-income workers) would spread the burden of supporting universal coverage.

Increased support for community-based service agencies is

seen as a priority because of their pivotal role in Asian Pacific communities (Guillermo, 1994). For example, native Hawaiian health care centers should be supported in any health care reform program. They play a key role in facilitating access to the larger health care delivery system for small, rural and underserved communities. While universal coverage may facilitate access to health care services, it does not address the issue of utilization. Here is where culturally responsive, community-based clinics offer a safety net. These clinics: a) are easy to access and negotiate, b) can understand the needs of the Asian Pacific client, and c) are staffed by personnel who share the same background as the clients. In addition, these clinics serve the underserved, particularly those who would otherwise be ineligible for health care. Thus, they control the costs for the greater health care system. The very smallness of these community-based clinics puts them at risk for closure, if a place is not allocated to them in any future health reform program.

Asian Pacific Americans also have a stake in reforming the health professions. Most Asian nurses, like nurses in general, are hospital-based. There is a great need to retool hospital nurses to work in communities, outpatient settings, and primary care environments. There is also a need to educate youth to recognize the value of a nursing career if we are to have well-educated nurses to care for Asian Pacific Americans. A study of high school students in an eastern state showed that of all ethnic groups, Asian females were less likely to perceive nursing as being appreciated, making a lot of money, working in safe places, and being respected by others (Reiskin and Haussler, 1994).

The cost of higher education can serve as a formidable barrier. It is important for Asian Pacific Americans to capitalize on the opportunity offered by the Clinton Plan, if it is adopted, to expand the number of Asian Pacific physician and nurse primary care providers as well as mental health care providers. The Clinton Plan will support additional training of advanced practice nurses who offer less expensive primary care services that promote health and prevent disease.

The training and retraining should include programs to ensure the cultural sensitivity and relevancy of health services and consumer education (Asian Pacific Health Care Venture,

Inc., 1993; Guillermo, 1993; Lin-Fu, 1994; Shibata, 1994). At present, the Asian Pacific American health care workforce is largely immigrant with 21 percent of all physicians being foreign medical graduates (Roback, Randolph and Seidman, 1992). One would expect more culturally sensitive care from Asian Pacific American providers. However, Asian Pacific Americans represent a very diverse, heterogeneous group who speak different languages and have different cultures. Many health care providers do not understand their own cultural orientation, nor the important role of culture in lifestyle and health behavior (Lin-Fu, 1993). Communication and cultural sensitivity between a recently immigrated, young Chinese doctor and an elderly Filipina may not be any better than that between an Anglo doctor and the same patient. Without training in culturally competent care, Asian Pacific providers may not be able to deliver culturally sensitive care to Asian Pacific American clients.

Training programs are needed to teach nurses, physicians, dentists, and other providers strategies for delivering culturally competent health care to Asian Pacific groups in urban and rural areas. These training programs may be funded by agencies in the Bureau of Health Professions of the Department of Health and Human Services. Providers need to be aware and use traditional medicines when appropriate, recognize folk medicines that pose a danger to the consumer, and learn how folk medicines may interact with Western drugs to the detriment of the patient. Asian Pacific Americans also urge the promotion of standards for translators working in the health care field. Reimbursement can be tied to the use of certified translators. This will likely increase the number of bilingual translators in health care agencies. Institutional barriers that jeopardize the care of Asian Pacific Americans include: long telephone waiting periods for appointments, extensive interview procedures to obtain services, restrictions in the use of emergency services, difficulties in arranging transportation, and general confusion when faced with negotiating a complex health care delivery system.

It is also important to provide consumers with health education material that is culturally and linguistically relevant.

It is especially important to innoculate Asian Pacific American consumers against unethical persons who may take money for health "insurance" or "services," and then provide no or substandard care. Also needed is educational material that addresses the unique health risks of diverse Asian Pacific groups and information regarding consumer rights and participation.

Finally, there is a need to improve quality management measures and racial/ethnic specific health data (Guillermo, 1994; Lin-Fu, 1994; Shibata, 1994). Asian Pacific Americans urge changes in standardized claim or other health forms and the data/information systems used by providers, insurance companies, health plans, state and federal governments so as to codify Asian Pacific Americans by major groups (Asian, Pacific Islander) and subgroups (e.g., Pilipino, Hmong, Korean). Since Asian Pacific Americans represent very heterogeneous subgroups, specificity in codification generates more useful data to describe health problems, service utilization, satisfaction with care, etc., by specific group and region. These data are essential to the development of effective health care guidelines for Asian Pacific American clients.

Concluding Remarks

It is important for Asian Pacific Americans to increase their participation in health care reform program development and governance (Asian Pacific Health Care Venture, Inc., 1993; Shibata, 1994). Asian Pacific Americans must lobby to be appointed to federal and state regulatory boards such as the proposed National Health Board and state boards (U.S. Office of the President, 1993). Any national regulatory board with the responsibility of setting federal standards and policies will have a major impact on health practices that affect the quality of care extended to Asian Pacific Americans. Likewise, any state board expected to monitor and assure compliance with federal guidelines will have a significant impact on health practices that affect Asian Pacific Americans. By participating in federal and state regulatory boards, Asian Pacific Americans can craft health reform programs to insure that reforms are responsive to the needs of Asian Pacific Americans in the following ways:

1) the plan covers the alternative health care services of herbalists, acupuncturists, nutritionists and other health care providers who meet the needs of Asian Pacific Americans;

2) the plan ensures access to care using outreach, follow-up, home visits, and transportation services for Asian Pacific American members when necessary;

3) the plan coordinates services of primary, secondary and tertiary care providers for Asian Pacific American clients.

While Asian Pacific Americans are overrepresented in the medical and nursing professions, they are underrepresented in administrative positions (see Chapter 7). It is important for Asian Pacific Americans to require that health care reform programs provide opportunities for Asian Pacific Americans to move into decision-making and policymaking positions to better serve their client counterparts.

Notes

1. For more information, see Starr (1982) in the chapter, "The Generalization of Doubt," especially pp. 408-411.
2. Chen (1993, p. 37) states that Asian Pacific Americans are "among the most neglected minority group with regards to health status surveillance..."

Chapter 12

High Technology Policies

Sheridan M. Tatsuno

The end of the Cold War and Asia's phenomenal growth have stimulated a fundamental rethinking of U.S. high technology policies and business practices. With the decline in military spending, the U.S. government is actively promoting defense conversion and export promotion programs. The Asian Pacific region, once relegated to bilateral security issues, is taking on growing importance for the U.S. high-tech industry. Not only is the Asia Pacific Economic Community (APEC) a major source of science and engineering talent, but its fast-growing markets offer new business opportunities for U.S. companies.

For Asian Americans involved in high technology industries, these changes present major opportunities and challenges. On the one hand, federal commercialization and export promotion policies favor U.S. high-tech companies expanding into Asian Pacific markets. Asian Americans with strong business contacts throughout the Asian Pacific region stand to benefit from this industry shift. On the other hand, the existence of "glass ceilings" in government, universities, and business, combined with widespread corporate layoffs, have reduced job opportunities domestically. While many Asian American scientists and engineers (S&Es) have responded by retraining and starting their own firms, increasing numbers of Asian-born S&Es are returning home where career opportunities are greater.

This chapter explores the impact of changing U.S. government high-tech policies, global high-tech industries, and workforce changes on Asian Americans in high technology sectors. It identifies emerging issues and recommends policies.[1]

Global High Techology Trends

The U.S. high technology industry is undergoing major structural changes in the post-Cold War era, paralleled only by the massive demobilization after World War II. As shown in Table 1, these changes require fresh, new thinking by educators, business leaders, and policymakers. Traditional notions about U.S. high-tech competitiveness are rooted in an era of plentiful funding and limited foreign competition. Today, faced with growing pressure from global competitors and defense cutbacks, U.S. high-tech companies can no longer afford to conduct "business as usual." They must rapidly evolve or face extinction. Corporate hierarchies are giving way to global networks of "virtual" corporations.

The decline in military spending has hit the high-tech industry particularly hard. Defense contractors, especially on the West and East Coasts where Asian Americans are concentrated, are laying off thousands of employees. These cutbacks will continue throughout the 1990s, sharply reducing career opportunities in aerospace, electronics, and other defense-related industries. Older professionals are retiring, while younger engineers are shifting to high-growth industries. To cushion the impact of defense cutbacks and base closures, the U.S. Department of Defense is encouraging defense contractors to commercialize their technologies and develop new dual-use technologies for commercial and military sectors. But finding new market opportunities is a slow, difficult process due to the specialized nature of military technologies. Many smaller contractors, especially in Southern California, are going out of business. Large numbers of Asian American professionals are affected by these cutbacks.

Fortunately, fast-growing Asian Pacific markets offer opportunities for U.S. high-tech companies that are diversifying from shrinking military programs and slow-growth markets in the U.S., Japan, and Europe. To assist U.S. high-tech companies to make the conversion from defense contracting, the National Institute for Standards and Technology (NIST) and Advanced Research Projects Agency (ARPA) are expanding their high technology research and development (R&D) funding, while the U.S. Department of Commerce is promoting exports, especially to Asia and Latin America.

Table 1. Science & Technology Trends

	Cold War (1950s-1980s)	Post-Cold War (1990s)
Global Trends		
Government	Increased defense spending SEATO military umbrella	Flat defense spending (US & Europe) Increased defense spending in Asia
University	Strong basic research Heavy military R&D Strong corporate support	Declining basic research funding Declining military R&D Declining corporate funding
Industry	Atlantic Basin focus (NATO) Hardware focus	Rise of Pacific Rim (APEC) Shift to software & services
U.S. Trends		
Government	Defense-oriented	Commercialization & dual-use
Universities	Rapid increase in Asians (1980s) Admission quotas	Heavy concentration of Asian Americans in science & engineering
Industry	High U.S. industry growth Rapid electronics growth	Slowing U.S. industry growth Shift to biotechnology & software
Corporations	Increasing percentage of Asian Americans Monocultural management	Heavy concentration of Asian Americans in engineering Diversity training
Asian American workforce	"Brain drain" to U.S. Mostly Japanese-, Chinese- and Filipino-Americans	"Reverse brain drain" to Asia Arrival of Korean, Thai, Vietnamese, and other Asian-Pacific workers
Labor status	Strong discrimination	Declining discrimination, but "glass ceiling" persists for key management positions
Entrepreneurialism	Few Asian American high-tech ventures	Proliferation of self-funded and Asian-funded ventures
Asian American women	Few scientists & engineers	Increasing number of professionals and students

These global trends are favorable for Asian Americans, especially those knowledgeable of Asian Pacific markets. Since the early 1980s, Asian American enrollment in university science and engineering departments has grown quickly. In 1990, Asian Americans accounted for 7 percent of all S&E students. At the corporate level, Asian American S&Es now account for over a quarter million high-tech employees. Increasingly, Asian Americans are opening their own high-tech startup companies. This influx of Asian American and U.S.-educated Asian scientists and engineers has enabled U.S. high-tech companies to maintain their global competitiveness.

However, the increasing "Asianification" of U.S. science and engineering is raising debate over questions of equal opportunity, diversity, and quotas. Although viewed as assets by companies pursuing Asian Pacific trade, Asian American S&Es now find themselves on the other side of the equal opportunity debate. This situation requires a fundamental rethinking of S&E policies, especially as the U.S. economy becomes more ethnically diverse and interdependent with foreign markets.

Government High Technology Policies

During World War II and the Cold War, the U.S. government pursued "supply-side" or mission-oriented high-technology policies. Federal laboratories were expanded to develop nuclear and non-nuclear weapons to strengthen national security. U.S. defense research and development (R&D) accounted for one-third of all public and private R&D conducted in OECD nations (Branscomb, 1993, p. 12). By the late 1980s, federal labs received about 70 percent of the $20 billion in federal research funding. This military effort became what former President Eisenhower called the "military-industrial complex" — a dense, interlocking network of defense contractors, suppliers, and advisors who became accustomed to large cost-plus contracts and top-secret research. U.S. research priorities were heavily influenced by U.S. participation in NATO, SEATO, and U.S.-Japan and other mutual security agreements. Commercialization of military technologies was actively discouraged to avoid giving advanced technologies to Communist Bloc nations.

In 1957, the launching of Sputnik accelerated the nuclear arms race. Fears of Russian nuclear missile attacks led to rapid mobilization of national security programs ranging from highway programs, student scholarships, and university-based contract research to heavy funding of top-secret military research and intelligence programs. Internet, which is now widely used by universities and businesses around the world, was initially funded by the Defense Area Research Project Agency (DARPA) to ensure back-up communications in the event of a nuclear attack.

In 1961, President John F. Kennedy's call for "putting a man on the moon" led to the formation of the National Aeronautics and Space Administration (NASA), which provided thousands of jobs for American scientists and engineers. Combined with the nuclear arms build-up and construction of the national highway system, these U.S. government programs fully mobilized scientists and engineers. Universities expanded their science and engineering programs to meet the demand from industry and government.

Although Asian American engineers and scientists joined high-tech companies, very few reached top-level management positions and policymaking positions. Citizenship requirements, tight security clearances and blatant racial discrimination effectively eliminated Asian Americans from positions of critical importance. Scientists and engineers with any family or personal ties with enemy nations such as China, Vietnam, or North Korea were viewed with suspicion, especially after the McCarthy "Communist witchhunt" hearings. Japanese Americans had experienced similar discrimination during World War II.

The few opportunities available were in non-military university positions in science and engineering departments, especially away from the anti-Asian climate along the West Coast. It was common knowledge that Asian American researchers could not find good jobs and advance very far in California during the 1950s and 1960s. Many Asian American scientists and researchers moved to the Midwest and the East Coast where they were usually concentrated in areas of basic research not requiring security clearances.

During the early 1970s, many Asian American scientists and

engineers began returning to the West Coast due to more liberal social attitudes and equal opportunity legislation. The liberalization of immigration laws in 1965 opened the door to Asian professionals whose numbers grew rapidly during the 1970s. By 1980, Asian Americans accounted for 4 percent of all scientists and engineers in the U.S. labor force. During the 1980s, President Reagan's rapid military build-up accelerated the immigration of top-flight researchers who were sought by the booming aerospace, defense and electronics industries. Taiwan, Hong Kong, South Korea, and the Philippines supplied most of the Asian-born researchers.

Since the fall of the Soviet Union, U.S. science and technology policies have been changing dramatically. Under the Clinton administration, defense spending is gradually being reduced and military bases are being closed. Defense contractors are being urged to commercialize their technologies and develop dual-use technologies to serve both commercial and military sectors. The U.S. government is taking a more activist stance in promoting high technologies. According to White House science advisor Jack Gibbons, President Clinton has discarded the Cold War generation's view that science funding produce "serendipitous" commercial development. Instead, administration officials are encouraging companies to develop and commercialize federally-funded R&D, especially defense contractors. This is a major reversal of federal R&D funding policies.

The Clinton administration's budget for the 1994-1997 period calls for a gradual decline in spending for defense, agriculture, community development and flat spending for science, space, technology, energy, environment and natural resources. By contrast, large increases are planned for commercial research programs managed by the National Institute for Standards and Technology (NIST), Area Research Projects Agency (ARPA), Technology Reinvestment Program (TRP), and the "information super-highway" or High-Performance Computing and Communications (HPCC). NIST and TRP, the nerve centers of U.S. industrial policy, will receive the biggest increase as the Clinton administration seeks to strengthen high-tech sectors and create new jobs (Davis, 1994.

What impact will changing U.S. science and technology

policies have on Asian Americans? Technology policies of the Clinton administration will have an impact on Asian Americans in four major areas (*New Technology Week*, 1993, p. 4). One, the federal government is directly supporting the development, commercialization, and deployment of new technologies. Asian Americans are eligible for the new federal R&D programs and university research grants related to defense conversion, such as the Technology Reinvestment Program (TRP). However, most funding is being awarded to large R&D consortia involving corporate, university, and government researchers. Since most Asian American-owned high-tech companies are small businesses aimed at commercial markets, they are usually unqualified to compete individually for these federal R&D programs. Greater effort should be made to educate Asian American researchers and companies about these programs and encourage them to join larger R&D consortia to improve their chances for federal funding. Conferences and on-line bulletin boards are two ways to spread the word.

Two, the administration is attempting to create a world-class business environment for innovation and private-sector investment. Asian Americans are heavily concentrated in high technology regions such as Silicon Valley, Los Angeles, Seattle, Denver, and New York City, which are closely tied to global financial markets. Many highly-skilled Asian American engineers and businesspeople have access to U.S. and Asian private investors, venture capital, loans from families and friends, and bank credit lines. Industry trade groups such as the Asian American Manufacturers' Association (AAMA) are instrumental in introducing prospective investors to Silicon Valley startup companies. However, seed capital is limited, often focused on tangible assets instead of intellectual property, and usually obtained through friends and family connections. Moreover, Asian American venture financing tends to be "ghettoized." To tap into large pools of talent and capital, Asian American financiers need to work with outside investors when establishing new venture capital funds. These funds could specialize in funneling investments from Asian Pacific and other international investors into domestic high-tech companies.

Three, there is a major push to develop an information super-highway. High-speed communication networks will open the doors for many Asian Americans, especially for trade with Asian Pacific markets, but lack of access among poorer families will remain a major problem. Asian American community groups should work closely with government, industry, and schools to ensure that all Asian Americans have equal access to computer networks. Moreover, proficiency in the English language and Asian languages should be promoted to enable Asian Americans to communicate with others over networks, both in the United States and Asia Pacific. Vice President Al Gore has stressed "universal access," but this concept needs to be made concrete and practical.

Four, as a part of "reinventing government," the administration is reforming government procurement policies. The shift toward dual-use technologies will create opportunities for leading-edge high technology companies supplying U.S. government agencies. During the 1980s, many Asian American-owned high-tech companies benefitted from Section 8a programs designed to help minority-owned businesses win federal procurement contracts. The federal government will award grants to R&D consortia under the Technology Reinvestment Program (TRP). To ensure that Asian American businesses have equal access to these programs, greater effort should be made through Asian American chambers of commerce, the Asian American Manufacturing Association (AAMA), and other trade associations to educate businesses about these opportunities.

Manpower Issues

Since the liberalization of immigration laws in 1965, Asian American enrollment in university science and engineering programs has been strongly influenced by the rapid increase in Asian immigrants. In 1990-91, 166,460 students from five Asian nations were enrolled in U.S. university S&E departments. Graduate enrollment was highest for students from China, India, Singapore, South Korea and Taiwan — countries where demand far exceeds available seats.

The large number of Asia-born S&E students has several implications for Asian Americans. First, their presence gives the impression of higher Asian American enrollment in S&E departments than is actually the case. As foreign-born enrollment increases, there may be growing public demands for quotas on Asian American enrollment. This situation could be exacerbated as universities actively recruit foreign students to compensate for declining U.S. student enrollment, since foreign students are usually charged higher tuition fees.

In the past, these U.S.-educated Asian scientists and engineers stayed in the United States after graduation because of better employment and housing opportunities. Due to slow U.S. job growth, the "glass ceiling," and rapid Asian economic growth, many Asian-born professionals are returning home, leading to a "reverse brain drain" of top-flight engineers, scientists, and technology managers. Most of these professionals have years of experience at leading U.S. high-tech companies, so their return is transferring leading-edge U.S. technologies to Asia. Once viewed as a one-way ticket to the United States, U.S. universities are increasingly viewed as training grounds for the next generation of Asian technocratic elites. In a recent report, the National Science Foundation outlined several implications of Asian S&E enrollment in U.S. universities (National Science Foundation, 1993):

Asian countries continue to rely on U.S. higher education since they cannot meet the demand for higher education fast enough.

Foreign enrollment will help maintain U.S. S&E doctoral programs, which are growing faster than non-science and engineering fields. In 1991, 3,204 foreign-born Asian students received doctoral degrees (China 940, Taiwan 906, South Korea 673, India 612, and Japan 73)

Asian countries will compete with the United States for the Asian-born graduates of U.S. universities. Though some will stay in the U.S. labor force, more will probably return to Asia.

Besides a "reverse brain drain," the United States also faces increasing high-tech competition from Asian nations due to their large university S&E enrollments. Asian nations granted three times more S&E bachelor degrees than the United States and nearly 70 percent more doctoral degrees. U.S. universities still lead the world in high-quality S&E education, but the large number of Asian S&E graduates will contribute to faster high-tech growth in Asia. Moreover, diminishing job opportunities in the U.S. high-tech sector are likely to depress U.S. S&E enrollment, further weakening U.S. high-tech competitiveness.

While "reverse brain drain" exists, it is a minor phenomenon. The vast majority of Asian American scientists and engineers work in the United States and contribute enormously to the development of technology in this country. Asian Americans are a growing portion of the U.S. high-tech workforce. They constituted 7 percent of all high-tech workers in 1990, up from 4 percent in 1980. Asian Americans represent a higher percentage of U.S. high-tech employees with higher levels of education, which accounts for the large number of Asian Americans in research positions.

By contrast, very few of these scientists and engineers have been promoted into upper management. In Chapter 8, Ong and Blumenberg report that Asian Americans are only two-thirds as likely to be in a management position as non-Hispanic whites. Although racial discrimination is often cited as the main reason for the "glass ceiling" phenomenon, there are other possible reasons. The majority of Asian American high-tech workers tend to be younger, more recent immigrants, thus lacking the work experience for these positions. Corporate downsizing is eliminating many mid-level management positions, eliminating promotion opportunities for Asian Americans. Asian Americans lack the "old boy" network of friends in top management positions or the know-how to develop a support network. Many Asian Americans, especially those not comfortable with American culture or fluent in English, are reluctant to seek management positions, which require extensive contact with outside investors, stockholders, the press, and the public. Even if considered candidates for management positions, many talented Asian Americans get impatient and quit to start their own ventures. Recently, excellent job opportunities in Asia are attracting top-level Asian-born scientists and engineers.

In many high-tech companies, Asian professionals often cluster together because of common background and interests. While it may ease their transition to American society, it also limits their promotion opportunities since they do not mix with predominantly Caucasian managers. Unless individuals make a special effort to overcome racial stereotyping and clustering, it is easy to remain in non-management roles. Part of this will change over time as Asia-born professionals become acculturated to the United States.

The meteoric rise of Asia raises serious questions about some of the assertions made for the lack of Asian Americans in high management. If Asians lack leadership skills, how does one account for the competitiveness of many Asian companies? Chinese high-tech entrepreneurs, for example, are major players in California and Asia (Kao, 1993). Although these companies operate mostly within Asian markets, these companies are compelling evidence that Asian American high-tech professionals can excel if given the opportunity.

Trade and Investments

Rapid economic growth in the Asia Pacific Economic Community (APEC) is perhaps the best opportunity for Asian American high-tech professionals. Two-way investments between the United States and APEC nations exceeded $300 billion in 1992. Since 20,000 to 30,000 high-tech jobs are created for each billion dollars invested in the U.S, the $147 billion in APEC direct investments in the United States in 1992 accounted for over two million jobs (new or retained). Although not limited to high-tech investments, these investments are indirectly creating job opportunities for scientists and engineers on both sides of the Pacific.

U.S.-APEC trade flows are significant. In 1991, exports from NAFTA (North American Free Trade Area) to APEC nations reached $136.9 billion, while imports were $219.3 billion. Exports to APEC thus accounted for about four to seven million jobs in 1992. These figures are forecast to grow rapidly in the future.

The rise of Asia creates numerous business opportunities for Asian American high-tech professionals. Whereas Asian Americans were dependent upon Caucasian-run companies in the past, many Asian Americans now have the option to start their own company, join an Asian company, work in Asia, or head an Asian Pacific operation in a large multinational corporation. Although the "glass ceiling" is still a problem at older high-tech companies, more management opportunities are available to Asian Americans because of trade in the Pacific Rim.

Growing U.S. high-tech trade with Asia is a two-edged sword for Asian American high-tech workers. On the one hand, Asian language and cultural capabilities are a major asset for doing business in Asian Pacific markets. High-tech joint ventures, technology exchanges, mutual licensing agreements, and joint R&D with Asian Pacific companies are proliferating. For native Asian language speakers, overseas jobs and technical marketing positions in export-oriented high-tech companies are plentiful. For U.S.-born Asian Americans fluent in the language of their ancestry, cultural familiarity makes it easier to do business. Asian Americans with strong family and personal connections in Asia have a clear advantage doing business there.

On the other hand, growing U.S.-Asian trade friction will heighten anti-Asian sentiment among people hurt by Asian imports. The Vincent Chin beating and Los Angeles riot attacks on Korean businesses are examples of anti-Asian crimes triggered by economic factors. As trade imbalances increase, trade friction and anti-Asian violence are likely to increase. This is particularly true with major exporting nations such as Japan, Taiwan, South Korea, China and India.

Rapid militarization in Asia resulting from increasing wealth will become a major issue for Asian Americans. For example, Japan's remilitarization or border clashes between China and India could heighten anti-Asian sentiment as well as antagonisms between Asian American communities. As Asian Americans become more politically active, these Asian rivalries will translate into public controversies and competing lobbying efforts in Washington D.C. These rivalries could be manipulated by local politicians and foreign governments for their own advantage to the detriment of Asian American communities involved.

Policy Recommendations

Asian Americans are frequently overlooked by policymakers and industry leaders because of prevailing "model minority" stereotypes and the belief that "Asians take care of themselves." These misconceptions ignore the enormous differences between Asian American groups and their different roles in high-technology sectors. Unlike other industries, high-tech industries are non-unionized so it is difficult for politically weak groups to organize. As a result, Asian American politicians and community organizations play a significant role in addressing policy issues affecting Asian Americans. The following sections address emerging policy issues facing Asian Americans.

RETRAINING AND CAREER PLANNING

Although there are no specific figures for the number of Asian Americans recently laid off due to corporate downsizing and defense cutbacks, high-tech industries along the West Coast and New England areas have been hit hard in recent years. Asian American groups particularly vulnerable to prolonged unemployment are semi-skilled, high-tech assembly workers whose jobs are being transferred to low-cost countries. Layoffs create enormous stress on families and communities. However, Asian Americans are often reluctant to take advantage of federal retraining and social programs for social, cultural, and legal reasons.

To overcome these problems, there must be an effort to identify the impact of layoffs on Asian American high-tech workers by region and determine the usage of federal and state retraining, unemployment, and social programs. Where there are serious problems, active campaigns need to be developed to educate Asian American high-tech workers about their program eligibility and rights. The analysis should also identify social and family problems caused by recent layoffs and develop community-based programs to help individuals and families during the transition to re-employment. The findings should serve as the basis to develop retraining and career planning programs tailored to specific Asian American communities affected by defense cutbacks and corporate downsizing.

MULTICULTURAL & MULTILINGUAL TRAINING

The rapid increase in Asian Pacific high technology trade promises major opportunities for Americans with multicultural and multilingual capabilities. This is particularly true at fast-growing high-tech companies partnering with Asian Pacific companies and marketing their products and services throughout the Pacific Rim. Although total fluency is not required to conduct business, a minimum level is necessary to maintain close customer ties. There are a large number of Asian immigrants and second-generation Asian Americans who have maintained their language capabilities to this level. For U.S. high-tech companies seeking employees able to work comfortably with Asian Pacific customers and partners, these Asian Americans provide the largest pool of potential candidates.

However, the precipitous decline in foreign language instruction and cultural training in U.S. public schools and universities has ill prepared the high-tech labor force for these opportunities in Asian Pacific. Many high schools and universities have reduced or eliminated altogether foreign language competency from their graduation requirements. It is difficult to find American-born high school graduates who are passably fluent in a foreign language, especially the more "difficult" Asian languages.

Even universities with Asian language departments generally do not offer technical language courses suitable for science and engineering students. The exceptions are leading universities such Stanford, UC Berkeley, MIT, Wisconsin, University of Texas, University of New Mexico, and Michigan, which are receiving U.S. government funding to provide technical Japanese language training under the Defense Conversion Act of 1991. However, there are no programs for other Asian languages and no guarantees that the technical Japanese language programs will continue.[2]

To bolster U.S. high-tech competitiveness in the Asian Pacific region, the U.S. government, local school districts, and universities should implement the following recommendations. One, they should offer Asia Pacific language courses at the primary, secondary and university levels. These courses could be co-sponsored with local Asian American community or-ganizations offering language instruction. Two, there is a need to institute technical Asian Pacific language instruction at all junior colleges, state universities, and private universities and to develop new computer-aided Asia Pacific language and cultural instruction using the latest technologies, including CD-

ROMs, voice recognition and synthesis, machine translation, and interactive video.

Also, there is a need to promote the use of Asian Pacific television programming in schools and universities as part of foreign language instruction. Funding from Asian Pacific corporations and foundations could be sought to implement these programs.

THE "GLASS CEILING"

The "glass ceiling" prevents many highly-qualified Asian Americans from fulfilling their career potential or reaching top management positions in high-tech companies. Asian Americans are usually excluded from top management positions despite their experience and qualifications. Cultural differences, leadership skills, and language difficulties are often cited by non-Asian executives as reasons for this low representation. These obstacles are especially true for Asian American women, who face a double barrier as women and minorities. Although U.S. companies are gradually adopting new management practices to cope with the highly-diverse multicultural work force, "diversity training" is still the exception, not the rule.

Changes will come about as Asian Americans become more proactive. Asian American civil rights organizations should maintain telephone hotlines to monitor and document cases of racial discrimination. Statistical records should be released to the press and open to public scrutiny. However, individual records should be kept confidential. Asian American organizations and training companies should provide multicultural awareness and assertiveness training for Asian American high-tech employees, especially new immigrants and women. Asian American organizations should encourage high-tech companies to implement diversity training programs and give awards to companies that show the greatest leadership in introducing innovative global, multicultural management methods.

TRANS-PACIFIC TIES

Rapid Asian economic growth and continuing layoffs in U.S. high-tech industries have encouraged many high-tech professionals, both Asian American and non-Asians, to seek employment in Asia. This reverse "brain drain" may be positive in the short-term for the U.S. high-tech labor markets, but it accelerates the flow of U.S. technologies abroad, thereby weakening long-term U.S. industrial competitiveness. Reversing labor mobility is difficult because of the numerous factors involved. At best, Asian American associations might develop informal "talent banks" of scientists and engineers to assist U.S. companies seeking Asia Pacific expertise.

Migration is not the only form of trans-Pacific ties that should be addressed. The number of Asian American engineers and scientists "commuting" between Asia and the United States is increasing. These trans-Pacific workers are known as "astronauts" among high-tech circles. Besides the physical and emotional stresses of separation, Asian American families in this situation are prone to more family problems: social isolation, juvenile delinquency and crime, school problems, divorce, etc. Over a period of time, this desire to have "the best of both worlds" is likely to lead to family breakdown. Asian American community groups should work closely with these families to prevent their isolation.

Concluding Remarks

Asian American scientists and engineers are rapidly becoming a major factor in U.S. high technology industries. No longer the minority in many companies, these professionals are in the enviable position of choosing their career paths. While the "glass ceiling" remains a barrier at more established companies, the rapid pace of high-tech industries ensures that new startup ventures are emerging weekly. Experienced, entrepreneurial Asian Americans have the opportunity to move quickly into key management positions. With the rise of Asia, employment opportunities look bright, especially for Asia-born engineers.

By contrast, Asian Americans in declining defense industries and manufacturing companies will find themselves in difficult times, especially older workers and less-educated assembly workers. Unless Asian American community organizations ensure that these people find retraining and new job opportunities, their families are likely to suffer.

Moreover, the success of Asian Americans and Asian

countries is likely to breed envy and resentment among other American workers hurt by Asian imports. Unless proactive steps are taken early, anti-Asian violence is likely to increase as Asia becomes more powerful. Thus, high technology is likely to become a two-edged sword. It can create wealth and jobs, but at the same time political friction and social discord.

Notes

1. There are related issues of importance that are not addressed in this paper. For example, there has been an increasing number of high-tech robberies in Silicon Valley committed by Asian American gangs. According to law enforcement officials, these gangs are predominantly Chinese and Vietnamese and believed to be overseas crime syndicates stretching from Silicon Valley to Hong Kong. The crimes are targeted at high-tech products because of their compactness, high value, and difficulty in tracing. These crime syndicates also deal in counterfeiting, prostitution, extortion, and drug dealing. In response to the growing crime wave, the U.S. attorney for Northern California is building a coalition of police and prosecutors on the West Coast to share information and crack down on Asian gangs (*San Jose Mercury News*, 1994).

2. These universities receive two-year federal grants that decline over time as an incentive to encourage industrial funding.

Chapter 13

Diversity Within a

Common Agenda

Paul Ong and Karen Umemoto

Throughout much of this book, the term diversity is used to highlight the internal heterogeneity within the Asian Pacific American population, but, as we discuss later, this term also has a much deeper political and philosophical meaning. Economic and political changes over the past several decades have spawned marked disparities within this population. International migration patterns, U.S. domestic and foreign policies, transnational capital flows, and mobilization of social resources have contributed to the emergence of sizable segments at both ends of the income and earnings spectrum. While some Asian Pacific American groups experience the highest public assistance usage rates among any ethnic groups in the United States, other Asian Pacific American groups have a disproportionately high number of health professionals, scientists and engineers. We cannot escape the challenge of meeting the needs of the rapidly growing and diverse Asian Pacific American population. While the internal diversity is important to our policy discussion, this final chapter is concerned with a different issue.

The term diversity has another meaning that brings into question what is the very nature of this country and what it should aspire to become. The moral fabric of the nation has been constructed upon the political philosophy of liberalism and the rights of individuals. However, the nation's polity and economy have historically distributed rights and rewards differentially among ethnic, racial, and gender groups. The legacies of historic inequalities and racial policies remain to this day. This divergence between political philosophy and historical practice creates a conundrum for public policy.

By the very nature of this book, which focuses on Asian Pacific American concerns, we are drawn into this broader debate. In exploring policy issues that Asian Pacific Americans face in various sectors of the U.S. economy, the writers incorporate ethnic factors into their analyses and recommendations. They document differences in history, culture, social resources, educational attainment and a host of other factors that have created a set of issues that have bearing on policy debates. And they argue for fuller membership for Asian Pacific Americans in the U.S. economy. In making these points, the writers implicitly, and in some cases explicitly, argue that group concerns and needs based on historic and contemporary experiences mediated by race and ethnicity should be considered in public policy.

The demand for incorporating ethnic concerns into public policy inevitably pulls the discussion into the arena of racial politics. Some key issues of this politics must be confronted if we are to move beyond polemics. Some argue that race-conscious policies are divisive. South Africa's system of apartheid and the bloody interethnic fighting in the Balkan states are certainly painful examples of how racial or ethnic-specific policies can undermine a country's moral legitimacy and tear away at human relations. We are not free from such divisions. There are racist groups in the United States that advocate for fragmenting this country.

Being conscious of race is not, fortunately, synonymous with racial divisions. It is an acceptance of the reality that race plays powerful roles in shaping individuals' life chances in our society. We have inherited institutions that produce and reproduce inequality by social grouping. Moreover, we have had a history of policies which has created a de jure and de facto system of privileges based on race. Although it has been fashionable to assert that recent policies have harmed white males, the historic record shows that government policies have done just the opposite over the life span of our nation.

So-called "color blind" policies ignore this unpleasant reality of race in the United States and run the risk of contributing to the maintenance of inequality. The moral question is whether this nation should take an active role in eliminating racial, ethnic, and gender inequality. The contributors to this volume have answered in the affirmative. The solution, however, is not as simple as conferring privileges upon marginalized groups. Such an approach proves to be short-sighted, generates perverse outcomes, and creates political backlash. We must insist on undertaking the more difficult task of transforming some very basic institutions and attitudes.

While sharing the above concern over rectifying racial inequality, policies that incorporate ethnic experiences have another goal: harnessing diversity for a common good. As the world becomes more integrated, our ability to interact constructively with other nations hinges on our own cultural resources. Given our diverse population, the United States has the potential of developing an understanding of multiculturalism — different ways of knowing, interacting, communicating, and governing — unmatched by other nations. The policy of embracing differences in language, values, and cultural practices as opposed to homogenizing everyone can be especially helpful in the arena of international trade and exchange. There are also domestic benefits derived from a cultural richness rooted in diversity in the arts, entertainment, food, and other areas of daily life. These benefits are difficult to quantify in economic terms but are recognized and appreciated by most. Ultimately, promoting diversity is not so much about preserving any one particular culture as it is about creating a positive multiethnic society.

Holding a rational discussion on ethnicity and diversity in the policy arena is often difficult. Many politicians shy away from a discussion of race for fear of being charged with catering to special interests. Some supporters of diversity have only a shallow understanding of the issues and are thus unable to articulate and defend their position. They become easy prey to those who make charges of "political correctness." The campaign for "political correctness" has served to undermine the support for cultural diversity and racial equality.

While we must accept the challenge of harnessing our multiethnic heritage, we must also be willing to discuss the core principles that we should share as a society. These principles provide the philosophical foundations upon which public policies are debated. This book has taken up this task in implicit and explicit forms. It would be a mistake to dismiss this book as an effort merely to promote narrow group interests, make claims on the government, or seek special privileges. The authors speak, at times passionately, about a broader national agenda and the underlying principles that should guide us. Their recommendations would help this nation achieve societal goals consistent with universal and fundamental principles shared by most Americans. Four principles, in particular, apply to economic policies.

The first is the principle of fairness — that is, everyone should have the same chance to participate in the economy and to enjoy the protection and benefits offered by the state. In practice, this means that demands, such as that to eliminate the glass ceiling, should not be based on a desire to promote individual gains but should be based on the desire to achieve fairness. Through legislation and the court system, this nation has adopted the position that discrimination based on race is undesirable and constitutionally illegal. What to do beyond legal proscriptions against discrimination has become controversial. There are disagreements regarding the extent to which government should act to rectify past actions and whether we should ensure equality of outcomes. There have been, no doubt, problems and shortcomings with some policies enacted to increase racial equality. However, whatever flaws that exist should not be used as justification for abandoning the fight for fairness.

The second principle of humanitarianism posits a concern about the economic welfare of all residents. This means that we should not accept the disgraceful rise of poverty, the existence of urban slums, and crushing hardships associated with low-wage work. These problems are grave among Asian Pacific Americans, and are particularly severe among African Americans and Latinos. Despite the slowdown of growth created by increased foreign competition and economic restructuring over the last two decades, we still remain one of the wealthiest nations in the world. This nation possesses the resources to tackle these problems. Unfortunately, this country is politically divided around the means to achieve this.

Compassion and sense of social responsibility are frequently checked by a fear of "welfare cheats" and by individual greed. The appropriate policy must balance the objectives of protecting the economic welfare of individuals and promoting individual responsibility in ways that allow people to maintain their dignity. The difficulties in achieving these oftentimes conflicting objectives should not dissuade us from pursuing this principle. As stated earlier, our willingness to eliminate gross economic injustices is a measure of our character as a caring nation.

The third principle is government efficiency, where we maximize the returns on our taxes in the interest of the public good. This requires that publicly supported programs are cost-effective and that mechanisms for determining priorities allow for public accountability. With our culturally diverse population, we must have programs that are sensitive to the needs and concerns of various groups. It is important that programs do not create artificial barriers as a result of language or other differences. Otherwise, many programs are doomed to failure or achieve only minimal success. Increasing government efficiency should not be limited to public-sector reform, as government cannot do all. Many goals can be achieved only through a partnership between government and other societal sectors, where the synergy between parties generates larger gains than can be produced separately. While the public-private partnership has received much attention, there must also be stronger partnerships between the government and social and community institutions.

The fourth principle is ensuring economic viability. Political and business leaders boast of U.S. economic industriousness and the drive of citizens to create a better material world for each successive generation. The economic greatness of the United States is being challenged as never before, not only by increased international competition but also by diminishing natural resources and growing environmental costs. Prospering in this new setting will require a more productive and innovative labor force. This can be achieved by ensuring that today's workers, Asian Pacific American and otherwise, receive the training needed to be competitive and that they are given the opportunity to make maximum use of their talents. At the same time, we must be willing to increase current investments in education, health and technology for the future.

Cynics would point out that the United States has more often violated these principles than has upheld them, particularly in the case of fairness and humanitarianism with respect to minority populations. Historically, only those considered full members of American society and worthy individuals enjoyed the opportunities and privileges of this nation. We have become more inclusive of minorities, but racial inequality is still with us. Should we, then, lose faith? If we use the utopian standard of full implementation of these lofty principles as our sole criterion, then we would be discouraged. A better position, however, is to realize that we have won many meaningful gains. We need to accept that the exceedingly difficult struggle for justice requires extraordinary collective and individual sacrifices. Most victories are small but nonetheless worthwhile. We need to see these noble principles as facilitating our fight for justice by creating a moral foundation for our cause.

Our task is to formulate policies that enable this nation to adhere to the high principles to which it aspires and that acknowledge both the ethnic diversity of this nation and the need for a common national agenda.

References

Abowd, J. and Freeman, R. (1991). *Immigration, Trade, and the Labor Market.* Chicago: University of Chicago Press.

American Health Association. (1993a). "American Medical Association Expresses Cautious Optimism Over Health-Reform Plan." *American Health Association News*, 29(38), 3.

American Health Association. (1993b). "Insurers Wave Cautious Flags Over Purchasing Alliances, Premium-Increase Caps." *American Health Association News*, 29(39), 3.

American Health Association. (1993c). "Providers, Business Groups, Consumers Offer Measured Support for Clinton Proposal." *American Health Association News*, 29(39), 2-3.

American Health Association. (1993d). "American Medical Association Mailing to Physicians Critiques Health-Reform Plan." *American Health Association News*, 29(40), 3.

American Nurses Association. (1993, Summer). *Primary Health Care.* Washington, D.C.: American Nurses Association, p. 13.

American Nurses Association. (1993, September 7). "American Nurses Association News Release." Washington, D.C.: American Nurses Association, p. 13.

American Nurses Association. (1993, September). "Consumers Willing to See a Nurse for Routine 'Doctoring,' according to Gallup Poll." News Release. Washington, D.C.: American Nurses Association.

Asian Pacific Health Care Venture, Inc. (1993). *A Perspective from the Asian Pacific Communities in Los Angeles: A Response to National Health Care Reform.* Los Angeles: Asian Pacific Health Care Venture, Inc.

Association of American Medical Colleges. (1987). *Minority Students in Medical Education: Facts and Figures*, 6 (December).

Atkinson, R. (1990). "Supply and Demand for Scientists and Engineers: A National Crisis in the Making." *Science*, 248, 49-54.

Bach, R. and Carroll-Seguin, R. (1986). "Labor Force Participation, Household Composition and Sponsorship among Southeast Asian Refugees." *International Migration Review*, 20(2).

Barringer, H. and Cho, S. (1989). *Koreans in the United States: A Fact Book.* Honolulu: Center for Korean Studies, University of Hawaii at Manoa.

Barringer, H., Gardner, R., and Levin, M. (1993). *Asians and Pacific Islanders in the United States.* New York: Russell Sage Foundation.

Berliner, H. (1993). "Changes in the Health Care Delivery System in New York City: 1980-1990." In Ginzberg, E., Berliner, H., and Ostow, M. (Eds.), *Changing U.S. Health Care: A Study of Four Metropolitan Areas.* Boulder, Colorado: Westview Press.

Berryman, S. E. (1991). *Designing Effecting Learning Environments: Cognitive Apprenticeship Models.* IEE Brief, Number 1. New York: Institute on Education and the Economy, Columbia University.

Betancur, J., Cordova, T., and Torres, M. (1993). "Economic Restructuring and the Process of Incorporation of Latinos Into the Chicago Economy." In Morales, R. and F. Bonilla (Eds.), *Latinos in a Changing U.S. Economy* (pp. 109-132). Newbury Park: Sage Publications.

Bindman A., Keane, D., and Lurie, N. (1993). "A Public Hospital Closes: Impact on Patients' Access to Care and Health Status." *Journal of American Medical Association,* 264 (22), 2899-904.

Blackburn, M., Bloom, D., and Freeman, R. (1990). "The Declining Economic Position of Less Skilled American Men." In Burtless, G. (Ed.), *A Future of Lousy Jobs?: The Changing Structure of U.S. Wages.* Washington, D.C.: Brookings Institution.

Blank, R. (1990). "Are Part-Time Jobs Bad Jobs?" In Burtless, G. (Ed.), *A Future of Lousy Jobs? The Changing Structure of U.S. Wages* (pp. 123-155). Washington, D.C.: Brookings Institution.

Blank, R. (1992), "The Employment Strategy: Public Policies to Increase Work and Earnings." Paper presented at Institute for Research on Poverty Conference, Madison, Wisconsin, May 28-30.

Bonacich, E. (1973). "A Theory of Middlemen Minorities." *American Sociological Review,* 38, 583-94.

Bonacich, E. (1993). "Asians in the Los Angeles Garment Industry." Unpublished manuscript, University of California, Riverside.

Bonacich, E. and Modell, J. (1980). *The Economic Basis of Ethnic Solidarity: Small Business in the Japanese American Community.* Berkeley: University of California Press.

Borjas, G. (1990). *Friends or Strangers: The Impact of Immigrants on the U.S. Economy.* New York: Basic Books, Inc.

Bowman, W. (1993). *Evaluating JTPA Programs for Economically Disadvantaged Adults: A Case Study of Utah and General Findings.* National Commission for Employment Policy. Washington, D.C.: U.S. Government Printing Office.

Branscomb, L. (1993). *Empowering Technology: Implementing a U.S. Strategy.* Cambridge, Massachusetts: MIT Press.

Braverman, H. (1974). *Labor and Monopoly Capital: The Degradation of Work in the Twentieth Century.* New York: Monthly Review Press.

Brown, E. and Cousineau, M. (1987). *Assessing Indigent Health Care Needs and Use of County Health Services.* Berkeley: Policy Seminar, University of California.

Brown, S. and Grimes, D. (1993). *A Meta-Analysis of Process of Care, Clinical Outcomes, and Cost Effectiveness of Nurses in Primary Care Roles: Nurse Practitioners and Nurse Mid-Wives.* Washington, D.C.: American Nurses Association.

Brownstein, R. (1993, September 30). "The Times Poll: By 2-1 Margin, Public Backs Health Care Plan." *Los Angeles Times,* pp. A1 and A22.

Business Week. (1992, July 13). "The Immigrants, How They're Helping to Revitalize the U.S. Economy," pp. 114-122.

Business Week. (1993, February 22). "How Much Good Will Training Do?" pp. 76-81.

Business Week. (1993, May 24). "Community College Educations Pay Off in the Labor Market," p. 22.

Business Week. (1994, January 24). "Are You Listening Mr. President?" p. 80.

Business Week. (1994, March 28). "Motorola: Training for the Millennium," pp. 158-163.

Cabezas, A. and Kawaguchi, G. (1988). "Empirical Evidence for Continuing Asian American Income Inequality: The Human Capital Model and Labor Market Segmentation." In Okihiro, G. (Ed.), *Reflections On Shattered Windows: Promises and Prospects for Asian American Studies* (pp. 144-164). Pullman, Washington: Washington State University Press.

Califano v. Wescott. (1979). 443 U.S. 76.

California Department of Social Services. (1991). *Final Statewide AFDC Tallies by Ethnic Origin.* Sacramento, California: Statistical Services Bureau.

California Department of Social Services. (1992). *Revised Statewide AFDC Tallies by Ethnic Origin.* Sacramento, California: Statistical Services Bureau.

California Department of Social Services. (1993). *Making Welfare Work: California's Welfare Reform Demonstration Project — Principles and Perspectives.* Sacramento, California: Statistical Services Bureau.

California Employment Development Division. (1980-1992). *Annual Planning Information.* California Labor Market Information Division. Sacramento: Economic Information Group.

Cannon, P. (1988). "Foreign Engineers in U.S. Industry: An Exploratory Assessment." In *Foreign and Foreign-Born Engineers in the United States, Infusing Talent, Raising Issues* (pp. 105-123). National Research Council, Committee on International Exchange and Movement of Engineers. Washington, D.C.: National Academy Press.

Carlson, S., Cowart, M., and Speake, D. (1992). "Perspectives of Nursing Personnel in the 1980s." In Cowart, M. and Serow, W. (Eds.), *Nurses in the Workplace.* pp. 1-27. Newbury Park, California: Sage Publications.

Carnevale, A. (1991). *America and the New Economy, How New Competitive Standards are Radically Changing American Workplaces.* San Francisco: Jossey-Bass Publishers.

Center for Disease Control. (1992). "Cigarette Smoking Among Southeast Asian Immigrants — Washington State." *Morbidity and Mortality Weekly Report,* 41, 854-855 and 862-863.

Center on Budget and Policy Priorities. (1993). *The Clinton EITC Proposal: How It Would Work and Why It Is Needed.* Washington, D.C.: U.S. Government Printing Office.

Chan, S. (1991). *Asian Americans: An Interpretive History.* Boston: Twayne Publishers.

Chang, Y., et al. (1988). *A Study of the Korean Population 1966.* Seoul, Korea: The Population and Development Studies Center, Seoul National University.

Chen, M. (1993a). "Cardiovascular Health Among Asian American/Pacific Islanders: An Examination of Health Status and Intervention Approaches." *American Journal of Health Promotion,* 7, 199-207.

Chen, M. (1993b). "A 1993 Status Report on the Health Status of

Asian Pacific Islander Americans: Comparisons with Health People 2000 Objectives." *Asian American and Pacific Islander Journal of Health*, 1(1), 37-55.

Chiswick, B. (1983). "An Analysis of the Earnings and Employment of Asian American Men." *Journal of Labor Economics*, 1, 197-214.

Commission on the Skills of the American Workforce. (1990). *America's Choice: High Skills or Low Wages!* Rochester, New York: National Center on Education and the Economy.

Commission on Workforce Quality and Labor Market Efficiency. (1989). *Investing in People, A Strategy to Address America's Workforce Crisis.* Washington, D.C.: U.S. Department of Labor.

Committee for Economic Development. (1990). *An America that Works: The Life-Cycle Approach to a Competitive Work Force.* Washington, D.C.: Research and Policy Committee.

Committee on Medical Care Costs. (1932). "The Committee on the Costs of Medical Care." *Journal of the American Medical Association*, 99, 1250-1251.

Council of Chief State School Officers/Resource Center on Educational Equity. (1990). *School Success for Limited-English-Proficient Students: The Challenge and State Response.* Washington, D.C.: Resource Center on Educational Equity.

Council on Graduate Medical Education. (1993, September 1). *Journal of the American Medical Association*, p. 270.

County of Los Angeles, Department of Health Services. (1992). *Los Angeles County Health: Uniting for a Common Goal.* Los Angeles: County of Los Angeles Printing Office.

Dallek, G. and Brown, E. (1987). *The Quality of Medical Care for the Poor in Los Angeles County's Health and Hospital System.* Los Angeles: Legal Aid Foundation of Los Angeles.

Daniels, R. (1988). *Asian America: Chinese and Japanese in the United States Since 1850.* Seattle: University of Washington Press.

Davis, B. (1994, February 8). "Science and Technology Programs to Get Big Boosts in Spending." *Wall Street Journal*, p. A12.

Davis, L., Easterin, R., and Parker, W. (1972). *American Economic Growth: An Economist's History of the United States.* New York: Harper Row.

Der, H. (1993). "Asian Pacific Islanders and the 'Glass Ceiling' — New Era of Civil Rights Activism? Affirmative Action Policy." In *The State of Asian Pacific America: Policy Issues to the Year 2020* (pp. 215-231). Los Angeles: LEAP Asian Pacific American

Public Policy Institute and UCLA Asian American Studies Center.

Dollar, D., and Wolff, E. (1993). *Competitiveness, Convergence, and International Specialization*. Cambridge, Massachusetts: The MIT Press.

Duboff, R. (1989). *Accumulation and Power: An Economic History of the United States*. Armonk, New York: M.E. Sharpe.

Duleep, H. and Sanders, S. (1992). "Discrimination at the Top: American-Born Asian and White Men." *Industrial Relations*, (31)3, 416-432.

Duleep, H. and Sanders, S. (1993). "The Decision to Work by Married Immigrant Women." *Industrial and Labor Relations Review*, 46, 677-690.

Education Week. (1994, January 26). "Vocational Education," p. 8.

Ehrenberg, R. (1992). "The Flow of New Doctorates." *Journal of Economic Literature*, 30(2), 830-875.

Eiler, M. and Loft, J. (1986). *Foreign Medical Graduates*. Chicago: American Medical Association.

Eitzen, D. and Zinn, M. (1989). *The Reshaping of America: Social Consequences of the Changing Economy*. Englewood Cliffs, New Jersey: Prentice Hall.

Ellwood, D. (1988). *Poor Support: Poverty in the American Family*. New York: Basic Books, Inc.

Falk, C.E. (1988). "Foreign Engineers and Engineering Students in the United States." In *Foreign and Foreign-Born Engineers in the United States, Infusing Talent, Raising Issues* (pp. 31-78). National Research Council, Committee on International Exchange and Movement of Engineers. Washington, D.C.: National Academy Press.

Fass, S. (1986). "Innovations in the Struggle for Self-Reliance: The Hmong Experience in the United States." *International Migration Review*, 20(2).

Finn, M. (1988). "Foreign Engineers in the U.S. Labor Force." In *Foreign and Foreign-Born Engineers in the United States. Infusing Talent, Raising Issues*. National Research Council, Committee on the International Exchange and Movement of Engineers. Washington, D.C.: National Academy Press.

Flanagan, L. (1976). *One Strong Voice*. Kansas City, Missouri: American Nurses Association.

Flexner, A. (1993). *Medical Education in the United States and*

Canada. New York: Carnegie Foundation for the Advancement of Teaching.

Forbes, S. (1984). *Residency Patterns and Secondary Migration of Refugees.* Washington, D.C.: Refugee Policy Group.

Freeman H., Blendon, R., Aiken, L., Sudman, S., Mullinex, C. and Corey, C. (1987). "Americans Report on Their Access to Health Care." *Health Affairs,* 6(1), 6-18.

Fritz, S. (1993, September 19). "The Uninsured." *Los Angeles Times,* p. A20.

Gearon, C. and Kostreski, F. (1993). "Critics Target Size and Power of Health Alliances." *AHA News,* 29(38), 1.

Ginzberg, E., Berliner, H., and Ostow, M. (1993). *Changing U.S. Health Care: A Study of Four Metropolitan Areas.* Boulder, Colorado: Westview Press.

Givens, H. (1939). "The Korean Community in Los Angeles County." M.A. thesis, University of Southern California.

Glenn, E. (1986). *Issei, Nisei, War Brides: Three Generations of Japanese American Women in Domestic Service.* Philadephia: Temple University Press.

Gold, S. (1993). "Chinese-Vietnamese Entrepreneurs in California." Unpublished manuscript, University of California at Los Angeles.

Goldberg, M. (1985). *The Chinese Connection: Getting Plugged in to Pacific Rim Real Estate, Trade, and Capital Markets.* Vancouver, Canada: University of British Columbia Press.

Goldsmith, W. and Blakely, E. (1992). *Separate Societies: Poverty and Inequality in U.S. Cities.* Philadelphia: Temple University Press.

Gordon, D., Edwards, R. and Reich, M. (1982). *Segmented Work, Divided Workers: The Historical Transformation of Labor in the United States.* Cambridge: Cambridge University Press.

Gordon, L. (1989). "National Surveys of Southeast Asian Refugees: Methods, Findings, Issues." In D. Haines (Ed.), *Refugees as Immigrants. Cambodians, Laotians, and Vietnamese in America.* Totowa, New Jersey: Rowman & Littlefield.

Greenberg, M. (1992). *Welfare Reform on a Budget: What's Happening in Jobs.* Washington, D.C.: Center for Law & Social Policy.

Greenwald, J. (1993, February 1). "The Job Freeze." *Time ,* pp. 52-53.

Grossman, G., and Helpman, E. (1991). *Innovation and Growth in the Global Economy.* Cambridge, Massachusetts: MIT Press.

Gruenwald, A. and Gordon, C. (1984). *Foreign Engineers in the United States: Immigration or Importation?* Manpower Committee, United States Activities Board. New York: Institute of Electrical and Electronics Engineers, Inc.

Guang, X., Veloski, J., Mohammadreza, H., Gonella, J., and Bacharach, B. (1993). "Longitudinal Comparison of the Academic Performance of Asian-American and White Medical Students." *Academic Medicine,* 68, 82-86.

Gueron, J. (1993). "Welfare and Poverty: Strategies to Increase Work." Paper prepared for a Conference on Reducing Poverty in America, Anderson Graduate School of Management, University of California, Los Angeles, January 15-16.

Gueron, J. and Pauly, E. (1991). *From Welfare to Work.* New York: Russell Sage Foundation.

Guillermo, T. (1993). "Health Care Needs and Service Delivery for Asian and Pacific Islander Americans: Health Policy." In *The State of Asian Pacific America: A Public Policy Report: Policy Issues to the Year 2020* (pp. 61-78). Los Angeles: LEAP Asian Pacific American Public Policy Institute and UCLA Asian American Studies Center.

Guillermo, T. (1994). "Testimony before the U.S. House of Representatives Committee on Energy and Commerce, Subcommittee on Health and the Environment." *Asian American and Pacific Islander Journal of Health,* 2(1), 62-65.

Haberfeld, Y. and Shenhav, Y. (1990). "Are Women and Blacks Closing the Gap? Salary Discrimination in American Science During the 1970s and 1980s." *Industrial and Labor Relations Review,* 44(1), 68-82.

Hafner-Eaton, C. (1993). "Physician Utilization Disparities Between the Uninsured and Insured." *JAMA,* 269(6), 787-792.

Haines, D. (Ed.) (1989). *Refugees as Immigrants. Cambodians, Laotians, and Vietnamese in America.* Totowa, New Jersey: Rowman & Littlefield.

Handler, J. and Hasenfeld, Y. (1991). *The Moral Construction of Poverty: Welfare Reform in America.* Newbury Park, California: Sage Publications.

Harrison, B. and Bluestone, B. (1988). *The Great U-Turn: Corporate Restructuring and the Polarizing of America.* New York: Basic Books.

Hasenfeld, Y. (1991). *The Implementation of G.A.I.N. in Los Angeles County: 1988-1990.* Los Angeles: School of Social Welfare, Center for Child and Family Policy Studies.

Hawkins J. and Higgins, L. (1989). *Nursing and the American Health Care Delivery System.* New York: The Tiresias Press.

Hirschman, C. and Wong, M. (1984). "Socioeconomic Gains of Asian Americans, Blacks, and Hispanics: 1960-1976." *American Journal of Sociology,* 90, 584-606.

Holley, D. (1986, October 27). "Refugees Build a Haven in Long Beach." *Los Angeles Times,* pp. B1 and B3.

Horton, J. (1992). "The Politics of Diversity in Monterey Park, California." In Lamphere, L. (Ed.), *Structuring Diversity: Ethnographic Perspectives on the New Immigration.* Chicago: University of Chicago Press.

Hoy, R. (1993). "A 'Model Minority' Speaks Out on Cultural Shyness." *Science,* 262, 1117-1118.

Hughes, J. and Cain, L. (1994). *American Economic History.* New York: Harper Collins.

Imahara, K. (1993). "Language Rights Issues to the Year 2020 and Beyond: Language Rights Policy." In *The State of Asian Pacific America: Policy Issues to the Year 2020* (pp. 233-251). Los Angeles: LEAP Asian Pacific American Public Policy Institute and UCLA Asian American Studies Center.

Interpreter Releases. (1989, December 4). Report and Analysis of Immigration and Nationality Law. Washington, D.C.: Federal Publications Inc. 66(35), 1009 and 1316.

Jencks, C. (1992). *Rethinking Social Policy: Race, Poverty, and the Underclass.* Cambridge: Harvard University Press.

Kain, J. (1968). "Residential Segregation, Negro Employment, and Metropolitan Decentralization." *Quarterly Journal of Economics,* 82, 175-97.

Kaiser Commission on the Future of Medicaid. (1992). *Medicaid at the Crossroads: Report of the Kaiser Commission on the Future of Medicaid.* Baltimore: The Commission.

Kato, L. (1993, June). Interview with Roy Hong, Director of Korean Immigrant Workers Advocates, Los Angeles, California.

Kansindorf, M. (1982, December 6). "Asian Americans: A Model Minority." *Newsweek,* pp. 39-51.

Kao, J. (1993, November). "The New Chinese Commonwealth." *Upside Magazine,* pp. 48-61.

Kasarda, J. (1989). "Urban Industrial Transition and the Underclass." *Annals of the American Academy of Political and Social Sciences*, 501, 26-47.

Kasarda, J. (1993). "Inner-city Poverty and Economic Access." In J. Sommer and D.A. Hicks (Eds.), *Rediscovering Urban America: Perspectives on the 1980s*. U.S. Department of Housing and Urban Development, Office of Policy Development and Research. Washington, D.C.: U.S. Government Printing Office.

Kent, N. (1983). *Hawaii: Islands Under the Influence*. New York: Monthly Review Press.

Kerpen, K. (1985, Winter). "Refugees on Welfare." *Public Welfare*, 43(1), 21-25.

Kiang, P. and Lee, V. (1993). "Exclusion or Contribution? Education K-12 Policy." In *The State of Asian Pacific America Policy Issues to the Year 2020* (pp. 25-48). Los Angeles: LEAP Asian Pacific American Public Policy Institute and UCLA Asian American Studies Center.

Kim, I. (1981). *New Urban Immigrants: The Korean Community in New York*. Princeton, New Jersey: Princeton University Press.

King, M. (1989). *Medical Indigency and Uncompensated Health Care Costs*. Washington, D.C.: National Conference of State Legislatures.

Kirschenman, J. and Neckerman, K. (1991). "We'd Love to Hire You, But...: The Meaning of Race for Employers." In Jencks, C. and Peterson, P. (Eds.), *The Urban Underclass*. Washington, D.C.: Brookings Institute.

Kwong, P. (1987). *The New Chinatown*. New York: Hill and Wang.

Law, S. (1983). "Women, Work, Welfare, and the Preservation of Patriarchy." *University of Pennsylvania Law Review*, 131, 1249-1339.

Le, N. (1993). "The Case of Southeast Asian Refugees: Policy for a Community 'At-Risk.'" In *The State of Asian Pacific America: Policy Issues to the Year 2020* (pp. 167-188). Los Angeles: LEAP Asian Pacific American Public Policy Institute and UCLA Asian American Studies Center.

Levitan, S. and Mangum, G. (1969). *Federal Training Programs in the Sixties*. Ann Arbor, Michigan: Institute of Labor and Industrial Relations.

Liao, C. and Hsieh, H. (nd.). *A Review of the Current International Migration Policies in Taiwan, the Republic of China*. Unpublished manuscript, Center for Pacific Rim Studies, University of California, Los Angeles.

Liebowitz, A. (1988). *The Role of Foreign Medical Graduates in the Delivery of Health Care in the United States: The Immigration Ramifications.* Washington D.C.: U.S. Department of Labor.

Light, I. (1972). *Ethnic Enterprise in America.* Berkeley, California: University of California Press.

Light, I. and Bonacich, E. (1988). *Immigrant Entrepreneurs: Koreans in Los Angeles, 1975-1982.* Berkeley: University of California Press.

Light, I. and Bhachu, P. (1993). *Immigration and Entrepreneurship: Culture, Capital, and Ethnic Networks.* New Brunswick: Transaction Publishers.

Lillard, L. and Tan, H. (1986). *Private Sector Training, Who Gets It and What Are Its Effects?* Santa Monica, California: RAND Corporation.

Lin-Fu, J. (1987). "Meeting the Needs of Southeast Asian Refugees in Maternal and Child Health and Primary Care Programs." In *Maternal and Child Health Technical Information Series.* Rockville, Maryland: Health Resources and Services Administration, U.S. Department of Health and Human Services.

Lin-Fu, J. (1993). "Asian and Pacific Islander Americans: An Overview of Demographic Characteristics and Health Care Issues." *Asian American and Pacific Islander Journal of Health,* 1(1), 20-36.

Lin-Fu, J. (1994). "Health Care Reform: A Caucus of Asian American Health Workers' Perspective." *Asian American and Pacific Islander Journal of Health,* 2(1), 13-17.

Litman, T. and Robins, L. (1984). *Health Politics and Policy.* New York: John Wiley and Sons.

Liu, J., Ong, P., and Rosenstein, C. (1991). "Dual Chain Migration: Post 1965 Filipino Immigration to the United States." *International Migration Review,* 25(3), 487-513.

Los Angeles Times. (1993, September 26). "Health Care Dictionary," p. Q6.

Lynn, L. (1993, Fall). "Ending Welfare Reform As We Know It." *The American Prospect,* pp.83-92.

Mar, D. (1991). "Another Look at the Enclave Economy Thesis: Chinese Immigrants in the Ethnic Labor Market." *Amerasia Journal,* 17, 5-21.

Markusen, A. (1984). *Military Spending and Urban Development in California*. Berkeley: Institute of Urban and Regional Development.

Marumoto, W. (1993). "Corporate Boards: The Final Frontier for Women and Minorities." Paper presented at District of Columbia Bar Association conference, Washington, D.C., Winter 1993.

Massey, D. and Denton, N. (1987). "Trends in Residential Segregation of Blacks, Hispanics, and Asians: 1970-1980." *American Sociological Review*, 52, 802-25.

Massey, D. and Denton, N. (1993). *American Apartheid: Segregation and the Making of the Underclass*. Cambridge: Harvard University Press.

Matsuoka, J. (1990). "The Utilization of Mental Health Programs and Services by Asian/Pacific Islanders: A National Study." Unpublished manuscript.

Mazumdar, S. (1993). "South Asians in the United States with a Focus on Asian Indians." In *The State of Asian Pacific America: Policy Issues to the Year 2020* (pp. 283-188). Los Angeles: LEAP and UCLA Asian American Studies Center.

McDonnell, L. and Hill, P. (1993). *Newcomers in American Schools*. Santa Monica, California: RAND Corporation.

McKibbin, R. (1990). *The Nursing Shortage and the 1990s*. Kansas City, Missouri: American Nurses Association.

Melendez, E., Rodriguez, C., and Figueroa, J. (Eds.). (1991). *Hispanics in the Labor Force: Issues and Policies*. New York: Plenum Press.

Melendy, H. (1984). *Chinese and Japanese Americans*. New York: Hippocrene Books.

Mieszkowski, P. and Mills, E. (1993). "The Causes of Metropolitan Suburbanization." *Journal of Economic Perspectives*, 7 (3), 135-148.

Miller, S. (1992, November 13). "Asian-Americans Bump Against Glass Ceilings." *Science*, 258, 1224-1228.

Millman, M. (Ed.). (1993). *Access to Health Care in America*. Institute of Medicine. Washington, D.C.: National Academy Press.

Mills, E. (1989). *Urban Economics*. Glenview, Illinois: Scott, Foresman.

Milo, N. (1983). *Promoting Health Through Public Policy*. Philadelphia: F.A. Davis Company.

Min, P. (1988). *Ethnic Business Enterprise: Korean Small Business in Atlanta*. New York: Center for Migration Studies.

Mincy, R. (forthcoming). "Ghetto Poverty: Black Problem or Harbinger of Things to Come?" In Boston, T. (Ed.), *African American Economic Thought, 2: Methodology and Policy*. New York: Routledge Press.

Mincy, R. and Wiener, S. (1993). "The Under Class in the 1980s: Changing Concept, Constant Reality." Working Paper, The Urban Institute. Washington, D.C.: The Urban Institute. Unpublished manuscript.

Mishel, L. and Frankel, D. (1991). *The State of Working America, 1990-91 Edition*. Economic Policy Institute. Armonk, New York: M.E. Sharpe.

Mollenkompf, J. and Castells, H. (Eds.), (1991). *Dual City: Restructuring In New York*. New York: Russell Sage Foundation.

Moore, J. (1989). "Is there an Hispanic Underclass?" *Social Science Quarterly*, 70(2), 265-84.

Morales, R. and Ong, P. (1993). "The Illusion of Progress: Latinos in Los Angeles." In Morales, R. and Bonilla, F. (Eds.), *Latinos in a Changing U.S. Economy* (pp. 55-84). Newbury Park, California: Sage Publications.

Morganthau, T. (1993, August 9). "America: Still a Melting Pot?" *Newsweek*, pp. 16-23.

Morganthau, T. and Hager, M. (1993, October 4). "The Clinton Cure: Reinventing Health Care." *Newsweek*, pp. 36-39 and 42-43.

Moss, P. and Tilly, C. (1993a). "Race Hurdles for Black Men: Evidence from Interviews with Employers." Unpublished manuscript, Department of Policy and Planning, University of Massachusetts, Lowell.

Moss, P. and Tilly, C. (1993b). "'Soft' Skills and Race: An Investigation of Black Men's Employment Problems." Unpublished manuscript, Department of Policy and Planning, University of Massachusetts, Lowell.

Murphy, K., and Welch, F. (1993). "Inequality and Relative Wages." *The American Economic Review*, 83(2), 104-109.

Murray, C. (1984). *Losing Ground: American Social Policy 1950-1980*. New York: Basic Books.

Nakanishi, D. T. and Hokoyama, J. D. (1993). "Preface." In *The*

State of Asian Pacific America: A Public Policy Report: Policy Issues to the Year 2020 (pp. xiii-xiv). Los Angeles: LEAP Asian Pacific American Public Policy Institute and UCLA Asian American Studies Center.

National Commission for Employment Policy. (1987). *The Job Training Partnership Act.* Washington, D.C.: National Commission for Employment Policy.

National Council of La Raza. (1994). *Welfare Reform Issue Brief.* Washington, D.C.: National Council of La Raza.

National Research Council. (1988). *Foreign and Foreign-Born Engineers in the United States: Infusing Talent, Raising Issues.* Committee on the International Exchange and Movement of Engineers. National Research Council. Washington, D.C.: National Academy Press.

National Science Foundation. (1986). "Survey of 300 U.S. Firms Finds One-half Employ Foreign Scientists and Engineers." *Highlights.*

National Science Foundation. (1991a). *Characteristics of Doctoral Scientists and Engineers in the United States: 1989.* Detailed Statistical Tables. Washington, D.C.: U.S. Government Printing Office.

National Science Foundation. (1991b). *Science and Engineering Doctorates: 1960-1990.* Surveys of Science Resources Series. Washington, D.C.: U.S. Government Printing Office.

National Science Foundation. (1993). *Human Resources for Science and Technology: The Asian Region.* Special Report. Washington, D.C.: U.S. Government Printing Office.

Nelson, R. and Wright, G. (1992). "The Rise and Fall of American Technological Leadership: The Postwar Era in Historical Perspective." *Journal of Economic Literature*, 30(4), 1921-1964.

New Technology Week Newsletter. (1993, March 8). "Technology is Centerpiece of Clinton Activism," p. 4.

Northrup, H. and Malin, M. (1985). *Personnel Policies for Engineers and Scientists.* Philadelphia: Industrial Research Unit, The Wharton School, University of Pennsylvania.

O'Brien, D. and Fugita, S. (1991). *The Japanese American Experience.* Bloomington, Indiana: Indiana University Press.

Okamoto, Phillip M. (1991). "Evolution of a Japanese American Enclave: Gardena, California — A Case Study of Ethnic Community Change and Continuity." M.A. thesis, University of California, Los Angeles.

Olson, L. (1994a). "Enrollments in Vocational Education Down from 1982-1990." *Education Week*, (January 19), pp. 1 and 19.

Olson, L. (1994b). "Bridging the Gap." *Education Week*, (January 26), pp. 20-26.

Olson, L. (1994c). "On the Career Track." *Education Week*, (February 23), pp. 28-31.

Olson, L. (1994d). "Young Dropouts Benefit Little from J.T.P.A., Study Finds." *Education Week*, (March 2), p. 23.

Olson, L. (1994e). "Skills Standards for High-Tech Workers Unveiled." *Education Week*, (March 2), pp. 12.

Omi, M. and Winant, H. (1983). "By the Rivers of Babylon: Race in the United States." *Socialist Review*, 72, 35-70.

Ong, P. (1981, Winter). "An Ethnic Trade: The Chinese Laundries in Early California." *The Journal of Ethnic Studies*, 8(4), 95-113.

Ong, P. (1984). "Chinatown Unemployment and Ethnic Labor Markets." *Amerasia Journal*, 11(1), 35-54.

Ong, P., Arguelles, D., Castro, S., Chow, B., Hirunpidok, C., Hum, T., Louie, W., Nakano, R., and Ramos, R. (1993). *Beyond Asian American Poverty: Community Economic Development Policies and Strategies*. Los Angeles: LEAP Asian Pacific American Public Policy Institute.

Ong, P. and Azores, T. (1994). "Asian Immigrants in Los Angeles: Diversity and Divisions." In P. Ong, Bonacich, E. and Cheng, L. (Eds.), *The New Asian Immigration*. Philadelphia: Temple University Press.

Ong, P. and Blumenberg, E. (1993). "Technical Notes on Southeast Asians and Welfare." Unpublished paper, University of California, Los Angeles.

Ong, P., Cheng, L., and Evans, L. (1992). "Migration of Highly Educated Asians and Global Dynamics." *Asian and Pacific Migration Journal*, 1, 3-4.

Ong, P. and Hee, S. (1993a). "The Growth of the Asian Pacific American Population: Twenty Million in 2020." In *The State of Asian Pacific America: Policy Issues to the Year 2020* (pp. 11-23). Los Angeles: LEAP and UCLA Asian American Studies Center.

Ong, P. and Hee, S. (1993b). "Lists of the Damaged Properties and the LA Riots/Rebellion and Korean Merchants." In Ong, P. and Hee, S., *Losses in the Los Angeles Civil Unrest: April 29 to May 1, 1992*. Los Angeles: Center for Pacific Rim Studies, University of California, Los Angeles.

Ong, P. and Hune, S. (1993). "Policy Recommendations." In *The State of Asian Pacific America: A Public Policy Report: Policy Issues to the Year 2020* (pp. xvii-xix). Los Angeles: LEAP Asian Pacific American Public Policy Institute and UCLA Asian American Studies Center.

Ong, P. and Lawrence, J. (1993). *The Unemployment Crisis in Aerospace.* Report. Los Angeles: Graduate School of Architecture and Urban Planning, University of California, Los Angeles.

Ong, P. and Lawrence, J. (1992). "Pluralism and Residential Patterns in Los Angeles." Discussion Papers, D9202. Los Angeles: Graduate School of Architecture and Urban Planning, University of California, Los Angeles.

Ong, P. and Liu, J. (1994). "U.S. Immigration Policies and Asian Migration." In P. Ong, Bonacich, E. and Cheng, L. (Eds.), *The New Asian Immigration.* Philadelphia: Temple University Press.

Ong, P. and Mar, D. (1992). "Post-Layoff Earnings Among Semiconductor Workers." *Industrial and Labor Relations Review,* 45(2), 366-379.

Ong, P. and Morales, R. (1989). "Mexican Labor in Los Angeles." In Romero, M., and Candelaria, C. (Eds.), *Community Empowerment and Chicano Scholarship* (pp. 63-84). Berkeley: National Association of Chicano Studies.

Ong, P., Park, K., and Tong, J. (1993). "The Korean-Black Conflict and the State." Unpublished manuscript, University of California, Los Angeles.

Park, E. (1992). "Asian Americans in Silicon Valley: Race and Ethnicity in the Postindustrial Economy." Ph.D. dissertation, Ethnic Studies, University of California, Berkeley.

Pavetti, L. (1993). "The Dynamics of Welfare and Work: Exploring the Process by Which Women Work Their Way Off Welfare." Ph.D. dissertation, John F. Kennedy School of Government, Harvard University.

Pido, A. (1986). *The Pilipinos in America.* New York: Center for Migration Studies.

Pollack, A. (1992, January 14). "It's Asians' Turn in Silicon Valley." *New York Times,* pp. D1 and D5.

Porter, M. (1990). *The Competitive Advantage of Nations.* New York: The Free Press.

Portes, A. and Bach, R. (1980). "Immigrant Earnings: Cuban and Mexican Immigrants in the United States." *International Migration Review*, 14, 15-41.

Portes, A. and Bach, R. (1985). *Latin Journey: Cuba and Mexican Immigrants in the U.S.* Berkeley: University of California Press.

Portes, A. and Jensen, L. (1987). "What's an Ethnic Enclave? The Case for Conceptual Clarity." *American Sociological Review*, 52, 768-70.

Portes, A. and Wilson, K. (1980). "Immigrant Enclaves: An Analysis of the Labor Market Experiences of Cubans in Miami." *American Journal of Sociology*, 86, 295-319.

Price, R. and Mills, E. (1985). "Race and Residence in Earnings Determination." *Journal of Urban Economics*, 17, 1-18.

Reich, M. (1981). *Racial Inequality: A Political-Economic Analysis.* Princeton, New Jersey: Princeton University Press.

Reich, R. (1992). *The Work of Nations.* New York: Vintage Books.

Reich, R. (1993, December 19). "Companies are Cutting Their Hearts Out." *The New York Times Magazine*, pp. 54-55.

Reiskin, H. and Haussler, S. (1994). "Multicultural Students' Perceptions of Nursing as a Career." *Image*, 26(1), 61-4.

Roback, G., Randolph, L., and Seidman, B. (1992). *Physician Characteristics and Distribution in the U.S.* Chicago: American Medical Association.

Rumbaut, R. (1989). "Portraits, Patterns, and Predictors of the Refugee Adaptation Process: Results and Reflections from the I.H.A.R.P. Study." In Haines D. (Ed.), *Refugees as Immigrants: Cambodians, Laotians, and Vietnamese in America.* Totowa, New Jersey: Rowman & Littlefield.

Rumbaut, R. and Weeks, J. (1986). "Fertility and Adaptation: Indochinese Refugees in the United States." *International Migration Review*, 20(2).

Ruthledge, P. (1992). *The Vietnamese Experience in America.* Bloomington, Indiana: Indiana University Press.

Safriet, B. (1992). "Health Care Dollars and Regulatory Sense: the Role of Advanced Practice Nursing." *Yale Journal on Regulation*, 9, 417-88.

Salmon, J. (1993). "Chicago Health Care: Private Growth Amidst Public Stagnation." In Ginzberg, E., Berliner, H., Ostow, M., Loe, H., Salmon, J. and Brown, E. (Eds.), *Changing U.S. Health Care: A Study of Four Metropolitan Areas.* Boulder, Colorado: Westview Press.

Salwen, K. (1994, March 10). "Clinton Unveils $13 Billion Proposal to Streamline Nation's Jobless System." *The Wall Street Journal*, pp. A2 and A8.

Samuelson, R. (1993). "Health Care: How We Got Into This Mess." *Newsweek*, pp. 30-32 and 34-35.

San Jose Mercury News. (1993, January 4). "Asian Gang's Growing Influence: Syndicates Seen Behind High-Tech Thievery," p. 1.

Sanders, J. and Nee, V. (1985). "The Road to Parity: Determinants of the Socioeconomic Achievements of Asian Americans." *Ethnic and Racial Studies*, 8, 75-93.

Sanders, J. and Nee, V. (1987). "Limits of Ethnic Solidarity in the Enclave Economy." *American Sociological Review*, 52, 745-67.

Sassen-Koob, S. (1988). *The Mobility of Labor and Capital*. Cambridge: Cambridge University Press.

Sassen-Koob, S. (1993). "Urban Transformation and Employment." In Morales, R. and Bonilla, F. (Eds.), *Latinos in a Changing U.S. Economy* (pp. 184-206). Newbury Park, California: Sage Publications.

Sawers, L. and Tabb, W. (Eds.). (1984). *Sunbelt/Snowbelt: Urban Development and Regional Restructuring*. New York: Oxford University Press.

Saxton, A. (1971). *The Indispensible Enemy: Labor and the Anti-Chinese Movement in California*. Berkeley: University of California Press.

Shibata, K. (1994). Testimony to the U.S. House of Representatives Committee on Education and Labor, Subcommittee on Labor-Management Relations, January 12.

Siu, C.P. (1987). *The Chinese Laundryman: A Study of Social Isolation*. New York: New York University Press.

Smith, J. and Welch, F. (1989). "Black Economic Progress After Myrdal." *Journal of Economic Literature*, 27, 519-564.

Smith, M. and Tarallo, B. (1993). "California's Changing Faces, New Immigrant Survival Strategies and State Policy." Berkeley: California Policy Seminar, University of California, Berkeley.

Sommerfeld, M. (1993, March 17). "Study Finds Little Consistency in 'Tech Prep' Efforts." *Education Week*, p. 17.

Sowell, T. (1983). *The Economics and Politics of Race: An International Perspective*. New York: Morrow.

Spangler, Z. (1991). "Culture Care of Philippine and Anglo-American Nurses in a Hospital Context." In Leininger, M. (Ed.), *Culture Care Diversity and Universality: A Theory of Nursing* (pp. 119-46). New York: National League for Nursing Press.

Sponselli, C., McGurk, M., and Bronson-Gray, B. (1993, October 4). "Assessment: The Clinton Health Plan." *Nurseweek*, pp. 4-5, and 22.

Starr, P. (1982). *The Social Transformation of American Medicine.* New York: Basic Books, Inc.

Strand, P. (1989). "The Indochinese Refugee Experience: The Case of San Diego." In Haines, D. (Ed.), *Refugees as Immigrants: Cambodians, Laotians, and Vietnamese in America.* Totowa, New Jersey: Rowman & Littlefield.

Strand, P. and Jones, W., Jr. (1985). *Indochinese Refugees in America: Problems of Adaptation and Assimilation.* Durham: Duke University Press.

Studnicki, J., Saywell, R., and Wiecketck, W. (1976). "Foreign Medical Graduates and Maryland Medicaid." *New England Journal of Medicine*, 294, 1153.

Sue, S. (1993). "The Changing Asian American Population: Mental Health Policy." In *The State of Asian Pacific America A Public Policy Report: Policy Issues to the Year 2020* (pp. 79-93). Los Angeles: LEAP Asian Pacific American Public Policy Institute and UCLA Asian American Studies Center.

Sue, S. and Morishima. J. (1982). *The Mental Health of Asian Americans.* San Francisco: Jossey Bass.

Sue, S. and Sue, D. (1974). "MMPI Comparisons Between Asian- and Non-Asian-American Students Utilizing a University Psychiatric Clinic." *Journal of Counseling Psychology*, 21, 423-7.

Suzuki, B. (1977). "Education and the Socialization of Asian Americans: The Revisionist Analysis of the Model Minority Thesis." *Amerasia Journal*, 4 (2), 23-51.

Swearingen, C. and Perrin, J. (1977). "Foreign Medical Graduates in Rural Primary Care: The Case of Western New York State." *Medical Care*, 15, 331.

Taggart, R. (1981). *A Fisherman's Guide, An Assessment of Training and Remediation Strategies.* Kalamazoo, Mississippi: W.E. Upjohn Institute for Employment Research.

Takaki, R. (1983). *Pau Hana: Plantation Life and Labor in Hawaii.*

Honolulu: University of Hawaii Press.

Tracey, T., Leong, F., and Glidden, C. (1986). "Help Seeking a Problem Perception Among Asian Americans." *Journal of Counseling Psychology*, 33(3), 331-6.

Tobin, M. (1993). "Sensitivity Analyses of the Growth and Composition of the Underclass and Concentrated Poverty." Unpublished manuscript, The Urban Institute, Washington, D.C.

Trotter-Betts, V. (1993). *Memorandum to State Nurses Association Presidents and Executive Directors.* Washington, D.C.: American Nurses Association.

Trotter-Betts, V. (1993). "The Best Buy in Health Care." *American Journal of Nursing*, (November), p. 7.

Trounson, R. (1981, December 26 and 27). "8,000 Refugees Make Long Beach Cambodian Capital of U.S." *Los Angeles Times — Long Beach Edition*, p. B1.

U.S. Bureau of the Census. (1973). *1970 Census of the Population. Subject Reports, Occupational Characteristics, PC(2)-7A.* Washington, D.C.: U.S. Government Printing Office.

U.S. Bureau of the Census. (1991). *1987 Economic Census: Characteristics of Business Owners.* Washington, D.C.: U.S. Government Printing Office.

U.S. Bureau of the Census. (1974-75). *1972 Survey of Minority-Owned Business Enterprises.* Washington, D.C.: U.S. Government Printing Office.

U.S. Bureau of the Census. (1985-86). *1982 Survey of Minority-Owned Business Enterprises.* Washington, D.C.: U.S. Government Printing Office.

U.S. Bureau of the Census. (1991). *1987 Economic Census. Survey of Minority-Owned Business Enterprises.* Washington, D.C.: U.S. Government Printing Office.

U.S. Bureau of the Census. (1992). *Current Population Reports, P20-459, The Asian and Pacific Islander Population in the United States: March 1991 and 1990.* Washington, D.C.: U.S. Government Printing Office.

U.S. Bureau of the Census. (1992). *Current Population Reports, P25-1092, Population Projections of the United States, by Sex, Race, and Hispanic Origin: 1992 to 2050.* Washington, D.C.: U.S. Government Printing Office.

U.S. Bureau of the Census. (1992). *Statistical Abstract of the United*

States: 1992. Washington, D.C.: U.S. Government Printing Office.

U.S. Bureau of the Census. (1993). *Current Population Reports, School Enrollment — Social and Economic Characteristics of Students: October 1991.* Series P20, No. 469. Washington, D.C.: U.S. Government Printing Office.

U.S. Bureau of the Census. (1993). *1990 Census of the Population, Asian and Pacific Islanders in the United States.* Washington, D.C.: U.S. Government Printing Office.

U.S. Commission on Civil Rights. (1975). *A Dream Unfulfilled: Korean and Pilipino Health Professionals in California.* A Report of the California Advisory Committee to the U.S. Civil Rights Commission. Washington, D.C.: U.S. Government Printing Office.

U.S. Commission on Civil Rights. (1980). *Asian Americans: An Agenda for Action.* A conference summary report of the New York State Advisory Committee to the U.S. Civil Rights Commission. Washington, D.C.: U.S. Government Printing Office.

U.S. Commission on Civil Rights. (1992). *Civil Rights Issues Facing Asian Americans in the 1990s.* Washington, D.C.: U.S. Government Printing Office.

U.S. Committee on Ways and Means. (1992). *Overview of Entitlement Programs: The Green Book.* U.S. House of Representatives. Washington D.C.: U.S. Government Printing Office.

U.S. Congress. (1986). *Nurse Practitioners, Physician Assistants, and Certified Nurse Midwives: A Policy Analysis.* Washington, D.C.: Office of Technology Assessment, U.S. Government Printing Office.

U.S. Congress. (1989). *Consultation on Refugee Admissions For Fiscal Year 1990: Hearing before the Committee on the Judiciary United States Senate.* Washington, D.C.: U.S. Government Printing Office.

U.S. Congress. (1989). *Immigration Nursing Relief Act of 1989: Hearings on H.R. 1507 and H.R. 2111.* House of Representatives. Committee on the Judiciary. Subcommittee on Immigration, Refugees, and International Law. Washington, D.C.: U.S. Government Printing Office.

U.S. Congress. (1990). *U.S. Refugee Programs for 1991: Hearing before the Committee on the Judiciary United States Senate.* Washington, D.C.: U.S. Government Printing Office.

U.S. Congress. (1991). *U.S. Refugee Programs for 1992: Annual Refugee Consultations: Hearing Before the Committee on the Judiciary United States Senate.* Washington, D.C.: U.S. Government Printing Office.

U.S. Congress. (1992). *U.S. Refugee Program for 1993: Annual Refugee Consultations: Hearing Before the Committee on the Judiciary United States Senate.* Washington, D.C.: U.S. Government Printing Office.

U.S. Congress. (1993). *Economic Report of the President.* Washington, D.C.: U.S. Government Printing Office.

U.S. Congress. (1993). *Health Security, The President's Report to the American People.* Washington, D.C.: U.S. Government Printing Office.

U.S. Congress Joint Economic Committee. (1990). *The 1990 Economic Report of the President: Hearings Before the Joint Economic Committee.* Congress of the United States, One Hundred First Congress, Second Session, January 24 and 30, February 2 and 8, and March 15. Washington, D.C.: U.S. Government Printing Office.

U.S. Congress Joint Economic Committee. (1993). *The 1993 Economic Report of the President: Hearings Before the Joint Economic Committee.* Congress of the United States. Washington, D.C.: U.S. Government Printing Office.

U.S. Congressional Budget Office and National Commission for Employment Policy. (1982). *CETA Training Programs: Do They Work For Adults?* Washington, D.C.: Congressional Budget Office.

U.S. Department of Health and Human Services. (1983). *The Impact of Foreign-Trained Doctors on the Supply of Physicians.* Hyattsville, Maryland: U.S. Department of Health and Human Services.

U.S. Department of Health and Human Services, Bureau of Health Professions. (1987). *Minorities & Women in the Health Fields.* Bethesda, Maryland: U.S. Department of Health and Human Services.

U.S. Department of Health and Human Services. (1990). *The

Registered Nurse Population: Findings from the National Sample Survey of RNs. Washington, D.C.: Public Health Services, Bureau of Health Professions.

U.S. Department of Health and Human Services. (1990). "Healthy People 2000." In *National Health Promotion and Disease Prevention Objectives.* Washington, D.C.: U.S. Department of Health and Human Services.

U.S. Department of Health and Human Services. (1993). *Health Status of Minorities and Low-Income Groups.* Hyattsville, Maryland: U.S. Department of Health and Human Services.

U.S. Department of Health and Human Services, Office of Refugee Resettlement. (1990). *Refugee Resettlement Program.* Report to Congress. Hyattsville, Maryland: U.S. Department of Health and Human Services, Social Security Administration, Office of Refugee Resettlement.

U.S. General Accounting Office. (1990). *Budget Deficit: Appendixes on Outlook, Implications, and Choices.* Office of the Controller General. GAO/OCG-90-5A. Gaithersburg, Maryland: U.S. General Accounting Office.

U.S. General Accounting Office. (1991). *Workers At Risk.* Washington, D.C.: U.S. Government Printing Office.

U.S. General Accounting Office. (1992). *Medicare Claims.* GAO/HR-93-6. Gaithersburg, Maryland: U.S. General Accounting Office.

U.S. General Accounting Office, Office of the Controller General. (1992). "Health Care Reform." In *U.S. General Accounting Office Transition Series.* GAO/OCG-93-8TR. Gaithersburg, Maryland: U.S. General Accounting Office.

U.S. Immigration and Naturalization Service. (1989). *Statistical Yearbook of the Immigration and Naturalization Service.* Washington, D.C.: U.S. Government Printing Office.

U.S. News and World Report. (1993, September 20). "Desperate for Doctors," pp. 30-35.

U.S. Office of the President. (1993). *Health Security Act.* Washington, D.C.: U.S. Government Printing Office.

U.S. Office of the President. (1994a). *Opening and Closing Remarks by the President at Department of Labor Conference on Reemployment.* Washington, D.C.: U.S. Government Printing Office.

U.S. Office of the President (1994b). Press Briefing by Secretary of Labor Robert Reich. The White House, Office of the Press Secretary, February 2.

U.S. Office of the President (1994c). Press Briefing by Secretary of Labor Robert Reich. The White House, Office of the Press Secretary, March 9.

Vaughan, R. (1990, August). "Education, Training, and Labor Markets: A Policy Perspective." In *NCEE Brief*. New York: National Center on Education and Employment, Columbia University.

Vaughan, R. and Berryman, S. (1989). "Employer-Sponsored Training: Current Status, Future Possibilities." *NCEE Brief.* New York: Columbia University.

Vose, C. (1959). *Caucasians Only.* Berkeley: University of California Press.

Waldinger, R., Ward, R., and Aldrich, H. (1985). "Ethnic Business and Occupational Mobility in Advanced Societies." *Sociology*, 19(4), 586-97.

Wall Street Journal. (1993, November 9). "Labor Letter, A Special News Report on People and Their Jobs in Offices, Fields, and Factories," p. 1.

Walsh, J. (1993, Fall). "The Perils of Success: Asians Have Become Exemplary Immigrants, But at a Price." *Time*, pp. 55-56.

Ward, D. (1971). *Cities and Immigrants.* New York: Oxford University Press.

Warner, J. and Bass, S. (1972). *The Urban Wilderness: A History of the American City.* New York: Harper & Row.

Weinberger, C. (1993). *College Major and the Gender Gap in Wages: Beyond Recomposition.* Berkeley: University of California Press.

Weintraub, D. (1993). "Legal Immigration to State Up by 23%, Report Finds." *Los Angeles Times*, p. A30.

Weisfeld, V. (Ed.). (1987). "Access to Health Care in the U.S.: Results of a 1986 Survey." *Special Report No. 2.* Princeton, New Jersey: Robert Wood Johnson Foundation.

Wielawski, I. (1993). "Health Systems in Bind on Care for Illegal Immigrants." *Los Angeles Times*, pp. A1, and A12.

Williams, W. (1969). *The Roots of the Modern American Empire.* New York: Random House.

Wilson, W. (1987). *The Truly Disadvantaged: The Inner City, the*

Underclass, and Public Policy. Chicago: University of Chicago Press.

Winnick, L. (1990). "America's Model Minority." *Commentary,* 90(2), 22-9.

Wong, P. and Nagasawa, R. (1991). "Asian American Scientists and Engineers: Is There a Glass Ceiling for Career Advancement?" *Chinese American Forum,* 6(3), 3-6.

Wu, Y. (1980). "Income and Occupational Patterns: Three Decades of Change." In Wu, Y. (Ed.), *The Economic Condition of Chinese Americans.* Chicago: Pacific/Asian American Mental Health Research Center.

Zhou, M. (1992). *Chinatown: The Socioeconomic Potential of an Urban Enclave.* Philadelphia: Temple University Press.

Zhou, M. and Logan, J. (1991). "Returns on Human Capital in Ethnic Enclaves: New York City's Chinatown." *American Sociological Review,* 54, 809-20.

Zikopoulos, M. (Ed.). (1991a). "Open Doors, 1990-1991." In *Report on International Education Exchange.* New York: Institute of International Education.

Zikopoulos, M., (Ed.). (1991b). "Profiles, 1989-1990." In *Detailed Analyses of the Foreign Student Population.* New York: Institute of International Education.

Computer Data Files

U.S. Bureau of the Census. (1991). Survey of Natural and Social Scientists and Engineers (SSE), 1989 [computer file]. Washington, D.C.: U.S. Department of Commerce, Bureau of the Census [producer], 1990. Ann Arbor: Inter-university Consortium for Political and Social Research [distributor].

U.S. Bureau of the Census. (1992). 1990 Census of the Population, STF 2 [computer file]. Washington, D.C.: U.S. Government Printing Office.

U.S. Bureau of the Census. (1992). 1990 Census of Population and Housing: Equal Employment Opportunity File [CD Rom]. Washington, D.C.: U.S. Government Printing Office.

U.S. Bureau of the Census. (1992). Census of Population and Housing, 1990: PUMS Sample: 1% Sample [computer file]. Washington, D.C.: U.S. Government Printing Office.

U.S. Bureau of the Census. (1992). Census of Population and Housing, 1990: PUMS Sample: 5% Sample [computer file].

Washington, D.C.: U.S. Government Printing Office.

U.S. Bureau of the Census. (1993). Current Population Survey: Annual Demographic File, 1992 [computer file]. Washington, D.C.: U.S. Department of Commerce, Bureau of the Census, 1993 [producer]. Ann Arbor: Inter-university Consortium for Political and Social Research [distributor].

U.S. Department of Health and Human Services, PHS Division of Nursing. (1988). National Sample Survey of Registered Nurses [computer file]. Washington,D.C.: Bureau of Health Professions.

U.S. Immigration and Naturalization Service. (1989, 1990, 1991). Immigrant Public Use Tape [computer file]. Washington, D.C.: Statistics Division, U.S. Immigration and Naturalization Service [producer].

Contributors

Tania Azores is a lecturer at the University of California, Los Angeles Department of Linguistics and at Loyola Marymount University in the Department of Modern Languages. Azores served as the chair of the Asian Pacific American Advisory Committee for the 1980 Census. She received a Ph.D. in urban planning from the University of California, Los Angeles.

Dennis G. Arguelles is a planner at the County of Los Angeles Community Development Commission. He received his M.A. in urban planning from the University of California, Los Angeles. He is active in Search to Involve Pilipino Americans. He is co-author of *Beyond Asian American Poverty: Community Economic Development Policies and Strategies* (LEAP, 1993).

Evelyn Blumenberg is a doctoral candidate in urban planning at the University of California, Los Angeles. Prior to entering graduate school, she worked as a political organizer in low-income communities in California. Her research focuses on issues of gender and racial inequality, labor markets and employment, and welfare policy.

Bonnie Faherty is a lecturer at the University of California, Los Angeles School of Nursing and coordinates the Master's Degree option in Chronic Care. Her expertise includes public policy, gerontology and home health care. Dr. Faherty holds degrees in nursing, public health and public administration from the University of California, Los Angeles and the University of Southern California.

Joel F. Handler is professor of law at the University of California, Los Angeles. He teaches and writes in the areas of poverty law and social welfare administration. He recently chaired the National Research Council's report, *Losing Generations: Adolescents in High Risk Settings*.

Suzanne J. Hee is a research associate for Leadership Education for Asian Pacifics (LEAP) and the LEAP Asian Pacific American Public Policy Institute. She received her M.A. in Asian American Studies from the University of California, Los Angeles. Her research focuses on Asian Americans, racial inequality, and public policy.

Chanchanit (Chancee) Hirunpidok is Executive Director of the American Thai Education and Research Institute, a community-based nonprofit organization in Southern California. She received her M.A. in urban planning from the University of California, Los Angeles. She is co-author of *Beyond Asian American Poverty: Community Economic Development Policies and Strategies* (LEAP, 1993).

Marlene Kim is assistant professor of labor studies at Rutgers University. She received a Ph.D. in economics from the University of California, Berkeley. Her research focuses on the effectiveness of comparable worth in improving the labor market status of women.

Don Mar is associate professor of economics at San Francisco State University. He received a Ph.D. in economics from the University of California, Berkeley. His research focuses on racial differences in labor market outcomes.

Erich Nakano manages housing and community development projects at Little Tokyo Service Center in Los Angeles. He received his M.A. in urban planning from the University of California, Los Angeles. He is chair of the Housing and Economic Development Committee of the Asian Pacific Planning Council and is co-author of *Beyond Asian American Poverty: Community Economic Development Policies and Strategies* (LEAP, 1993).

Paul Ong is associate professor of urban planning and the chair of the Interdepartmental Program in Asian American Studies at the University of California, Los Angeles. His work focuses on the labor market conditions of minorities and immigrants. He received a Ph.D. in economics from the University of California, Berkeley.

Geraldine V. Padilla is professor and associate dean for research at the University of California, Los Angeles School of

Nursing and teaches graduate students. Her research focuses on quality of life as affected by disease, treatment and style of care in white and minority populations. She received her Ph.D. in psychology from the University of California, Los Angeles.

Sheridan Tatsuno is president of Dreamscape Productions, an interactive media research, consulting and production company in Aptos, Calfornia. He has a B.A. in political science from Yale University and an M.A. in public policy and planning from Harvard's Kennedy School of Government. He is the author of *The Technopolis Strategy* (Prentice-Hall, 1986) and *Created in Japan* (Harper Business, 1990).

Karen Umemoto is a doctoral candidate in urban studies and planning at the Massachusetts Institute of Technology. She received her M.A. in Asian American Studies from the University of California, Los Angeles. Her research focuses on race relations, urban ethnic conflict, and public policy.

Linda C. Wing is lecturer at the Harvard Graduate School of Education where she is also coordinator of the Urban Superintendents Program. She earned a Ph.D. in educational policy analysis from the University of California at Berkeley. Her latest works include *Policy Issues in Employment Testing* (Kluwer, 1994) and *Teaching, Learning, and Technology*, an interactive computer-based multimedia kit designed to help educators restructure their schools.

Leadership Education for Asian Pacifics (LEAP), Inc.

Leadership Education for Asian Pacifics (LEAP) is a nonprofit, non-partisan, educational, community organization founded in 1982 to develop, strengthen, and expand the leadership roles played by Asian Pacific Americans within their own communities as well as in mainstream institutions.

LEAP's mission to achieve full participation and equality for Asian Pacific Americans through leadership, empowerment, and policy is being realized through the creation of the nationally recognized Asian Pacific Amerian Public Policy Institute (APA•PPI), the innovative Leadership Management Institute (LMI), and the newly created Community Development Institute (CDI).

Leadership Education for Asian Pacifics (LEAP), Inc.
327 East Second Street, Suite 226
Los Angeles, CA 90012-4210
Tel.: (213) 485-1422
Fax: (213) 485-0050
E-mail: LEAP90012@AOL.COM

Board of Directors

William H. "Mo" Marumoto, *Chair*
Shirley Komoto Maimoni, *Vice Chair*
Gay Yuen Wong, *Vice Chair*
Glenn Kawafuchi, *Vice Chair*
Tim T. L. Dong, *Vice Chair*
Florence S. Ochi, *Secretary*
Enrique B. de la Cruz, *Chief Financial Officer*
John T. Nagai, *Legal Counsel (ex officio)*

David R. Barclay	Irene Natividad
Marilynn Fong-Choy	Nampet Panichpant-M
Ernest M. Hiroshige	Ki Suh Park
Yoon Hee Kim	Frank J. Quevedo
Janice T. Koyama	Prany Sananikone
Stewart Kwoh	Bill Sing
Ngoan Thi Le	Buddy T. Takata
Robert Lee	Nghia Trung Tran
David W. Louie	Peter Wiersma

J. D. Hokoyama, *President & Executive Director*

Staff

Linda Akutagawa, *Administrative Assistant*
Suzanne J. Hee, *Research Associate*
Gena A. Lew, *Research Associate*

Consultants

Graham S. Finney
John Y. Tateishi

UCLA Asian American Studies Center

The Center, founded in 1969, is one of four ethnic studies centers at UCLA. The Center does research in the social sciences and the humanities, public policy and urban planning, immigrant and labor history, public health and social welfare, literature and film studies; administers undergraduate curriculum and graduate programs; develops and disseminates publications; works with student and community groups; and maintains one of the world's largest research archives in Asian American Studies.

UCLA Asian American Studies Center
3230 Campbell Hall, 405 Hilgard Ave.
Los Angeles, CA 90024-1546
tel.: (310) 825-2974
FAX: (310) 206-9844
e-mail: iyi4dtn@mvs.oac.ucla.edu

Don T. Nakanishi, *Director*

Center Staff

Cathy Castor, *Administrative Assistant of Center Management*
Enrique de la Cruz, *Assistant Director*
Grace Hong, *Publications Assistant*
Yuji Ichioka, *Research & Adjunct Professor in History*
Mary Kao, *Graphics and Production Assistant*
Marjorie Lee, *Librarian & Library Coordinator*
Russell C. Leong, *Editor, Amerasia Journal*
Brian Niiya, *Associate Librarian*
Glenn Omatsu, *Associate Editor, Amerasia Journal*
Sandra Shin, *Administrative Assistant, Center Management*
Meg Thornton, *Coordinator, Student/Community Projects*
Christine Wang, *Coordinator, Center Management*
Eric Wat, *Assistant Coordinator, Student/Community Projects*
Jean Pang Yip, *Publications Business Manager*

Faculty Advisory Committee

James Lubben (Chair), *Social Welfare*
Pauling Agbayani-Siewart, *Soc. Welf.*
Emil Berkanovic, *Public Health*
Lucie Cheng, *Sociology*
Clara Chu, *Library & Info. Science*
King-Kok Cheung, *English*
Cindy Fan, *Geography*
Shirley Hune, *Urban Planning*
Yuji Ichioka, *History*
Snehendu Kar, *Public Health*
Harry Kitano, *Social Welfare*
Jinqi Ling, *English*
David Wong Louie, *English*
Mitchell Maki, *Social Welfare*
Takashi Makinodan, *Medicine-GRECC*

Valerie Matsumoto, *History*
Ailee Moon, *Social Welfare*
Robert Nakamura, *Theater, Film & TV*
Kazuo Nihira, *Psych. & Biobeh. Sci.*
Paul Ong, *Urban Planning*
William Ouchi, *Management*
Geraldine Padilla, *Nursing*
Kyeyoung Park, *Anthropology*
Michael Salman, *History*
Gregory Sarris, *English*
Shu-mei Shih, *Comp. Literature*
Zhixin Justine Su, *Education*
Stanley Sue, *Psychology*
James Tong, *Political Science*
Cindy Yee-Bradbury, *Psychology*